25 Business Stories

25 Business Stories

A Practical Guide for English Learners

Andrew E. Bennett

Merriam-Webster, Incorporated
Springfield, Massachusetts, U.S.A.

A GENUINE MERRIAM-WEBSTER

The name *Webster* alone is no guarantee of excellence. It is used by a number of publishers and may serve mainly to mislead an unwary buyer.

Merriam-Webster™ is the name you should look for when you consider the purchase of dictionaries or other fine reference books. It carries the reputation of a company that has been publishing since 1831 and is your assurance of quality and authority.

ISBN: 978-087779-683-1

Library of Congress Cataloging-in-Publication Data

Bennett, Andrew E.
25 business stories : a practical guide for English learners / Andrew E. Bennett.
p. cm.
ISBN 978-0-87779-683-1
1. Readers—Business. 2. English language—Textbooks for foreign speakers. 3. English language—Business English. 4. Readers (Adult) I. Title. II. Title: Twenty-five business stories.
PE1127.B86B66 2008
428.6—dc22
2008033238

Made in the United States of America

12345QW/V1211100908

CONTENTS

PREFACE

One of the most challenging things about learning a new language is understanding business articles. Even after studying English for several years, it can be difficult to read an article in *Time*, *Fortune*, or the *Wall Street Journal*. Yet, often, that's what we really need. We need to be able to read and talk about the businesspeople and companies that shape our world—but we want to do so without having to look up half the words in a dictionary.

This is where *25 Business Stories* comes in. Written at an intermediate level, it bridges the gap between the language learner and the real business world.

25 Business Stories covers a wide range of topics in its five sections. In the section on business successes, you'll read about amazing companies like Apple. And in the section on business failures, you'll read about New Coke, one of the most famous mistakes in corporate history. These are just two of the many interesting—and sometimes exciting—stories waiting for you in the pages that follow.

Each unit opens with an interesting article about an important company or businessperson. Accompanying each passage is a graphic aid, such as a chart or table. These provide information about the topic while building your skills and confidence in dealing with this kind of material when it appears in magazines and newspapers.

After a brief exercise in reading comprehension, each unit provides definitions and example sentences for its vocabulary words and phrases. For one phrase in each unit, an explanation of its origin is given. These words and phrases were chosen for their usefulness in daily life as well as their likelihood of appearing in business articles.

The final two parts of each unit will help you take the step from reading about the topic to speaking about it. One is a set of sentence patterns, which will help you use certain key patterns. The other is a series of examples showing how ordinary people would talk about the topic. Thus, unit by unit, you will be expanding a set of "real-world" language tools that will help you in speaking and writing over and over in the years to come.

Every set of five units is followed by a vocabulary review, to refresh your memory about the words and phrases you've just learned. You might find it helpful to write these words and phrases down in a small notebook; reviewing them once in a while, along with writing practice sentences, will help fix them in your memory.

I hope you'll enjoy reading *25 Business Stories* as much as I enjoyed writing it!

Andrew E. Bennett

section 1
✦ FIVE BUSINESS SUCCESSES

TARGET VOCABULARY

acquisition *(n)*	Chap. 2: Lenovo
affect *(v)*	Chap. 5: BHP Billiton
asset *(n)*	Chap. 5: BHP Billiton
based *(adj)*	Chap. 4: MTN
boldly *(adv)*	Chap. 2: Lenovo
bottom line *(n)*	Chap. 4: MTN
capture *(v)*	Chap. 1: Starbucks
challenge *(n)*	Chap. 5: BHP Billiton
competitive *(adj)*	Chap. 1: Starbucks
concept *(n)*	Chap. 1: Starbucks
costly *(adj)*	Chap. 4: MTN
customer base *(n)*	Chap. 4: MTN
decade *(n)*	Chap. 1: Starbucks
deep *(adj)*	Chap. 5: BHP Billiton
determined *(adj)*	Chap. 2: Lenovo
domestically *(adv)*	Chap. 1: Starbucks
equation *(n)*	Chap. 3: Apple
expand *(v)*	Chap. 4: MTN
fashion statement *(n)*	Chap. 3: Apple
feature *(n)*	Chap. 3: Apple
flagship *(n)*	Chap. 3: Apple
fresh *(adj)*	Chap. 3: Apple
hip *(adj)*	Chap. 3: Apple
household name *(n)*	Chap. 2: Lenovo
huge *(adj)*	Chap. 2: Lenovo
impact *(n)*	Chap. 5: BHP Billiton
impressive *(adj)*	Chap. 3: Apple
know-how *(n)*	Chap. 2: Lenovo
largely *(adv)*	Chap. 2: Lenovo
lucrative *(adj)*	Chap. 1: Starbucks
manufacture *(v)*	Chap. 5: BHP Billiton
market share *(n)*	Chap. 3: Apple
merger *(n)*	Chap. 5: BHP Billiton
model *(adj)*	Chap. 4: MTN

natural resource *(n)*	Chap. 5: BHP Billiton	**remarkable** *(adj)*	Chap. 1: Starbucks
operate *(v)*	Chap. 4: MTN	**resistance** *(n)*	Chap. 2: Lenovo
player *(n)*	Chap. 5: BHP Billiton	**revenue** *(n)*	Chap. 1: Starbucks
powerhouse *(n)*	Chap. 1: Starbucks	**sponsor** *(v)*	Chap. 2: Lenovo
rapid *(adj)*	Chap. 4: MTN	**start-up** *(n)*	Chap. 2: Lenovo
record *(adj)*	Chap. 5: BHP Billiton	**superstar** *(n)*	Chap. 4: MTN
regain *(v)*	Chap. 3: Apple	**turnaround** *(n)*	Chap. 3: Apple
regularly *(adv)*	Chap. 4: MTN	**unique** *(adj)*	Chap. 1: Starbucks

TARGET PHRASES

along with	Chap. 2: Lenovo	**music to someone's ears**	Chap. 3: Apple
branch out	Chap. 5: BHP Billiton	**out of this world**	Chap. 4: MTN
change hands	Chap. 5: BHP Billiton	**raise eyebrows**	Chap. 2: Lenovo
drive up	Chap. 1: Starbucks	**regardless of**	Chap. 1: Starbucks
eat away at	Chap. 3: Apple	**shut down**	Chap. 5: BHP Billiton
flying high	Chap. 3: Apple	**the sky's the limit**	Chap. 1: Starbucks
for instance	Chap. 2: Lenovo	**stay in touch**	Chap. 4: MTN
head back	Chap. 4: MTN		

chapter 1
STARBUCKS AROUND THE WORLD

READING PASSAGE

Few companies in the food and drink industry have grown as widely and successfully as Starbucks. In just two **decades**, Starbucks has grown from a small chain of U.S. coffee shops into an international **powerhouse**. From Japan to England to Mexico, Starbucks is now one of the world's best-known brands, with thousands of shops around the world.

What's the secret of their amazing success? Actually, both the history and **concept** of Starbucks are very simple. It started in the 1970s as a small chain in Seattle, Washington, a crowded market with heavy competition. The owner, Howard Schultz, was looking for a way to make his shops **unique**. So he took a trip to Italy, where he studied the style and culture of Italian coffee shops.

Back in America, Schultz applied some of his findings. He made Starbucks shops more comfortable and sold a variety of high-quality European and American drinks. The "coffee culture" he created turned out to be very popular. Starbucks cafés became fun places to chat, read the morning paper, or hold a business meeting.

Behind this simple idea is a strong business model and excellent marketing, and the company's sales and profit numbers are **remarkable**. Starbucks went public in 1992. Over the next decade, sales grew an average of 20 percent per year, while profits grew an average of 30 percent yearly. As the company **expanded** overseas in the mid-1990s, its market share and profits continued to rise. Investors rewarded the stock by **driving up** the stock price (see chart).

Of course, every success produces competitors. Other coffee-shop chains have opened to try to **capture** some of the **lucrative** market. Also, Starbucks already has a large number of coffee shops in the U.S. (more than 11,000 in 2008). That means they're running out of places to open shops **domestically**.

Regardless of these issues, Starbucks continues to grow and impress. There's still plenty of room to expand overseas. Also, riding the strength of their brand, they now sell bottled coffee drinks, ice cream, coffee beans, and other products. With so many **revenue** sources and ongoing expansion plans, **the sky's the limit** for Starbucks.

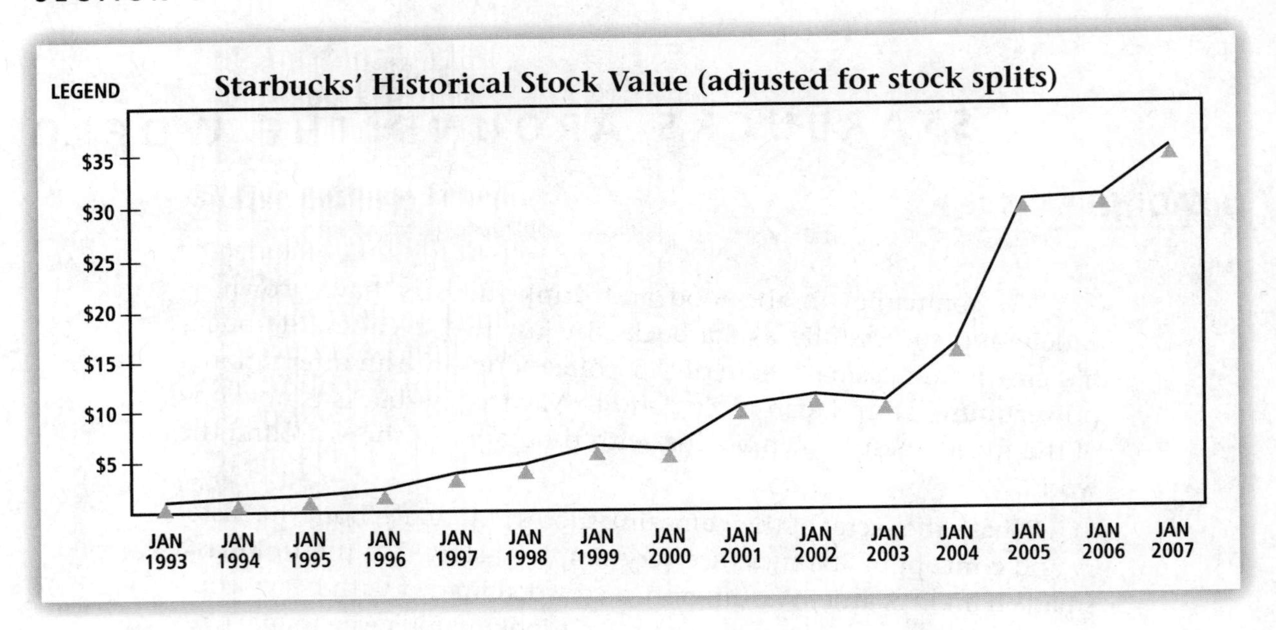

COMPREHENSION CHECK

1. ( ) What is the main idea of the reading passage?
   A. Starbucks sells delicious drinks.
   B. With a simple concept, anyone can open a successful company.
   C. Through good ideas and good management, Starbucks has become one of the world's most successful brands.
   D. Italian coffee culture is popular around the world.

2. ( ) When did Starbucks become a publicly traded company?
   A. In the mid 1980s
   B. In the early 1990s
   C. In the late 1990s
   D. At the start of the 21st century

3. ( ) Profits at Starbucks ___________.
   A. were highest in 1992
   B. were 20 percent higher in 2002 than in 1992
   C. grew more than 30 percent per year in the 1990s
   D. grew at a higher percentage than sales in the 1990s

4. ( ) What does "they're" in the fifth paragraph mean?
   A. overseas companies
   B. Starbucks
   C. Starbucks' competition
   D. U.S. coffee shops

5. ( ) Which of the following is *not* true about Starbucks?
   A. They sell their own ice cream and bottled drinks.
   B. They have many rivals trying to take market share.
   C. Domestic shops were opened before international shops were opened.
   D. Their stock doubled from 1992 to 1993.

VOCABULARY BUILDING

decade *(n)* — a period of 10 years
✦ We've lived in this house for more than a decade.

powerhouse *(n)* — something (such as a company) that is very powerful
✦ In the bottled-soda industry, Coca-Cola is a powerhouse.

concept *(n)* — an idea
✦ It's a good concept, but creating the actual product would be expensive.

competitive *(adj)* — having a lot of competition
✦ The restaurant business is so competitive that I don't think I want to get into it now.

unique *(adj)* — special and different from others
✦ I didn't find the ad unique at all. It looked just like all their other ads.

remarkable *(adj)* — incredible
✦ What a remarkable drawing! Did you do it yourself?

capture *(v)* — take
✦ In the third quarter, we captured 5 percent of the market.

lucrative *(adj)* — profitable
✦ The market for digital cameras is lucrative, but there's a lot of competition.

domestically *(adv)* — in one's home market
✦ Sometimes movies do poorly domestically but make a lot of money overseas.

revenue *(n)* — income
✦ Few companies rely on just one product for all their revenue.

PHRASE BUILDING

drive up — cause to increase
✦ High oil prices are driving up the cost of airplane tickets.

regardless of — despite
✦ Regardless of what Mary said, you should tell the boss what happened.

the sky's the limit — there's no limit

✦ You're young, smart, and hardworking—the sky's the limit for what you can accomplish.

WHY DO WE SAY THAT?

the sky's the limit — We use this phrase to refer to something that has great potential. When we look up at the sky, we can see for many, many miles. In fact, the distance is so great that it's almost impossible to imagine. So when we say "the sky's the limit," we mean that a person, project, company, etc., has the potential to go very far and be very successful.

SENTENCE PATTERNS

What's the *secret of* / *reason for* / *cause behind* their amazing success?

During that time, / *At that time,* / *At the same time,* profits grew an average of 30 percent per year.

WHAT PEOPLE ARE SAYING ABOUT STARBUCKS

Maria I absolutely love Starbucks! I get a double espresso every morning before work. My friends and I like hanging out there on the weekend. It's always clean, and the service is good.

Hiroko Starbucks is becoming popular in Japan. Although drinks like cappuccino and mocha are new to Japan, I think more and more people are starting to like them. However, I only go to Starbucks once in a while. We have so many other coffee shops here, like Dante and Doutor. I have to say, they're cheaper than Starbucks, too.

Steve I used to like Starbucks, but not so much anymore. You know, in the beginning it was really cool going there. Now they've got so many stores, it just feels like a big corporation. Plus their drinks are so expensive! Four dollars for a cup of coffee? That's crazy. I don't know about you, but I can't afford to go there every day. I'd rather make coffee at home.

chapter 2

LENOVO: CHINA'S PC POWERHOUSE

READING PASSAGE

Lenovo is one of the great success stories of the modern Chinese economy. Once mainly known as China's personal computer (PC) market leader, it became a **household name** worldwide with its purchase of IBM's PC division.

The company, originally called Legend, began like many other technology companies—as a small **start-up**. In 1984, 11 computer scientists started the firm in a small building in Beijing. Their research and **know-how** were important tools as they built low-cost computers for the domestic market.

By the mid-1990s, Legend had grown into the top-selling PC maker in China's home and office markets. The following decade, the company changed its name to Lenovo (see table). Along with the name change came a big move that really **raised eyebrows.**

In 2005, Lenovo completed the **acquisition** of IBM's PC division, including its desktop and notebook lines. This was **huge** news. After all, IBM had been **largely** responsible for the birth of the home PC market 20 years earlier. It had invented the laptop computer, and its ThinkPad line was one of the world's top brands. Lenovo had **boldly** announced to the world that it was a serious force in the PC industry.

Lenovo quickly made changes to the ThinkPad line. **For instance,** it started selling ThinkPads (which had always been black) in titanium. It also sold versions of the notebooks with wider screens. These changes were met with some **resistance**, yet Lenovo was **determined** to make the line its own as it left IBM's shadow.

Taking its place as an industry leader, the company has been praised for its support in the fight against piracy. In April 2006, Lenovo signed a $1.2 billion deal with Microsoft, agreeing to install Windows operating systems on its new computers. The company has also helped build its brand by **sponsoring** the Olympics.

After the IBM deal, Lenovo took its place as the world's third-largest PC seller. **Along with** computers, Lenovo develops cell phones, computer equipment, and other electronic products. With over 20 years in the business, $13 billion in revenues, and 20,000 employees, it's a powerhouse that we'll surely be hearing from for many years to come.

Key Moments in Legend/Lenovo's History

YEAR	EVENT
1984	Legend founded with $25,000 in start-up capital
1994	Legend starts publicly trading on Hong Kong Stock Exchange
1998	Total PC sales reach one million computers
2004	Name changed from Legend to Lenovo
2005	Lenovo completes purchase of IBM's PC division

COMPREHENSION CHECK

1. ( ) What was Lenovo's situation like before the IBM deal?
   A. It only had 11 employees.
   B. It was known for its top-end PCs.
   C. The company was the market leader in China.
   D. As the inventor of the notebook computer, Lenovo was in great shape.

2. ( ) The article suggests that Lenovo's deal with IBM was _________.
   A. planned many years in advance
   B. strongly welcomed after Lenovo started changing the ThinkPad line
   C. limited to IBM's notebook lines
   D. a major development in the industry

3. ( ) Which of these events took place first?
   A. Lenovo sold its one millionth computer.
   B. Lenovo and Microsoft signed a deal.
   C. Lenovo became a public company.
   D. Lenovo changed its name.

4. ( ) Which of the following is *not* mentioned as an example of Lenovo's leadership?
   A. Its wide range of low-cost cell phones
   B. Its deal to install Windows on its computers
   C. Its sponsorship of major sporting events
   D. Its actions against piracy

5. ( ) What does the article suggest about Lenovo's future?
   A. The company will soon be the world's top PC seller.
   B. It's in a strong position to continue making headlines.
   C. Lenovo will soon begin selling cell phones and other products.
   D. The deal with Microsoft may be met with resistance.

VOCABULARY BUILDING

household name *(n)* — a name that everybody knows
✦ IBM is a household name in many countries.

start-up *(n)* — a new company
✦ Sometimes a start-up includes just one person working from home.

know-how *(n)* — knowledge
✦ Sure, we have the know-how to open a restaurant, but do we have the money?

acquisition *(n)* — a purchase
✦ The acquisition of the shipping firm was seen as a good move for the transportation giant.

huge *(adj)* — very big
✦ CEOs' salaries are usually huge compared to the salaries of other employees.

largely *(adv)* — mostly
✦ The fall in production was largely due to poor weather.

boldly *(adv)* — confidently and bravely
✦ Erica boldly walked into her boss's office and demanded a raise.

resistance *(n)* — opposition
✦ Plans to build new highways are often met with resistance from local residents.

determined *(adj)* — firmly intent on doing something
✦ My friend Tamuki is determined to retire before he's 40.

sponsor *(v)* — support (often with money or other types of aid)
✦ Companies often sponsor sporting events as part of their marketing strategy.

PHRASE BUILDING

raise eyebrows — attract attention
✦ A price increase of 3 percent isn't a very big deal, but a 10 or 15 percent increase would definitely raise eyebrows.

for instance — for example
✦ This city has a lot of problems, but it also has its good points; for instance, every neighborhood has at least one large park.

along with — besides
✦ Along with changing the design, I recommend we change the product's name.

WHY DO WE SAY THAT?

raise eyebrows — When we hear surprising news or pay close attention to something, we often raise our eyebrows. So, we say something "raises eyebrows" when it attracts attention.

SENTENCE PATTERNS

Along with the name change came a big move that really *raised eyebrows.*
caught people's attention.
made news.

Lenovo had boldly announced to the world that it was *a major player.*
here to stay.
an industry leader.

WHAT PEOPLE ARE SAYING ABOUT LENOVO

Mei Lin I bought my first computer from Lenovo in 2001, when it was still called Legend. Most of the other companies were a lot more expensive. The quality of the computer was good, and the price was great. Since then, I've recommended Lenovo to a lot of friends.

Frederick I was really surprised to hear that Lenovo bought IBM's PC division. Everyone in my family uses a ThinkPad. I guess some people aren't sure if the quality of future ThinkPads will stay the same. But I'm willing to give Lenovo a chance.

Martha Personally, I like Macs, so Lenovo, Dell, and the other PC makers are all the same to me!

chapter 3

APPLE'S IPOD: BIG PROFITS COME IN SMALL PACKAGES

READING PASSAGE

Sometimes it just takes one product—one *very special* product—for a company to make it big. In Apple's case, the release of the iPod in 2001 helped the company **regain** its former glory. While making the company **hip** again, the iPod delivered billions in revenues.

In the 1980s, with its **flagship** Macintosh computer, the company was **flying high**. Yet competition from IBM and low-cost computer makers **ate away at** Apple's **market share**. Later, as cheap PCs running Microsoft's software became popular, Apple slid even further.

The return of company founder Steve Jobs in the late 1990s was the beginning of Apple's **turnaround**. Its new iMac computers became a big hit. Yet that was nothing compared to the success of the tiny iPod.

The first iPod was an easy-to-use digital music player. It wasn't a new concept, but the look and **features** of Apple's offering made it more attractive than other devices. The first iPod could store 1,000 songs, a huge amount at the time. And its modern design and soft white color turned the music player into a **fashion statement**.

In the years that followed, the iPod's popularity grew. Apple released version after version, keeping the product **fresh** and up-to-date with the newest technology. New features were added over time, including color screens, photo viewing, and the ability to watch videos.

Apple's iTunes software made it easy to transfer songs from a computer to an iPod. The company also started selling songs and videos on the Internet, another successful part of the iPod **equation**. In fact, by January 2008, more than four billion songs had been purchased from the iTunes Web site.

The numbers for the iPod are also **impressive.** In just a few short years, from 2001 to late 2007, more than 150 million iPods were sold. Sales of the product grew to represent more than half of all of Apple's revenues. In just the first quarter (Q1) of 2007, that meant $3.4 billion in revenues (see chart). Now that's **music to a company's ears.**

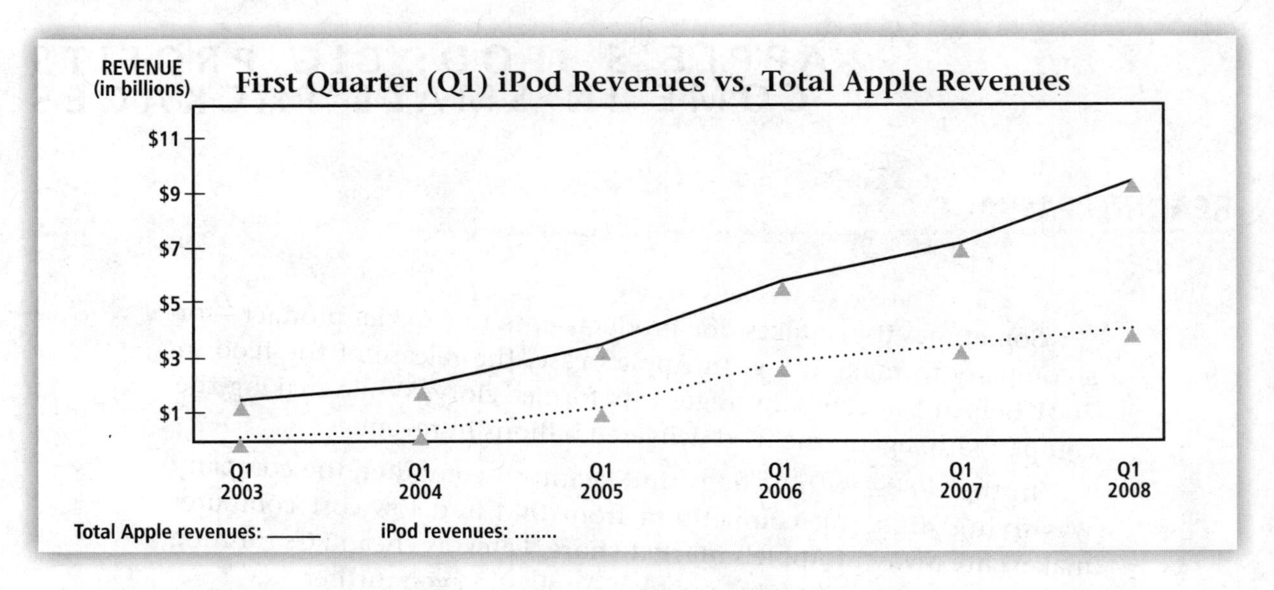

COMPREHENSION CHECK

1. ( ) According to the article, what was causing Apple to lose business?
   A. The loss of Steve Jobs as CEO
   B. The popularity of cheap PCs
   C. The poor reaction to the first Macintosh
   D. Competition from low-cost digital music players

2. ( ) How has Apple been able to keep the iPod hip and cool?
   A. By regularly improving the product
   B. By copying the features of other music players
   C. By including a video-watching feature with the first iPod
   D. By keeping the price stable

3. ( ) What does "store" in the fourth paragraph mean?
   A. shop
   B. place
   C. supply
   D. hold

4. ( ) What can be concluded about Apple's revenues?
   A. The company always had revenue problems before the iPod's release.
   B. From 2003 to 2007 total revenues and iPod revenues both grew quickly.
   C. They more than doubled from Q1 2004 to Q1 2005.
   D. They totaled about $1.55 billion in 2003.

5. ( ) What does the article imply about the iPod?
   A. It is responsible for all of Apple's profits.
   B. It is the only portable digital music player on the market.
   C. It was an important part of Apple's turnaround.
   D. It was the first digital music player on the market.

VOCABULARY BUILDING

regain *(v)* — get something back again
✦ By cutting prices, the car-parts supplier was able to regain its lost market share.

hip *(adj)* — cool and fashionable
✦ Many clothing and shoe companies work hard to maintain a hip, young image.

flagship *(n)* — the leading item in a group (such as a product or store)
✦ Apple has a flagship store in the center of New York City.

market share *(n)* — the portion of a market that is held by a company
✦ In the small-sized refrigerator business, our market share is 12 percent.

turnaround *(n)* — a change of direction, improvement
✦ We may need to hire someone from outside the firm to lead the turnaround.

fashion statement *(n)* — something that stands out and says something about the user
✦ When Gina wore a bright orange dress, she was making a fashion statement.

fresh *(adj)* — modern and new
✦ What you need is a fresh new logo and a new company image.

feature *(n)* — a special characteristic or key function
✦ Few people use all the features built into their digital cameras.

equation *(n)* — a situation with various elements
✦ One part of the equation I didn't consider was the cost of buying new equipment.

impressive *(adj)* — causing admiration
✦ This year's sales were impressive, but we can do even better next year!

PHRASE BUILDING

flying high — feeling great; in an excellent position
✦ After her victory in the tournament, the athlete was flying high.

eat away at — cause something to gradually reduce
✦ All these expenses are eating away at our profits.

music to someone's ears — a great piece of news or information
✦ When I heard we were getting a holiday bonus, it was music to my ears.

WHY DO WE SAY THAT?

music to someone's ears — Most of us like to listen to music, and we especially like to hear our favorite kind of music. So something that is music to your ears is something that you're very happy to hear. The news that you are getting a raise, for example, would be music to your ears.

SENTENCE PATTERNS

In the years that followed, the iPod's popularity grew.
Over time,
Slowly but surely,

In just the first quarter of 2007, that meant $3.4 billion in revenues.
Within a year,
Over the course of three months,

WHAT PEOPLE ARE SAYING ABOUT THE IPOD

Claudia I don't have an iPod, but a lot of my friends do. I like to listen to music, but I don't need a portable player to take everywhere. So for now, I'll just keep listening to my CDs at home.

Jorge I'm totally in love with my iPod. I remember what a hassle it was to carry around my CD player and all those CDs. I used to keep at least 100 CDs in my car. Now I've got all (and I mean all!) my music on my iPod. It doesn't weigh anything, and I can plug it into my car speaker. So I can leave my CDs at home and don't have to worry about them getting stolen!

Vladimir I just think iPods are too expensive. There are a lot of other players that do the same job for a lot less money. Plus I see so many people with iPods, they're like a fashion statement. I like to be different from the rest of the crowd.

chapter 4

MTN: CONNECTING AFRICA

READING PASSAGE

Communication. It's key to doing business. The telephone is one of the most powerful tools in connecting people across distances. However, in most African countries, there are not nearly enough landlines, which are **costly** to lay down and maintain. That's where cheap wireless technology comes in, allowing people in cities, on farms, and even on fishing boats to have a phone. Leading the way in connecting Africa is MTN, Africa's largest cell-phone company.

MTN started offering cell-phone services in South Africa, where the company is **based**, in 1994. Three years later, it began **expanding** to other African countries, starting with Uganda, Rwanda, and Swaziland. By 2004, MTN was serving more than 11 million people (see chart). Considering that the company started with a ten-year goal of signing up 500,000 customers, that level of success is **out of this world**.

But MTN was just getting started. In 2005, it made its first moves into the Middle East, paying for a license to **operate** in Iran. Then, in May 2006, MTN made one of the biggest moves in the history of African business. For $5.53 billion, it bought Investcom, a Dubai-based cell-phone company that operated in three Middle Eastern and six African countries. That increased MTN's **customer base** to 28 million people across 21 countries.

This **rapid** growth in cell-phone use has had many positive effects. Of course, it's great for MTN's **bottom line**. But it also changes people's lives. Before **heading back** to port, fishermen can phone ahead to find the best place to bring their catch. Farmers can ask around to find the best price for their crops. And people can **stay in touch** with relatives in distant places.

But voice communication is just the beginning. MTN also offers Internet access, which will continue to grow as wireless technology improves. Considered a **model** company, MTN is **regularly** voted as one of the best companies to work for in South Africa. On its 10th birthday, MTN was praised by Nelson Mandela, South Africa's former president, as a model African business. Indeed, the future looks bright for this cell-phone **superstar**.

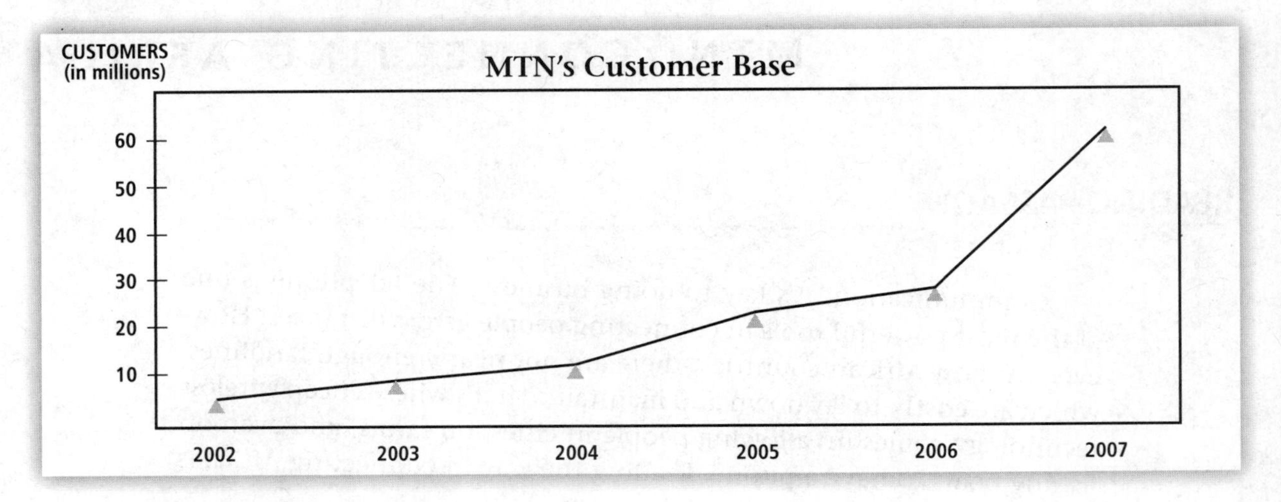

COMPREHENSION CHECK

1. ( ) MTN's expansion into Uganda __________.
   A. came after the company's licensing deal in Iran
   B. took place as MTN was celebrating 10 years in business
   C. was one of many expansion moves in Africa
   D. brought 11 million customers to MTN

2. ( ) What does the article suggest about MTN on its 10th birthday?
   A. The company went well past its growth target.
   B. The company was disappointed with its growth.
   C. The company was not well known in South Africa.
   D. The company had already expanded into the Middle East.

3. ( ) What resulted from the Investcom deal?
   A. MTN's customer base doubled.
   B. MTN's customer base increased by 28 million people.
   C. MTN gained a customer base in several Middle Eastern countries.
   D. MTN more than doubled the number of countries it operated in.

4. ( ) What does the article imply about cell phones in Africa?
   A. Cell phones are too costly for most people.
   B. MTN is Africa's only cell-phone service provider.
   C. They can change the way people do business.
   D. Services for cell phones cost as much to maintain as landline services.

5. ( ) Which of the following is true about MTN?
   A. It was the first multinational South African business.
   B. It offers more than basic cell-phone services.
   C. It expanded into the Middle East before expanding in Africa.
   D. It does not have a positive image in its home country.

VOCABULARY BUILDING

costly *(adj)* — expensive
- ✦ Since the new equipment is costly, we need approval before buying it.

based *(adj)* — located
- ✦ We're based in London, but we work with partners in 20 countries.

expand *(v)* — grow
- ✦ Mr. Finch thinks this is a good time to expand in Asia.

operate *(v)* — manage, run
- ✦ The company operates a chain of 100 stores worldwide.

customer base *(n)* — a company's group of customers
- ✦ If you want to grow your company's customer base, you need to let more people know about your products.

rapid *(adj)* — fast
- ✦ Rapid changes in the computer industry mean today's winners may be tomorrow's losers.

bottom line *(n)* — a point of profit or loss
- ✦ Ms. Hampton is very concerned about our bottom line. She won't touch any project that risks losing money.

model *(adj)* — a great example of something or someone
- ✦ Chuck, you're a model employee. You're always on time, you work hard, and you get along with everyone.

regularly *(adv)* — done on a usual basis
- ✦ The printer is regularly cleaned to keep it running in top condition.

superstar *(n)* — an excellent performer
- ✦ Cynthia is a superstar here. She wins the Salesperson of the Year award every year.

PHRASE BUILDING

out of this world — incredible
- ✦ Your cooking is out of this world! You'll have to teach me sometime!

head back — return to a place
- ✦ Let's head back to the farm before it gets too dark.

stay in touch — maintain contact

✦ E-mail makes it easy for people to stay in touch with each other, no matter where they are.

WHY DO WE SAY THAT?

out of this world — The things we see in our daily lives are common; they're all around us, and not hard to find. In contrast, something that is "out of this world" is very special, as if it came from another planet. So this idiom refers to something that is truly amazing.

SENTENCE PATTERNS

This rapid growth in cell-phone use	*has many positive effects.* *will be great for the local economy.* *is due to a number of factors.*

Indeed, *Without doubt,* *There's no question,*	the future looks bright for this cell-phone superstar.

WHAT PEOPLE ARE SAYING ABOUT MTN

Kwende I live in South Africa and I am an MTN subscriber. I talk to my friends every day on my cell phone. The coverage is good, and the phone lines are very clear. We need more companies like MTN!

Lydia As a businessperson in Kenya, I can't imagine not having a cell phone. I use it to talk to clients and go onto the Internet. But the rates for going onto the Net with my cell phone are still too high, in my opinion. Plus it's not very fast, so those are things MTN could improve on.

Amina I've been an Investcom customer for a while, and they've been quite reliable. I hope things stay the same under the new management.

chapter 5

BHP BILLITON: THE NATURAL RESOURCES LEADER

READING PASSAGE

Running factories, **manufacturing** products, and shipping goods all require **natural resources** such as iron, copper, and oil. As the world economy has grown, such goods have been in high demand, driving up prices. Leading the way in supplying natural resources is BHP Billiton, the world's largest mining company.

BHP Billiton was formed in 2001 as a **merger** of two large companies: BHP (an Australian firm) and Billiton (a British firm). Both had long histories. BHP was founded in 1885. Starting with a single mine in Australia, it later **branched out** into steel production, ship building, gold mining, and other areas.

The other half of the merger, Billiton, also brought a proud past to the team. From its start in 1860, the company was an international **player**, as its first mine was in Indonesia. The company became very strong in mining metals such as lead, copper, and silver.

Along with its **deep** experience, BHP Billiton's size is a key advantage. In the natural-resources industry, mines and companies often **change hands**. Large companies can buy new **assets** and **fight off** hungry competitors. In fact, from 1983 to 1986, a competitor tried (and failed) to buy BHP four different times. It no longer seems likely that BHP Billiton, with a stock value of more than $175 billion, will be devoured by another company.

Another key concern is bad weather, which can **shut down** mines. With assets worldwide, BHP Billiton can reduce the **impact** of poor weather. Consider the nine-month period ending in March 2006—one of the best ever for the company. Despite serious weather problems, nickel production was still at a **record** high (see chart). While one nickel mine was **affected** by heavy rains, another mine increased production.

The recent rise in resource prices has meant amazing profits for BHP Billiton. (It earned profits of $13.7 billion in 2007.) However, just as prices can rise, so can they fall. Also, the company must deal with environmental groups demanding cleaner and safer mines. With operations in 25 countries, BHP Billiton is in a strong position to face these **challenges** while holding onto the top spot in its industry.

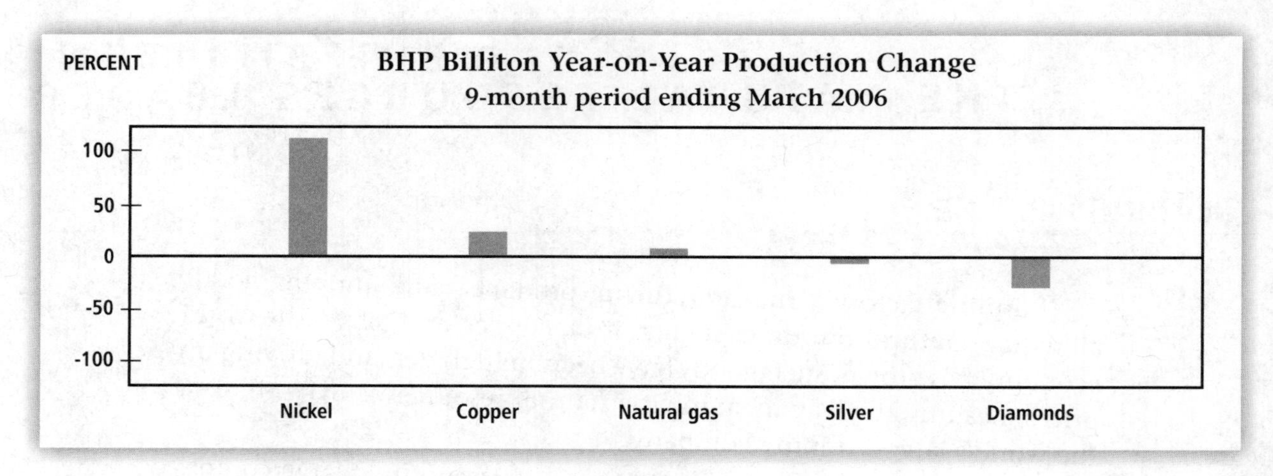

COMPREHENSION CHECK

1. ( ) What is the article's tone?
   A. Doubtful B. Negative
   C. Critical D. Praising

2. ( ) Before the merger, BHP and Billiton ________.
   A. were small companies that were having trouble surviving
   B. were both very well established
   C. both focused on mining operations in Australia
   D. tried to acquire each other several times

3. ( ) Large companies enjoy key advantages. Which of these advantages is *not* mentioned in the article?
   A. The means to keep costs down
   B. An ability to purchase new mines
   C. Security against takeover attempts
   D. Purchasing power to acquire other companies

4. ( ) Which of the following is true about the company's nine-month period ending March 2006?
   A. Even with record profits, there were some areas that performed poorly.
   B. Production increased for all the natural resources sold by the company.
   C. Poor weather affected almost every BHP Billiton operation.
   D. Silver production fell more than diamond production.

5. ( ) According to the article, why does BHP Billiton need to continue working hard?
   A. It's likely that an even larger mining company will try to take it over.
   B. Hard work will be needed before the company can turn a profit.
   C. The prices of natural resources are not stable.
   D. The size of the company makes it difficult to manage operations.

VOCABULARY BUILDING

natural resource *(n)* — a raw material from the earth (such as oil or copper)
✦ This area is poor in natural resources, so we have to import almost everything.

challenge *(n)* — a problem that requires focus and hard work to deal with
✦ Their biggest challenge that year was moving the company's offices to a new city.

merger *(n)* — the joining of two companies or groups into a single organization
✦ It took two years for the fast-food companies to complete their merger.

player *(n)* — an important person or company in a group or industry
✦ Nestlé is an important player in the chocolate business.

deep *(adj)* — wide and impressive
✦ Professor Wilson's deep knowledge of African history is amazing.

asset *(n)* — an item owned by a person or company
✦ After the firm went out of business, its assets were sold to pay off its debts.

impact *(n)* — an influence or effect on something else
✦ Nobody knows what impact higher prices will have on the market.

record *(adj)* — highest or largest ever
✦ A record number of people have studied Chinese in recent years.

affect *(v)* — change or influence
✦ Their bread business had been strongly affected by high wheat prices.

manufacture *(v)* — make something (often in a factory)
✦ We don't do much manufacturing in South America yet, but we're planning to do so soon.

PHRASE BUILDING

branch out — expand into a new area or business field
✦ Before we branch out into delivering food, I think we should open several more restaurants.

change hands — change owners
✦ This warehouse has already changed hands three or four times.

shut down — close
✦ The health inspector forced the unsafe factory to shut down.

WHY DO WE SAY THAT?

change hands — When you give something to someone, you usually hand it to him or her. The item goes from your hands to the other person's hands—it changes hands. So, when we talk about a change of ownership for a company, asset, or other item, we say the thing "changes hands."

SENTENCE PATTERNS

In	*the natural resources industry,* *this business,* *our competitive field,*	mines and companies often change hands.

Along with its deep experience, BHP Billiton's size is	*a key advantage.* *a major benefit.* *another strength.*

WHAT PEOPLE ARE SAYING ABOUT BHP BILLITON

Phillip I worked for BHP for 25 years before the merger with Billiton. Now I still work for them. My father and his father before him also worked for BHP. The company has always taken care of my family. I can't imagine working anywhere else.

Yuan-feng I run a medium-sized business in Guangdong, China. We use a lot of raw materials to manufacture steel and other goods. I like buying from BHP Billiton. They can supply me with just about everything I need, which saves time and reduces shipping costs.

Tonya The world is using too many natural resources, too quickly. Companies like BHP Billiton are mining the world dry, and pretty soon there won't be anything left to dig up. And their operations disrupt the lives of native peoples while destroying the local environment. More needs to be done to balance profit-making with protecting the earth.

section 1
VOCABULARY AND PHRASE REVIEW

A. Complete each sentence, using the best word(s) from the box.

based	**revenue**	**decade**
asset	**unique**	**customer base**
costly	**bottom line**	**know-how**

1. The project will be _________, but I think the investment will be worth it.
2. Paul, you've been in the restaurant business for more than a(n) _________. What advice would you give someone who wants to open their own place?
3. Sales _________________ exceeded 10 million dollars this year, and profits are up 15 percent over last year.
4. Companies that are _________ in Berlin are in a good position to expand throughout Europe.
5. The Web site says it's a(n) _________________ design. They say they're the only company selling a car that can drive underwater.
6. After working in the field for 18 years, I've got all the _________ I need to open a computer store. I've learned a lot about running a successful business.
7. We appreciate your coming to us with your idea, but we have to consider our _____________, and it doesn't look like your project will be profitable for us.
8. This shopping mall is our biggest ____________. It's worth about $4 million.

B. Choose the best word(s) to complete each sentence.

1. Craig knows running his own hair salon will be hard, but he's _________ to succeed. He says he won't give up, no matter how many hours he has to work every day.

   A. determined B. competitive C. lucrative D. impressive

2. The _________ of the two construction giants will give the new company a 62 percent market share. Analysts believe it will be good for both companies.

   A. powerhouse B. acquisition C. merger D. turnaround

3. I'm not sure if it's the right time to _________ into Europe. We're using most of our resources to grow our domestic market share.

   A. expand B. capture C. affect D. sponsor

4. This radio is our ________ product. It's been our top seller for 12 years.

   A. impact B. equation C. concept D. flagship

5. Some movie stars eat here ________. Tourists always look in the window to try to see a celebrity.

   A. regularly B. largely C. boldly D. domestically

C. Match the beginning and ending of each sentence.

1. We've been trying for years to	such a huge house?
2. The TV's best feature is	it will certainly affect our business.
3. If the oil news is bad,	push our market share past 8 percent.
4. How were you able to afford	how can they keep from going out of business?
5. After those record losses,	that it lets you watch two shows at the same time.

D. Choose the best response to what the first person says.

1. **Tom:** We might have to raise prices by $25.

   A. Kate: Branching out into that type of product is a good idea.

   B. Kate: If high steel prices keep driving up our production costs, we won't have a choice.

   C. Kate: It's a good way to stay in touch with our customers.

2. **Li-fen:** Systemtech posted excellent profits again!

   A. Sam: Whatever happened to them? That company used to be flying high in the '90s.

   B. Sam: Ah, so that's why they had to shut down another factory.

   C. Sam: That's music to my ears. I have 1,000 shares of stock in the company.

3. **José:** Look at all these bills: electricity, insurance, supplies—they're eating away at my profits!

   A. Mandy: Good for you! The sky's the limit for you guys!

   B. Mandy: It might be time to head back to the office.

   C. Mandy: Is there anything you can do to lower those costs?

section 2
✦ FIVE BUSINESS FAILURES

TARGET VOCABULARY

account *(n)*	Chap. 8: Barings Bank
accurate *(adj)*	Chap. 10: Andersen
accused *(adj)*	Chap. 10: Andersen
appoint *(v)*	Chap. 8: Barings Bank
assure *(v)*	Chap. 10: Andersen
balance sheet *(n)*	Chap. 9: Enron
bankrupt *(adj)*	Chap. 7: Big Airlines
boost *(v)*	Chap. 9: Enron
burden *(n)*	Chap. 7: Big Airlines
collapse *(v)*	Chap. 9: Enron
consultant *(n)*	Chap. 10: Andersen
consumer *(n)*	Chap. 6: New Coke
disastrous *(adj)*	Chap. 9: Enron
disturbing *(adj)*	Chap. 6: New Coke
dramatic *(adj)*	Chap. 7: Big Airlines
emerge *(v)*	Chap. 7: Big Airlines
even *(adj)*	Chap. 6: New Coke
firm *(n)*	Chap. 8: Barings Bank
fold *(v)*	Chap. 7: Big Airlines
fond *(adj)*	Chap. 6: New Coke
forbidden *(adj)*	Chap. 9: Enron
global *(adj)*	Chap. 9: Enron
greed *(n)*	Chap. 8: Barings Bank
guilty *(adj)*	Chap. 8: Barings Bank
handful *(n)*	Chap. 7: Big Airlines
interfere *(v)*	Chap. 10: Andersen
investigate *(v)*	Chap. 10: Andersen
linked *(adj)*	Chap. 9: Enron

loyalty *(n)*	Chap. 6: New Coke
mark *(v)*	Chap. 6: New Coke
pension plan *(n)*	Chap. 7: Big Airlines
portfolio *(n)*	Chap. 9: Enron
profitable *(adj)*	Chap. 8: Barings Bank
rebound *(v)*	Chap. 9: Enron
reputation *(n)*	Chap. 8: Barings Bank
rival *(n)*	Chap. 6: New Coke
role *(n)*	Chap. 10: Andersen
ruin *(v)*	Chap. 8: Barings Bank
scandal *(n)*	Chap. 10: Andersen
securities *(n)*	Chap. 8: Barings Bank
settle *(v)*	Chap. 10: Andersen
sharply *(adv)*	Chap. 7: Big Airlines
strengthen *(v)*	Chap. 6: New Coke
struggle *(v)*	Chap. 7: Big Airlines
synonymous *(adj)*	Chap. 10: Andersen
thrilled *(adj)*	Chap. 6: New Coke
tragedy *(n)*	Chap. 9: Enron
trend *(n)*	Chap. 6: New Coke
unauthorized *(adj)*	Chap. 8: Barings Bank
undergo *(v)*	Chap. 7: Big Airlines

TARGET PHRASES

bow to	Chap. 6: New Coke
bring down	Chap. 8: Barings Bank
bring something to its knees	Chap. 6: New Coke
conflict of interest	Chap. 10: Andersen
cover up	Chap. 10: Andersen
cut back on	Chap. 7: Big Airlines
in short	Chap. 6: New Coke
in the red	Chap. 9: Enron
lead to	Chap. 9: Enron
lose ground	Chap. 8: Barings Bank
on the verge of	Chap. 9: Enron
step onto the stage	Chap. 7: Big Airlines
step up	Chap. 7: Big Airlines
turn sour	Chap. 10: Andersen
wake-up call	Chap. 8: Barings Bank

NEW COKE

READING PASSAGE

1985 was not a good year for Coca-Cola. It **marked** one of the greatest marketing failures in history: the replacement of the original Coke formula with a new one, usually called "New Coke." The reaction of American **consumers** was so strong that the mighty company was almost **brought to its knees**.

The change was no small decision by Coca-Cola. For 99 years, the Coke formula had stayed the same. Yet, beginning in the 1970s, the company started losing market share to its biggest **rival**, Pepsi. By 1984, sales of Coke and Pepsi were almost **even**.

In response to these **disturbing trends**, Coca-Cola developed a new, sweeter formula. It held almost 200,000 taste tests, with mostly positive results.

On April 23, 1985, the new formula hit the market. Many people liked the taste, but a growing number of consumers were upset that "their" Coca-Cola had been changed. Thousands of people wrote angry letters and telephoned the company, demanding that the original formula be brought back (see table). In songs, TV shows, newspapers, and magazines, people expressed their unhappiness with New Coke. In the meantime, Pepsi took over as the top soft drink in the country.

What happened? In blind taste tests, people preferred the new formula. What Coca-Cola did not consider was how strongly people were attached to the original taste and brand. Millions of consumers grew up drinking Coke, and they had **fond** memories of sharing the drink with friends and family members. **In short**, the original Coke was an important part of their lives, and people had an emotional attachment to the drink.

On July 10, less than three months after the release of New Coke, Coca-Cola admitted defeat and started selling the original formula (now called "Coca-Cola Classic") once again. Consumers were **thrilled** that such a large company had **bowed to** their wishes. They were also excited to have the old Coke back.

Coca-Cola Classic quickly rose to the top spot in the "cola wars" of the 1980s. And so, even though New Coke was a terrible disaster, it actually **strengthened** people's **loyalty** to the Coca-Cola brand. This was one case where admitting a mistake was clearly the best thing to do.

New Coke Fact Sheet

No. of years (before 1985) that Coca-Cola had slowly lost market share to Pepsi	15
No. of days that original Coke was off the market	79
Average daily no. of phone calls received by the Coca-Cola hotline before New Coke was released	400
Average daily no. of calls received in June 1985	1,500
No. of calls received in the two days after original Coke was brought back	31,600

COMPREHENSION CHECK

1. ( ) Why did Coca-Cola start selling New Coke?
   A. People were bored with the original drink.
   B. Consumers demanded that the company stop selling the original formula.
   C. It needed to do something to win back market share.
   D. In the early 1980s, Pepsi won about 200,000 new customers.

2. ( ) What happened shortly after New Coke hit the market?
   A. The drink became a top seller.
   B. It was clear that nobody liked the new taste.
   C. Many people went onto the Internet to complain about the drink.
   D. For a period of time, Coca-Cola's biggest competitor became the market leader.

3. ( ) The Coca-Cola hotline received ________.
   A. several hundred calls per day before 1985
   B. hundreds of thousands of calls two months after New Coke's release
   C. about 3,000 calls after bringing back the original formula
   D. the same number of calls before and after New Coke's release

4. ( ) What did Coca-Cola fail to consider before the release of New Coke?
   A. The growing popularity of other soft drinks
   B. The importance of the original formula to Coca-Cola drinkers
   C. The results of blind taste tests
   D. The loss of market share to Pepsi

5. ( ) What resulted from the release and failure of New Coke?
   A. Coca-Cola executives learned that taste tests weren't important.
   B. Most people gave up on drinking Coca-Cola products.
   C. The return of the original formula helped Coca-Cola win the cola wars.
   D. The company learned it should never admit its mistakes.

VOCABULARY BUILDING

mark *(v)* — signal a point when something happens
✦ Next Wednesday marks the start of our fifth year in business.

consumer *(n)* — someone who buys something
✦ Consumers usually look for the best product for the lowest price.

rival *(n)* — an opponent, competitor
✦ Our biggest rival, selling many of the same things we do, is a South American firm.

even *(adj)* — at the same level or amount
✦ Last year my sales totals were even with Greg's, but this year I'm ahead.

disturbing *(adj)* — causing bother or worry
✦ The state of the economy is disturbing, and consumer spending is still falling.

trend *(n)* — general direction
✦ With high oil prices, the trend is to build lighter, smaller cars.

fond *(adj)* — pleasant
✦ Many people have fond memories of their years as university students.

thrilled *(adj)* — very happy
✦ When Sherry heard the good news, she was thrilled.

strengthen *(v)* — make stronger
✦ Hiring a marketing expert will strengthen our sales team.

loyalty *(n)* — feeling of duty and faithfulness
✦ After 30 years at the company, Martin felt a sense of loyalty toward his boss.

PHRASE BUILDING

bring something/someone to its/his/her knees — cause to fail, lose, or give up
✦ Sometimes an excellent product from a small company can bring a larger rival to its knees.

in short — speaking briefly
✦ We need to make major changes here. In short, some jobs need to be cut.

bow to — do what someone else wants; give up; accept someone else's will or demand
✦ The airline bowed to customer demands and lowered prices.

WHY DO WE SAY THAT?

bring something/someone to its/his/her knees — When someone loses a fight, he or she may fall to his or her knees. The action is a sign of failure. So, when something brings a person, company, etc., to its knees, it causes the other side to fail. An example would be one company clearly beating another in a certain market.

SENTENCE PATTERNS

1985 was	*not a good year*	for Coca-Cola.
	a terrible year	
	a major turning point	

This was one case in which	admitting a mistake was clearly the best thing to do.
Given the situation,	
At the time,	

WHAT PEOPLE ARE SAYING ABOUT NEW COKE

Denise I remember when New Coke came out. People really hated it, and there were all sorts of jokes and news reports about how bad it was. I didn't think it was too bad, but I'm glad they brought back the original formula.

Paul My family and I were upset when Coca-Cola changed from old Coke to New Coke. I grew up drinking Coke with my parents and brother. It wasn't just a drink—it was more like a part of our family memories. The company was stupid to mess with the drink in the first place. They did the right thing when they started selling Coke Classic again.

Romeo I've always been a Pepsi drinker. I thought it was so funny to see Coke mess up so badly with New Coke. To tell the truth, I actually kind of liked it. It was sweeter than the original Coke. But I still preferred Pepsi.

chapter 7

BIG AIRLINES IN BIG TROUBLE

READING PASSAGE

In recent years, the business world has **undergone** major changes. Giants in the banking, electronics, and other industries that once stood as tall as mountains have fallen. One of the most **dramatic** scenes has been the fight for the skies. **Bankrupt** and beaten down, many of America's oldest airline companies (often called "legacy airlines") are **struggling** to survive.

At one time, a **handful** of these airlines, including United, Delta, and Northwest, were the kings of the skies. Confident and powerful, they brought in healthy profits as air travel spread.

The late 20th century, however, wasn't so kind to the legacy airlines. Their management, labor, and cost structures were becoming major **burdens**. At the same time, several smart, younger companies, like Southwest and JetBlue, **stepped onto the stage**.

Running an airline is no easy task. Besides buying and maintaining airplanes, renting space at airports, and paying for security, airlines spend a lot of money on fuel and labor. Oil prices have risen **sharply** since 1998 (see chart). Meanwhile, legacy airlines have labor costs and **pension plans** that total billions of dollars per year. Add in the competition from low-cost airlines, and things start to look really bad. Indeed, between 2001 and 2004, U.S. airlines lost a combined $32.3 billion. When losses are that large, companies start to **fold**.

In 2002, both US Airways and United Airlines went bankrupt. US Airways soon **emerged** from its debts, but it filed for bankruptcy again in 2004. The following year, with oil at $70 a barrel, Northwest and Delta both declared bankruptcy.

Trying to regain their financial health, the legacy airlines have made a number of moves. Changes include cutting salaries, simplifying the ticket pricing system, and installing "self-check-in" counters at airports. Airlines are also **cutting back on** the amount of food and drink that passengers are given during flights.

Will these moves be enough to save the big airlines from completely disappearing? Or will one or more of the smaller airlines **step up** to become the new kings of the sky? In these troubling times, there are no easy answers.

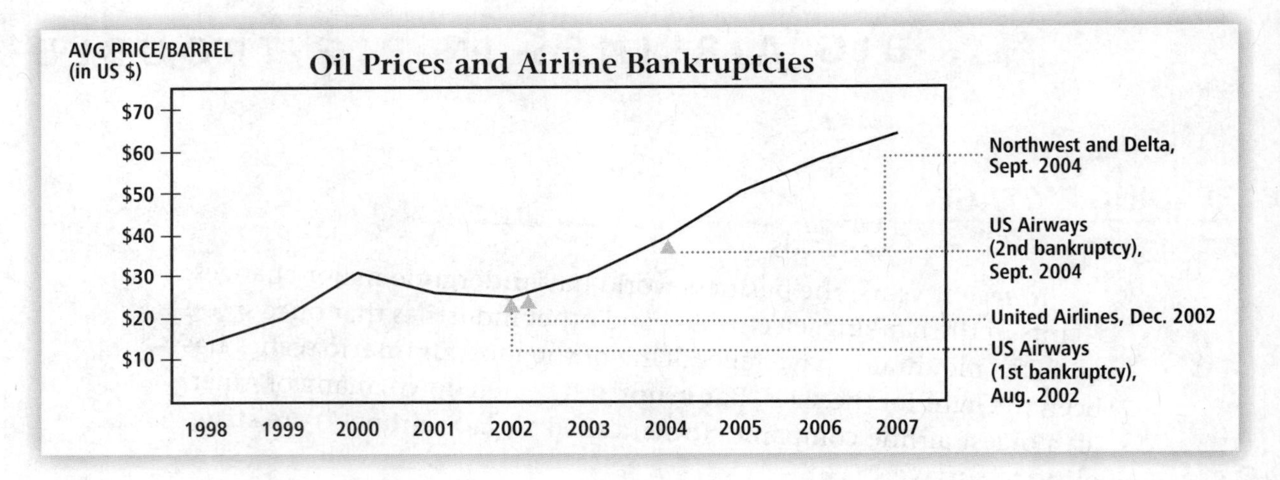

COMPREHENSION CHECK

1. ( ) What is the main idea?
   A. Southwest is a more efficient company than Northwest.
   B. These days, no company is safe, no matter how old it is.
   C. Legacy airlines must meet a number of challenges to stay in business.
   D. The high price of oil is a problem for companies in many industries.

2. ( ) What does "cutting" in the second sentence of paragraph six mean?
   A. inserting
   B. taking apart
   C. separating
   D. reducing

3. ( ) In the year of US Airways' second bankruptcy, _________.
   A. oil cost about 30 percent more than it did the previous year
   B. United Airlines also went bankrupt
   C. oil cost more than $50 per barrel
   D. it was not the only airline to go bankrupt

4. ( ) Which of the following changes by legacy airlines is not mentioned?
   A. Giving passengers less to eat
   B. Allowing passengers to check in at home
   C. Making the ticket pricing method less complicated
   D. Lowering wages

5. ( ) What does the article suggest about the future?
   A. It's hard to say whether the big airlines will be able to stay alive.
   B. It's likely the smaller carriers will become the new market leaders.
   C. If oil prices stay very high, several legacy airlines will disappear.
   D. Cost cutting by the legacy airlines will allow them to stay in business.

VOCABULARY BUILDING

undergo *(v)* — experience; go through
✦ Next year, the entrance test will undergo a complete revision.

bankrupt *(adj)* — without any money
✦ If a troubled company is not able to borrow money, it may go bankrupt.

struggle *(v)* — work hard to deal with a difficult problem
✦ Poor families often struggle to pay their monthly bills.

handful *(n)* — a small amount or number
✦ Only a handful of people earn a billion dollars a year.

burden *(n)* — a great weight or source of trouble
✦ High management salaries can be a burden to companies of any size.

dramatic *(adj)* — sudden or surprising
✦ The improvement of Russia's economy in recent years has been dramatic.

sharply *(adv)* — suddenly and seriously
✦ After the CEO admitted he was stealing from the company, the company's stock fell sharply.

pension plan *(n)* — a system of retirement benefits
✦ A company may require that you work for 20 years to qualify for its pension plan.

fold *(v)* — go out of business
✦ When a large company folds, thousands of people may lose their jobs.

emerge *(v)* — come out (from)
✦ It could take years for the economy to emerge from its troubled state.

PHRASE BUILDING

cut back on — reduce
✦ By turning off lights when you leave a room, you can cut back on energy use.

step up — take a more active or leading role
✦ After Laura's father retired, she stepped up to direct more of the company's operations.

step onto the stage — begin participating in an area or field
✦ A wealthy businessperson who steps onto the stage in a small field can have a big impact on the industry.

WHY DO WE SAY THAT?

step onto the stage — In a play, when an actor or actress enters a scene, he or she walks onto a stage. So, when we say a person (or company) steps onto the stage, we mean he or she starts participating actively in a field, business, or industry.

SENTENCE PATTERNS

In recent years, the business world has *undergone* major changes.
experienced
gone through

Running an airline is no easy task.
Starting a business
Earning a million dollars

WHAT PEOPLE ARE SAYING ABOUT BIG AIRLINES

Joon Han I often fly on Northwest and I have a lot of frequent-flyer miles that I haven't used yet. My biggest worry is that they'll cancel the frequent-flyer program. I'm trying to get time off from work so I can actually use these miles while I can!

Oscar I'm not loyal to any airline. Whenever I fly, I look for the cheapest ticket I can get. So personally it doesn't bother me when an airline goes under. But I do feel bad for all the people who lost their jobs.

Francis I don't like the way all the airlines are getting so cheap with everything. The last flight I took, all I got to eat was a pack of peanuts. I understand they're trying to save money, but sometimes they go too far. Of course, the small airlines do this as well. I guess flying isn't what it used to be.

chapter 8

THE FALL OF BARINGS BANK

READING PASSAGE

Is it possible for one employee to **bring down** an entire bank? Indeed it is. In 1995, England's Barings Bank, founded in 1762, was **ruined** by the actions of one trader: Nick Leeson. It's an amazing story of **greed**, poor management, and risky business.

Leeson started working at Barings' Singapore office in 1992. A rising star in the company, he was **appointed** general manager of the office. He also became the head trader, giving him a lot of power—perhaps too much. The young star quickly earned a **reputation** as an excellent **securities** trader who delivered big profits.

Leeson reported profits of nearly £9 million in 1993, which earned him a bonus of £130,000. The numbers were even better in 1994, and Barings considered giving him a bonus of £450,000. Everything looked great on paper. Unfortunately, the profits reported by Leeson didn't exist. Unknown to Barings, Leeson's trading activity was actually losing the bank millions of pounds (see table).

What was going on? Shortly after arriving in Singapore, Leeson had started making **unauthorized**, high-risk trades in the Japanese market. He quickly lost money, but he hid the losses in an **account**—Error Account 88888—instead of reporting them. Leeson then made trades between that account and three other Barings accounts. This type of "cross-trade" made those three accounts look **profitable**.

By the end of 1994, Leeson had lost hundreds of millions of pounds. Things got even worse the following year, as the Japanese stock market continued to **lose ground**. By February 1995, Barings had finally discovered what was going on, but it was too late. Their total losses from Leeson's activities were £827 million, more than the bank could cover.

Leeson was found **guilty** of fraud and spent 3½ years in a Singapore prison. Barings, the 233-year-old bank whose customers included the Queen of England, went out of business. The bank was later bought for just £1 by ING, a Dutch bank. It was a sad ending for the once-proud **firm**. It was also a **wake-up call** to other banks to improve the way they managed risks and traders.

Nick Leeson's Reported vs. Actual Profits and Losses

YEAR	REPORTED PROFIT/LOSS	ACTUAL PROFIT/LOSS
1993	+ £8.83 million	– £21 million
1994	+ £28.53 million	– £185 million
1995	+ £18.57 million	– £619 million

COMPREHENSION CHECK

1. ( ) When Leeson started working in Singapore, ________.
   A. he was highly thought of by his company
   B. Barings was careful to limit the amount of power he had
   C. he reported directly to the office's general manager
   D. the bank did not expect him to report profits anytime soon

2. ( ) What does the article suggest about the amount of power given to Leeson?
   A. He was a suitable person to handle so many responsibilities.
   B. He may have been given too much power.
   C. As Leeson was a rising star, he needed to have a lot of power.
   D. Leeson deserved a chance to perform his various tasks.

3. ( ) Why did Barings consider giving Leeson a £450,000 bonus?
   A. The bank thought a loss of £180 million was acceptable.
   B. Leeson had done a good job telling the bank about its heavy losses.
   C. The bank thought he had earned nearly £30 million for them that year.
   D. Leeson had hidden the fact that he lost £21 million in 1994.

4. ( ) Which of the following is true?
   A. ING went bankrupt from the losses caused by Leeson.
   B. At the end of 1994, Leeson told Barings the truth about his losses.
   C. Leeson went to jail for his crime.
   D. Leeson reported his actual losses on a yearly basis.

5. ( ) According to the article, what might other banks learn from the Barings scandal?
   A. Everything about the banking business is risky these days.
   B. Banks need to keep a closer watch on the actions of their traders.
   C. Many traders are trying to cheat their employers.
   D. Banks should not be concerned about making a profit.

VOCABULARY BUILDING

account *(n)* — a set of financial records for a single customer, or the customer itself
✦ He had spent the entire afternoon checking his clients' accounts for errors.

ruin *(v)* — destroy
✦ If a bicycle is left outside, bad weather can ruin it over time.

appoint *(v)* — assign
✦ Who should we appoint to act as the secretary?

reputation *(n)* — the general way a person is regarded
✦ Luis has a reputation for working quickly yet accurately.

securities *(n)* — financial products such as stocks and bonds
✦ These days, it's easy to buy and sell securities on the Internet.

unauthorized *(adj)* — not allowed
✦ Police think someone gained unauthorized access to the building.

profitable *(adj)* — earning money
✦ To remain profitable, a business needs to control its monthly expenses.

greed *(n)* — a very strong desire for money
✦ Almost all business scandals are the result of greed.

guilty *(adj)* — at fault for something
✦ If he isn't guilty, why did he have a gun in his car?

firm *(n)* — a company or business
✦ There are two firms in this city that import furniture from India.

PHRASE BUILDING

bring down — cause to fail
✦ It usually takes more than one unsuccessful product to bring down a company.

lose ground — decrease in performance level
✦ I guarantee you: Unless we cut prices to match the competition, we will lose ground to them.

wake-up call — a sign that it's time to take action
✦ The poor quarterly results were a wake-up call for the firm to improve its marketing efforts.

WHY DO WE SAY THAT?

wake-up call — At a hotel, you ask for a wake-up call so you can get up on time. So when we talk about a "wake-up call" anywhere else, we're referring to something that makes you aware of a problem or danger, and tells you to do something about it. Perhaps you were delaying or ignoring something, but now it's time to act.

SENTENCE PATTERNS

Everything looked great	*on paper.*
	until we closely examined the numbers.
	at first glance.

It was	*a sad*	ending for the once proud firm.
	an unfortunate	
	a sorry	

WHAT PEOPLE ARE SAYING ABOUT BARINGS BANK

Ben I find it hard to believe that one trader could do so much damage. But it's not only his fault. The way I see it, there should have been a better system of management, to prevent or handle that kind of problem before it got out of control.

Sonia The story about that guy made me so angry. He made all that money from bonuses, but he was doing a terrible job while lying to his company. It's like he doesn't have a conscience. He caused a lot of people to lose their jobs. I don't know how he can sleep at night.

Kwan Yip Less than four years in jail for causing a company to lose a billion dollars and go bankrupt . . . That's a pretty light punishment, if you ask me. If punishments for major crimes are so light, other criminals won't be afraid of committing similar crimes themselves.

chapter 9

A BANKRUPTCY OF TRUST, 1: ENRON

READING PASSAGE

Trust. It's a big part of our lives. We place trust in our doctors, teachers, and employers, and when a bond of trust is broken the results can be **disastrous**. When that happened at Enron, once one of the world's largest companies, thousands of employees and investors saw their lives ruined. This is a true story of corporate greed that ended in bankruptcy and **tragedy**.

Enron was once a leader in the **global** energy business, with assets in the billions. In the 1990s, however, some of the company's divisions were losing money. Enron executives feared the stock price would fall if the truth about the losses became known.

To make their **balance sheets** look better, executives moved losses and debts over to a large number of partnerships. This made it look like Enron was earning a lot more money than it actually was, which helped **boost** Enron's stock price. The trickery also **led to** large executive bonuses, which were **linked** to the company's stock price. In 2000 and 2001, while the company was **in the red**, executives took home some $400 million worth of bonuses!

The story gets worse. As the stock started falling in 2001 from a high point of $90, executives sold more than $1 billion worth of stock. Yet employees were **forbidden** to sell the Enron stock in their retirement **portfolios**. Executives even encouraged employees to buy more Enron stock, telling them it was **on the verge of rebounding**!

But it wasn't. On December 2, 2001, Enron filed for bankruptcy. With assets of $62.8 billion, it was (at the time) the largest bankruptcy in U.S. history, and the company's stock lost almost all its value (see chart). Thousands of employees who held Enron stock lost their life savings, as well as their pensions. Investors also suffered from the stock's **collapse**.

The fall of Enron was a complete failure: to the company, its employees, and its investors. It made the public and government mistrustful of the way corporations report their earnings and the way they pay their executives. In fact, as Enron fell, it also brought down its accounting firm: Arthur Andersen. For that story, read Part 2 of "A Bankruptcy of Trust."

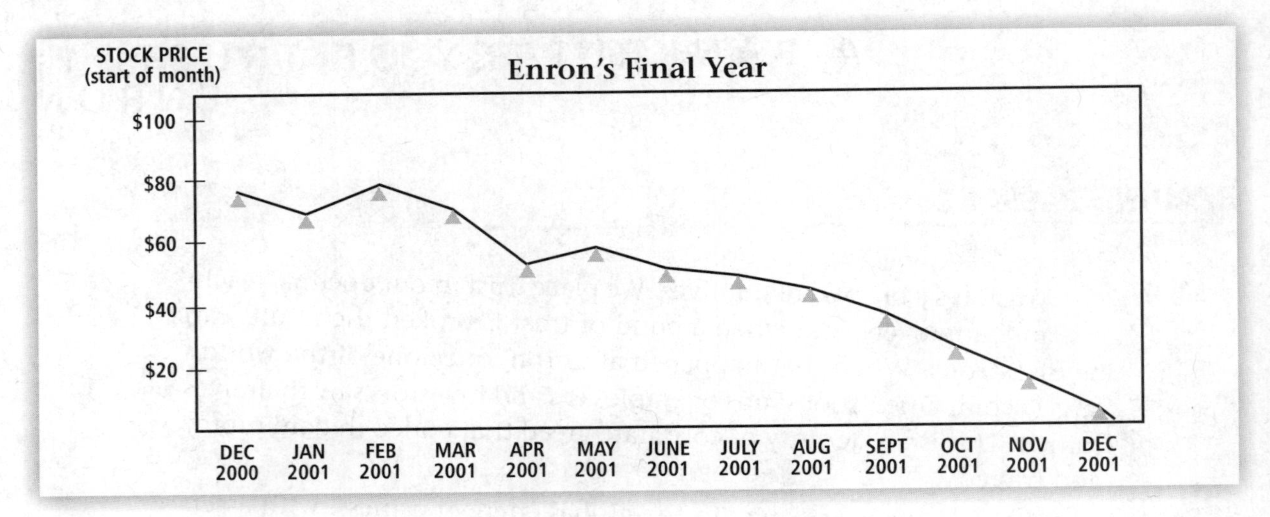

COMPREHENSION CHECK

1. ( ) Why did Enron executives start moving debts to partnerships?
   A. All of the company's divisions were in the red.
   B. It's a common practice by executives in large companies.
   C. They were worried about Enron's stock price.
   D. They were afraid of losing their jobs.

2. ( ) How were Enron executives able to earn $400 million worth of bonuses?
   A. By keeping the company out of the red
   B. By maintaining a high stock price
   C. By selling large lots of Enron shares
   D. By being honest about the company's financial health

3. ( ) Which of the following is true about Enron's stock?
   A. Between the start of June 2001 and November 2001, it fell by $34.
   B. Enron employees were encouraged to sell it when it hit $79.
   C. It fell every month from January 2001 to December 2001.
   D. Its sharpest month-to-month fall was from September 2001 to October 2001.

4. ( ) Which group of people is not mentioned as suffering from Enron's collapse?
   A. Employees with pension plans at Enron
   B. Enron executives who had received bonuses
   C. Investors in Enron
   D. Employees who had bought Enron stock

5. ( ) According to the article, what was a result of the Enron scandal?
   A. Companies stopped giving executives bonuses.
   B. It made people question the earnings reports of other corporations.
   C. It caused investors to be mistrustful of the government.
   D. Arthur Andersen took control of Enron.

VOCABULARY BUILDING

disastrous *(adj)* — terrible; extremely bad
✦ The trip to Europe was disastrous. Nothing went as planned.

tragedy *(n)* — a very sad event
✦ If Rita quit, it would be a tragedy. Nobody could replace her.

global *(adj)* — worldwide
✦ Global companies succeed by having local sales forces in many countries.

balance sheet *(n)* — a statement showing a company's profits, losses, assets, and debts
✦ Twice a year, we send investors a copy of our balance sheet.

boost *(v)* — cause to increase
✦ Good managers know how to help boost employees' confidence.

linked *(adj)* — connected
✦ Since your accounts are linked, you can transfer money between them.

forbidden *(adj)* — not allowed
✦ Access to that room is forbidden to everyone but senior management.

rebound *(v)* — recover; return to a better situation
✦ After falling for three straight years, the stock market finally rebounded.

collapse *(v)* — fall sharply; fail
✦ I don't think the dollar will collapse, but it might lose some of its value.

portfolio *(n)* — a group of investments (such as stocks and bonds)
✦ Experts suggest we should hold a mix of small and large companies in our portfolios.

PHRASE BUILDING

lead to — result in
✦ News of the accident led to a review of the factory's safety procedures.

in the red — losing money
✦ We're not in the red, but we're not making a huge amount of money either.

on the verge of — close to
✦ Experts believe Radioland is on the verge of going bankrupt.

WHY DO WE SAY THAT?

in the red — When recording numbers in an accounts book, it's common to use red ink to write negative numbers. So, if a company is "in the red," that means it's losing money. (We say a company is "in the black" if it's earning money.)

SENTENCE PATTERNS

The	*story gets*	worse.
	situation is going from bad to	
	problem might even become	

Investors	*also suffered from*	the stock's collapse.
	were hit hard by	
	did not expect	

WHAT PEOPLE ARE SAYING ABOUT ENRON

Trent My cousin knew somebody who worked at Enron. The guy even told my cousin to buy Enron stock right before the company went bankrupt. Fortunately he didn't!

Phoebe It just goes to show you can't trust big corporations. They're only interested in making a lot of money and keeping their stock price high. They don't care about the people who work there, and they sure don't care about things like honesty and responsibility.

Ernesto I noticed that, after the Enron case, companies were a lot more careful about how they reported their earnings. Investors also became more careful about putting their money in high-quality companies. Of course, there's no way of knowing if there are more Enrons waiting to happen. But I have to think it's less likely now.

chapter 10

A BANKRUPTCY OF TRUST, 2: ARTHUR ANDERSEN

READING PASSAGE

Accounting firms often audit the records of public companies, making sure the balance sheets are in order. This **assures** investors that the company's figures are **accurate**. But what happens when the accountant itself loses the public's trust? That's what happened with Arthur Andersen. Once a very successful accounting firm, it was brought to ruin by its involvement with Enron (see previous story to read about Enron's fall).

When Arthur Andersen himself ran the company in the early 20th century, its reputation was built on trust and honesty. And for many years after Mr. Andersen's death in 1947, the firm continued to be highly respected.

Things started to **turn sour** in the 1990s, with legal trouble related to clients' accounting problems. After the collapse of Sunbeam Corporation in 1998, Andersen paid $110 million to **settle** lawsuits. Then in 2001, Andersen paid $7 million to settle suits involving another client, Waste Management. But those were nothing compared to the Enron **scandal**.

In October 2001, as the U.S. government started to **investigate** Enron, staff at Arthur Andersen destroyed thousands of Enron-related files (see timetable). The government charged Arthur Andersen with obstruction of justice (**interfering** with an investigation). The firm was **accused** of **covering up** its involvement with Enron's activities.

A key issue in the scandal was Arthur Andersen's two **roles** at Enron. Andersen had not only acted as Enron's accountant; it was also a **consultant** for the energy giant. Many people saw this as a **conflict of interest**. How can you work as an independent accountant while advising the client about ways to save or earn money?

In June 2002, Arthur Andersen was found guilty of obstruction of justice. The firm had to give up its license to perform audits for public companies. It soon lost most of its clients, and most of its 28,000 U.S. employees lost their jobs.

Several years later, in May 2005, the decision against Arthur Andersen was overturned by the U.S. Supreme Court. By then, however, the firm was down to just 200 employees, and its reputation was ruined. Arthur Andersen's name, once **synonymous** with corporate trust, was now, to many people, synonymous with corporate greed.

Four Weeks of Scandal in 2001	
Oct. 12	Andersen employees receive e-mail that they believe is a signal to start destroying Enron-related files
Oct. 22	Securities and Exchange Commission (SEC) starts investigation of Enron
Oct. 23	Andersen employees speed up destruction of files
Oct. 31	SEC investigation of Enron is made public
Nov. 9	Andersen tells employees not to destroy any more files

COMPREHENSION CHECK

1. ( ) What does the article reveal about the Enron scandal?
   A. It was not the first time Andersen had been in legal trouble.
   B. For Andersen, it was not as serious as the collapse of Sunbeam Corporation.
   C. It was Andersen's biggest scandal in the 1990s.
   D. It was the first of a series of scandals involving Andersen.

2. ( ) The government accused Andersen of ________.
   A. destroying documents to protect Enron
   B. covering up the government's involvement with Enron
   C. starting its own investigation of Enron
   D. trying to hide its role in the Enron scandal

3. ( ) When were Andersen employees told to stop destroying Enron-related files?
   A. A couple of weeks after the file destruction began
   B. Several days after the SEC started investigating Enron
   C. One week after employees began speeding up the destruction of files
   D. Nearly a month after the file destruction began

4. ( ) What does "charged" in the fourth paragraph mean?
   A. accused
   B. ran at
   C. filled with electricity
   D. asked

5. ( ) What resulted from the Supreme Court's reversal of the ruling against Andersen?
   A. The company's 28,000 employees got their jobs back.
   B. Most of Andersen's previous clients hired the firm back.
   C. Very little, since the company had already been seriously hurt.
   D. Andersen once again had an excellent reputation.

VOCABULARY BUILDING

assure *(v)* — convince someone about a matter
✦ I assure you we're doing everything we can to solve the problem.

accurate *(adj)* — correct
✦ What he told you is accurate: The restaurant will be moving to another location.

settle *(v)* — resolve
✦ Lawyers help people settle legal matters that they can't resolve on their own.

scandal *(n)* — a shocking event that causes people to be surprised or upset
✦ When the movie star had an affair with someone else's wife, it was a huge scandal.

investigate *(v)* — research; look into
✦ The building manager called someone to investigate the strange sounds.

interfere *(v)* — disrupt or get involved in someone else's matters
✦ I know you're his friend, but you shouldn't interfere in his personal life.

accused *(adj)* — charged with doing something
✦ Loretta was accused of cheating on the test, but she said she didn't do anything wrong.

role *(n)* — a position, including a set of responsibilities
✦ My main role is company treasurer, but I have several other duties as well.

consultant *(n)* — a person who gives advice to a person, company, etc.
✦ The consultant we hired advised us to improve our product packaging.

synonymous *(adj)* — meaning the same thing
✦ "Big" and "wide" are not synonymous.

PHRASE BUILDING

turn sour — go bad
✦ Things at Liston Construction turned sour after Bob Liston Jr. took over the company.

cover up — hide the truth about something bad
✦ When people hear about a company covering up bad news, they usually punish the company's stock prices.

conflict of interest — a situation in which a person holds more than one job, and one of the jobs may influence the other

✦ Government workers don't usually keep private jobs, since they could easily be accused of having a conflict of interest.

WHY DO WE SAY THAT?

turn sour — When a drink such as milk goes bad, we say it becomes sour. So, when a situation in life goes bad, we may say it "turns sour."

SENTENCE PATTERNS

This assures investors that	*the company's figures are*	accurate.
	all the information is	
	the reports they received are	

But what	*happens*	when the accountant itself loses the public's trust?
	do you do	
	about	

WHAT PEOPLE ARE SAYING ABOUT ARTHUR ANDERSEN

Samantha It was one thing when Enron went bankrupt, but the Arthur Andersen scandal was something else altogether. I mean, we don't trust corporations anyway, which is why they use outside auditors. Then we find out the auditors themselves are dirty. Who's left to trust?

Ichiro It seems people these days only care about money. I understand companies have pressure on them to make money, but they shouldn't forget their values. Maybe I'm old-fashioned, but I think companies like Arthur Andersen have a deep responsibility to society. They shouldn't only focus on getting rich.

Julio I don't think people should blame everyone who worked at Arthur Andersen. It was probably just a few managers making bad decisions. Most people are good at heart. I just hope all those people who lost their jobs were able to find work again quickly.

VOCABULARY AND PHRASE REVIEW

A. Complete each sentence, using the best word from the box.

appoint	**guilty**	**portfolio**
tragedy	**dramatic**	**accurate**
handful	**account**	**interfere**

1. That's a private matter between Jake and Caroline. I don't think you should _______________ in it.
2. There are only a(n) _______________ of cans left, so if you want one, you'd better buy it now.
3. I have a few large companies in my _______________, but I mostly invest in smaller firms.
4. The car accident was a(n) _______________. What a terrible loss for the family.
5. Are you sure these numbers are _______________? It was my understanding that our debt had fallen below $100,000.
6. There are some interesting possibilities for us in Turkey. I'd like to _______________ Steve to research the market there.
7. She had wasted most of every workday that week dealing with the problems in one small _______________.
8. We all noticed a _______________ improvement in her dress and appearance.

B. Choose the best word to complete each sentence.

1. When we studied the records, several accounting errors _______________.

   A. settled B. ruined C. interfered D. collapsed

2. Once the news is released, it's going to have a(n) __________ effect on the stock price. I wouldn't be surprised to see it fall 20 percent in one day.

   A. profitable B. bankrupt C. disastrous D. unauthorized

3. Personally, I feel we should go with Weston Building. They've got a great __________ for doing top-quality work.

   A. loyalty B. burden C. scandal D. reputation

4. Mr. Landon, I __________ you we're doing everything we can to find your missing dog.

   A. emerge B. assure C. strengthen D. struggle

5. Basically, my _________ here is to find out what our customers are saying on the Internet and decide how to use that information to improve our products.

   A. role B. consumer C. rival D. trend

C. Match the beginning and ending of each sentence.

1. We have to work here for 30 years	to enter this area.
2. I'm sorry, but visitors are forbidden	are investigating the fire.
3. Maybe we should hire a consultant	you decided to come work with us.
4. I've been told the police	to advise us what to do.
5. We're all so thrilled that	to qualify for the pension plan.

D. Choose the best response to what the first person says.

1. **Melissa:** Our second-quarter results were down. That makes three quarters of losses in a row.

   A. Susan: That sounds like a serious conflict of interest.

   B. Susan: Things are good now, but they could turn sour anytime.

   C. Susan: So, we're still in the red.

2. **Ryan:** The research stage is nearly complete. Hopefully we can move on to product development later this year.

   A. Fernando: If this works out, we could be on the verge of a very important breakthrough.

   B. Fernando: That's a real wake-up call. Nobody knew things were this bad.

   C. Fernando: Are you sure you can manage that type of cover-up?

3. **Kenji:** The X350 is incredible. The system is going to sell so well, it will bring the competition to its knees!

   A. Christopher: Finally they won't have to bow to us anymore.

   B. Christopher: Do you really think we can bring down Alpha Systems? The X350 is going to be amazing, for sure, but Alpha is a huge company.

   C. Christopher: We can't keep losing ground like this. Our investors are worried we don't have any hot products.

section 3
✦ FIVE BUSINESS PEOPLE

TARGET VOCABULARY

accomplishment *(n)*	Chap. 11: R. Branson	**elegant** *(adj)*	Chap. 12: Donna Karan
achieve *(v)*	Chap. 11: R. Branson	**empire** *(n)*	Chap. 13: Wang Y.-c.
affluent *(adj)*	Chap. 11: R. Branson	**enormous** *(adj)*	Chap. 11: R. Branson
ambitious *(adj)*	Chap. 11: R. Branson	**ethical** *(adj)*	Chap. 14: A. Roddick
bear *(v)*	Chap. 12: Donna Karan	**eventually** *(adv)*	Chap. 14: A. Roddick
booming *(adj)*	Chap. 15: Azim Premji	**fiscal year** *(n)*	Chap. 15: Azim Premji
charity *(n)*	Chap. 11: R. Branson	**focus** *(v)*	Chap. 15: Azim Premji
community *(n)*	Chap. 14: A. Roddick	**franchise** *(n)*	Chap. 14: A. Roddick
concerned *(adj)*	Chap. 15: Azim Premji	**frugal** *(adj)*	Chap. 13: Wang Y.-c.
contribute *(v)*	Chap. 14: A. Roddick	**ingenuity** *(n)*	Chap. 15: Azim Premji
core *(adj)*	Chap. 14: A. Roddick	**ingredient** *(n)*	Chap. 14: A. Roddick
diverse *(adj)*	Chap. 13: Wang Y.-c.	**inspiration** *(n)*	Chap. 12: Donna Karan
diversify *(v)*	Chap. 15: Azim Premji	**launch** *(v)*	Chap. 12: Donna Karan
efficient *(adj)*	Chap. 12: Donna Karan	**mission** *(n)*	Chap. 12: Donna Karan

native *(adj)*	Chap. 14: A. Roddick	**significant** *(adj)*	Chap. 11: R. Branson
numerous *(adj)*	Chap. 13: Wang Y.-c.	**slew** *(n)*	Chap. 12: Donna Karan
opportunity *(n)*	Chap. 13: Wang Y.-c.	**steer** *(v)*	Chap. 15: Azim Premji
oppose *(v)*	Chap. 14: A. Roddick	**symbolize** *(v)*	Chap. 12: Donna Karan
outsource *(v)*	Chap. 15: Azim Premji	**teenager** *(n)*	Chap. 11: R. Branson
poverty *(n)*	Chap. 13: Wang Y.-c.	**tireless** *(adj)*	Chap. 13: Wang Y.-c.
release *(v)*	Chap. 11: R. Branson	**track record** *(n)*	Chap. 13: Wang Y.-c.
rural *(adj)*	Chap. 14: A. Roddick	**trademark** *(n)*	Chap. 12: Donna Karan
scramble *(v)*	Chap. 15: Azim Premji	**tremendously** *(adv)*	Chap. 13: Wang Y.-c.
shareholder *(n)*	Chap. 15: Azim Premji	**venture** *(n)*	Chap. 13: Wang Y.-c.
shooting star *(n)*	Chap. 12: Donna Karan		

TARGET PHRASES

a string of	Chap. 11: R. Branson	**jump at**	Chap. 13: Wang Y.-c.
appeal to	Chap. 12: Donna Karan	**on one's mind**	Chap. 12: Donna Karan
at the helm	Chap. 15: Azim Premji	**on the other hand**	Chap. 11: R. Branson
carry out	Chap. 14: A. Roddick	**put up**	Chap. 15: Azim Premji
deal with	Chap. 14: A. Roddick	**rise through the ranks**	Chap. 12: Donna Karan
get a foothold in	Chap. 13: Wang Y.-c.	**set up**	Chap. 13: Wang Y.-c.
go on to	Chap. 11: R. Branson	**under way**	Chap. 11: R. Branson
go out of one's way	Chap. 14: A. Roddick		
have nothing to do with	Chap. 15: Azim Premji		

chapter 11

RICHARD BRANSON: THE BOLD BILLIONAIRE

READING PASSAGE

Not many people can say they've "done it all." Richard Branson, **on the other hand**, quite possibly has. He has **achieved** an amazing level of personal and professional success, and he has done it all with a smile.

Branson, born in England in 1950, seemed to be in a hurry to get his career **under way**. In the late 1960s, as a **teenager**, he started *Student Magazine*. Just a few years later, he founded Virgin Records. That was Branson's first major success, as the very first record **released** by the company sold more than 5 million copies! Over the years, the company signed superstar after superstar and **went on to** become one of the world's most successful record labels.

Virgin Records was only the beginning for the **ambitious** young Brit. In 1984, he founded Virgin Atlantic Airways. By providing excellent service at low prices, the company quickly grew to become one of England's largest.

Following his many interests, Branson has opened **a string of** companies (more than 200 so far!) selling everything from books to wine to vacation packages (see table). One of his most ambitious companies, Virgin Galactic, has plans to take people on trips into space!

Speaking of the sky, Branson's personal interests are also related to flying. He has invested a **significant** amount of time and money (while risking his personal safety) chasing some of aviation's greatest goals. In 1987, he became the first person to cross the Atlantic Ocean in a hot-air balloon. In 1991, he crossed the Pacific Ocean in a balloon, traveling at speeds faster than any balloon in history. These are just two of a long list of aviation **accomplishments**. Not bad for one of the world's most **affluent** people!

Just when you think you've seen it all from Richard Branson, there's something more to discover. His **charity** work with the Virgin Healthcare Foundation and the International Rescue Corps is impressive. He has written several books and has even been knighted by the Queen of England. With a list of achievements like that, it's not surprising that, in nearly every photo of this bold billionaire, he has an **enormous** smile on his face.

Some Pieces of the Virgin Puzzle		
ENTERTAINMENT	**TRAVEL**	**FINANCE**
Virgin Megastores (retail stores) Virgin Books (book publishing) Virgin Radio (radio station)	Virgin Atlantic (air travel) Virgin Vacations (vacation planning) Virgin Galactic (space travel) Virgin Balloon Flights (rides in hot-air balloons)	Virgin Credit Card (credit cards) Virgin Money (loans, life insurance, etc.)

COMPREHENSION CHECK

1. ( ) The article suggests that Richard Branson is a ________ person.
   A. cautious
   B. selfish
   C. daring
   D. frustrated

2. ( ) How did Branson react to his early success with Virgin Records?
   A. He slowed down his business efforts.
   B. He expanded his activities into new areas.
   C. He became more careful about the way he invested his money.
   D. He felt he didn't have anything left to accomplish.

3. ( ) What does the article imply about Branson's achievements as a pilot?
   A. He only had two important aviation accomplishments.
   B. He only had so much success because he was rich.
   C. He was more concerned about his safety than anything else.
   D. He had other successes besides those listed in the article.

4. ( ) What does "signed" in the second paragraph mean?
   A. wrote
   B. contracted
   C. listed
   D. indicated

5. ( ) Which of the following is *not* true?
   A. Virgin Atlantic quickly grew because of its luxury services.
   B. One of the Virgin Group's companies provides loan services.
   C. The Virgin Group's travel services are not limited to airplane tickets.
   D. Richard Branson has flown across more than one ocean.

VOCABULARY BUILDING

achieve *(v)* — obtain; reach a point or level
✦ To achieve success in school, it's important to attend classes and study hard.

teenager *(n)* — a person between 13 and 19 years of age
✦ This mall is popular with local teenagers.

release *(v)* — begin selling; put on the market
✦ Companies like to release hot new products a few months before Christmas.

ambitious *(adj)* — having big plans and goals; wanting to be successful
✦ Ambitious people often rise quickly in a company.

significant *(adj)* — very important
✦ Doctors say the research is significant and could lead to new treatments.

accomplishment *(n)* — an achievement; something you have done which is significant or makes you proud
✦ Running a successful business for 10 years has been my greatest accomplishment.

affluent *(adj)* — rich
✦ Experts say that knowing how to manage your money is key to becoming affluent.

charity *(n)* — a group that volunteers to help people, animals, or other causes
✦ Once a year, Sheila donates money to several charities.

enormous *(adj)* — very large
✦ There's an enormous mouse running loose in the kitchen!

PHRASE BUILDING

on the other hand — however
✦ This would be a great place for the party. On the other hand, it is expensive.

go on to — proceed to
✦ If you're ready, we can go on to the next stage of the experiment.

a string of — a series of
✦ A string of bad reviews hurt the movie in its opening weekend.

under way — started; moving
✦ The train is about to get under way, so please take your seat.

WHY DO WE SAY THAT?

a string of — When we place things next to each other (for example, plastic balls), they form a line. The line looks like a piece of string. Likewise, we may talk about a string of actions. A string of successes, for example, would be several successes coming one after the other: perhaps one this year, another the following year, and so on.

SENTENCE PATTERNS

These are just *two of a long list of* aviation accomplishments.
a couple of his many
a few of his

Not bad for *one of the world's most affluent people!*
someone from a poor background.
a person whom nobody expected to succeed.

WHAT PEOPLE ARE SAYING ABOUT RICHARD BRANSON

Clarence How can you not admire Richard Branson? He's so successful I can't help being somewhat jealous. I don't mean I would want to be him, since I'm sure he's under a lot of pressure (which I wouldn't want). But he really has done something special with his life.

Susanne I wonder how he has time to do so much. I barely have enough time to work 40 hours a week and keep my house clean. He probably has a company that does nothing but train new assistants for him!

Manuel Richard Branson is one of those people who want everything. He wants to be superrich, and he wants his face on TV every day. That's why he does all those crazy stunts. I think it's fine to want to be successful, but how much does one person need? I say appreciate what you have, and don't dream of becoming as rich as Richard.

chapter 12

DONNA KARAN: DESIGNING THE WORLD

READING PASSAGE

In many ways, Donna Karan **symbolizes** modern fashion. Talented and ambitious, she has spent the last three decades designing clothing, accessories, and other products for the modern person. Her range is impressive, going from high fashion (the Donna Karan Collection) to a popular ready-to-wear collection (DKNY). As part of her **mission** to create a broad lifestyle brand, labels **bearing** her name include bedding, eyewear, and a **slew** of other products.

Karan, born in 1948, did not just wake up one day and decide to become a fashion designer. Indeed, the New Yorker's mother was a model, and her father was a tailor. From a very young age, Karan had fashion **on her mind**, designing her first clothing collection when she was still in high school!

After attending Parsons School of Design, Karan soon became a star in the fashion world. Her first job was at Anne Klein, where she quickly **rose through the ranks**. In 1974, after Klein's death, Donna became co-designer of the Anne Klein Collection. A decade later, she opened her own company, Donna Karan New York. Karan had proved she wasn't just a **shooting star**; she was here to stay.

From the beginning, with the first line released in 1985, her collections were big hits. Karan developed a successful clothing system that included seven pieces. They could be worn in different combinations, at any time of the day or year. It was an **efficient** yet **elegant** method that **appealed to** many working women. Karan was also known for her tight-fitting bodysuits, which became a **trademark** fashion statement.

In 1989, Karan **launched** DKNY, a ready-to-wear line that was affordable yet stylish. Another huge success for Karan, DKNY expanded its product line to include eyewear, men's clothing, children's clothing, accessories, and many other items.

Riding this amazing wave of success, DKNY became a publicly traded company in 1996. A few years later, it was bought by the luxury giant LVMH. There are now Donna Karan Collection and DKNY outlets in many countries (see map). Karan continues to design and impress, finding **inspiration** in the world around her as she expands her personal world of design.

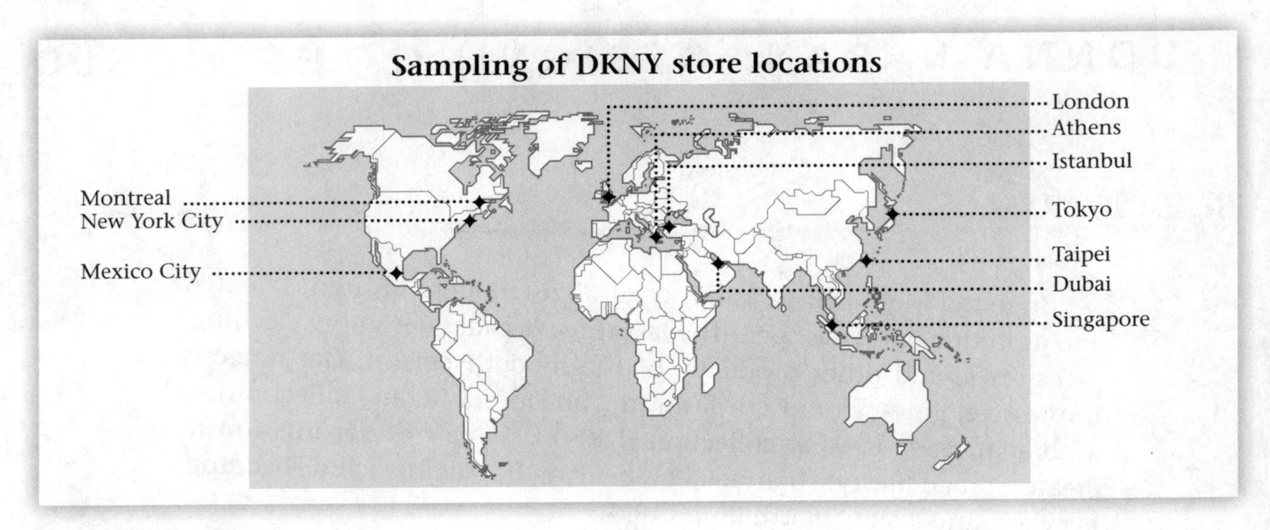

COMPREHENSION CHECK

1. ( ) Donna Karan started co-designing the Anne Klein Collection _________.
   A. while Anne Klein was still with the company
   B. when she was 26
   C. four years before opening her own company
   D. while she was attending Parsons School of Design

2. ( ) What is suggested about Karan's parents?
   A. They gave Donna her first design job.
   B. They didn't agree with her career plans.
   C. They were an important reason for Donna's interest in fashion.
   D. They were both in the clothing design business.

3. ( ) How would a pair of DKNY sunglasses fit into Karan's design world?
   A. As part of her collection for working women
   B. As part of her high-fashion collection
   C. As part of her seven-piece system
   D. As part of her ready-to-wear line

4. ( ) The map does *not* show DKNY stores in _________.
   A. North America
   B. Asia
   C. South America
   D. Europe

5. ( ) What do we know about the purchase of Karan's company by LVMH?
   A. It led to Karan's being named as the new CEO.
   B. It led to Karan's retirement.
   C. It led to a decrease in the number of DKNY outlets.
   D. It did not stop Karan from designing.

VOCABULARY BUILDING

symbolize *(v)* — represent; stand for
✦ When the CEO quit, it symbolized the serious trouble the company was in.

mission *(n)* — a purpose; goal
✦ Our mission is to help low-income people realize their dream of owning a home.

bear *(v)* — carry
✦ It's hard for one person to bear too much responsibility.

slew *(n)* — a large amount
✦ This year, a slew of new car models will hit the market.

shooting star *(n)* — a person who suddenly becomes successful but quickly fades away
✦ Aaron turned out to be a shooting star in the music industry. His only hits were in 2004.

efficient *(adj)* — effective and free of waste
✦ I'm impressed by your efficient management style.

elegant *(adj)* — sophisticated and stylish
✦ Fashion magazines feature articles about the latest, most elegant clothes.

trademark *(n)* — something that a person or company is well known for
✦ Jeff's long hair is his trademark. If he gets it cut, people won't recognize him!

launch *(v)* — release to the market
✦ Do you know what day they plan to launch the new DVD system?

inspiration *(n)* — a source of ideas; motivation
✦ The artist said his parents were his greatest inspiration.

PHRASE BUILDING

on one's mind — being thought about by someone
✦ If you always have work on your mind, it can interfere with your social life.

rise through the ranks — gain higher positions steadily
✦ To rise through the ranks in a large company, it helps to have a good personality.

appeal to — attract
✦ Few TV shows appeal to both young and old viewers.

WHY DO WE SAY THAT?

rise through the ranks — In the army, each person has a rank, such as captain or general. When a person is promoted, he or she receives a higher rank. In other words, he or she rises through the ranks. We also use this phrase to talk about a person in a private company rising to a higher position.

SENTENCE PATTERNS

Karan *developed* / *came up with* / *put together* a successful clothing system that included seven pieces.

There are now Donna Karan Collection and DKNY outlets *in many countries.* / *all over the world.* / *worldwide.*

WHAT PEOPLE ARE SAYING ABOUT DONNA KARAN

Fiona I love Donna Karan's work. For a businesswoman like me, it isn't easy finding clothes that are professional and stylish. I have four or five of her outfits, and I get compliments on them all the time.

Seth I respect Karan for what she's done, but personally her stuff doesn't appeal to me. Maybe my style is wilder than most people's. I like to take a chance with what I wear—you know, stand out in a crowd.

Keiko Donna Karan is one of my idols. We studied her work in one of my design classes. Trust me, it's not easy designing a single piece of clothing. Designing an outfit is even harder. I can't imagine how hard it is to design an entire collection! Next month I'm traveling to New York. I can't wait to go to the big DKNY store there!

chapter 13

WANG YUNG-CHING: FROM POVERTY TO PENTHOUSE

READING PASSAGE

Wang Yung-ching, Taiwan's second-richest person, is the founder of the Formosa Plastics Group. The group includes companies making everything from plastics to electronics. In many ways, the **diverse** group is like its founder. From a very early age, Wang looked for **opportunities** wherever he could find them. In doing so, he rose from **poverty** to become one of the world's most powerful businesspeople.

Wang was born near Taipei in 1917. One of eight brothers and sisters, he grew up poor, and his mother had to do farm work to support the family. When he was 15 years old, Wang moved to another city to sell rice. His talent for business quickly emerged. In a few short years, he went from selling rice to opening his own store to opening a rice factory. He won customers' loyalty by delivering rice to their homes.

Wang went from **venture** to venture, increasing his wealth and knowledge all along. He **set up** a brick factory, and then a wood-processing factory. By the time he was 37, he had the largest savings-account balance in Taiwan. Because of his successful **track record**, he was offered a chance to go into the PVC business. At the time, Wang knew nothing about plastics, but he saw another excellent opportunity and **jumped at** the chance.

Thus, the Formosa Plastics Corporation was born in 1954. Shortly after opening his first PVC factory, Wang founded a production company to make goods using his PVC. He then branched out into transportation (to move the goods), textiles, and **numerous** other areas (see table). As he grew his **empire** into a worldwide success, Wang's efforts became an important element in Taiwan's economic growth.

Wang Yung-ching has great skill at using what he has learned in one industry to **get a foothold in** related industries. Though his efforts have made him **tremendously** rich (ranked 178th in the world in 2008) he is well known for being **frugal** with money. (One of his sweaters has lasted more than 25 years!) This **tireless** businessman, who turned 91 in 2008, continues to impress the world.

Formosa Plastics Group: Select List of Companies		
COMPANY	FUNCTION	YEAR FOUNDED
Formosa Plastics Corp.	Producing PVC resin	1954
Carlin Plastics Product Corp.	Producing plastic products	1963
Formosa Plastics Transport Corp.	Transporting goods	1965
Formosa Chemicals & Fiber Corp.	Producing textile products	1965
PFG Fiber Glass Corp.	Producing glass fibers	1987
Chang Gung Biotechnology Corp.	Producing health-related biotech products	1999
Formosa Plasma Display Corp.	Producing plasma displays	2002

COMPREHENSION CHECK

1. ( ) What do we learn here about Wang's childhood?
   A. His family had money problems.
   B. He was able to attend the best schools.
   C. He had to do farm work throughout his childhood.
   D. He learned about PVC by working at a factory.

2. ( ) When Wang decided to go into the PVC business, ________.
   A. it was because he was an expert in the field
   B. his textile business had already made him rich
   C. he was not knowledgeable about the industry
   D. he had to stop what he was doing in other industries

3. ( ) What has led Wang to expand from industry to industry?
   A. He is constantly offered chances to start new businesses.
   B. Without entering new industries, his profits cannot grow.
   C. No outside companies can meet the needs of the Formosa Plastics Group.
   D. By applying knowledge of industries he understands, he branches into new ones.

4. ( ) What does "a few short years" in the second paragraph mean?
   A. A number of decades
   B. Several years
   C. Years with fewer than 365 days in them
   D. Less than three years

5. ( ) Which of the following is true?
   A. Nearly 50 years passed between the founding of the Formosa Plastics Corporation and the start of the Group's plasma-display business.
   B. The size of Wang's bank account helped him get an offer to open a rice factory.
   C. Wang's first job was growing and packaging rice.
   D. The Formosa Plastics Group entered the transportation business before the PVC business.

VOCABULARY BUILDING

diverse *(adj)* — varied; including many different sides
✦ It was a highly diverse community, with immigrants from fifteen countries.

opportunity *(n)* — a chance
✦ It sounds like a great opportunity, but I haven't got the money.

poverty *(n)* — the condition of being poor
✦ There's nothing sadder than seeing a child living in poverty.

venture *(n)* — a deal or project
✦ Some businesspeople prefer ventures that present high risk but offer large rewards.

track record *(n)* — performance history
✦ CEOs with good track records can earn millions of dollars per year.

numerous *(adj)* — many
✦ There are numerous reasons why this city needs a subway system.

empire *(n)* — in business, a company or group of companies with wide-reaching power
✦ The merger of the two companies formed a business empire reaching across 150 countries.

tremendously *(adv)* — extremely
✦ The guidebook had been tremendously helpful, and may even have saved their lives.

frugal *(adj)* — very careful with money
✦ If you're not frugal today, you may not have any money tomorrow.

tireless *(adj)* — full of energy; never stopping or quitting
✦ My dad is tireless; he works 15 hours a day.

PHRASE BUILDING

set up — establish, found, create
✦ I want to start selling things on the Internet, but I need someone to help me set up a Web site.

jump at — act quickly to grab an opportunity
✦ George says we may lose our chance if we don't jump at this deal.

get a foothold in — take action to get established in a field or industry
✦ I'm thinking of buying a small café to get a foothold in the restaurant business.

WHY DO WE SAY THAT?

get a foothold in — When you are hiking or rock climbing, you need to watch your step. When you place your front foot firmly on the ground or on the side of a mountain, that gives you a "foothold." It lets you prepare for the next step. So, when we "get a foothold in" an industry or field, it means we take that first action to get established. Once we have a foothold, we can move on or expand.

SENTENCE PATTERNS

His talent for business quickly emerged.
Her skill at painting
Their trading ability

By *the time he was 37,* he had the largest savings-account balance in Taiwan.
his 25th birthday,
his 10th year in business,

WHAT PEOPLE ARE SAYING ABOUT WANG YUNG-CHING

Jia-rong A lot of people in Taiwan look up to Wang Yung-ching. He's in the newspapers quite a lot. I remember he used to jog all the time, but I'm not sure if he still does. But it wouldn't surprise me!

Lillian I'm impressed by the way he has founded so many companies. Instead of finding an outside company to transport his products, he just went ahead and started a new one to do the job! These days it seems he's interested in just about every type of industry. I'm just a bit concerned about the amount of pollution coming from all his factories.

Serena I have to say, Mr. Wang certainly is a natural-born businessman! It would be easy for him to sit back and enjoy all his money, but he just keeps going and going. He must really have a passion for his work!

chapter 14

ANITA RODDICK: THE BUSINESS OF BETTERING THE WORLD

READING PASSAGE

Most companies and businesspeople say they want to make the world a better, cleaner, and safer place. Anita Roddick, founder of The Body Shop, actually built her business around these values. Using all-natural products, while supporting many social and environmental causes, she grew the cosmetics company into a worldwide success . . . with a heart.

Before Roddick opened the first Body Shop in 1976, the British **native** traveled widely. Spending time in **rural** areas, she saw with her own eyes how people lived and how they **dealt with** the problems they faced. She was also introduced to many interesting locally grown products.

Her first store in England sold only a handful of personal-care items, which used **ingredients** such as aloe vera and cocoa butter. Such ingredients, which are now fairly well known, were uncommon at the time. The store did well, and Roddick opened her second store just six months later. The Body Shop continued to grow by selling **franchises**, first in Europe and then elsewhere, **eventually** totaling more than 2,000 stores worldwide.

Roddick built a number of **core ethical** principles into The Body Shop. For instance, the company **opposed** testing products on animals, supported human rights, and encouraged **community** trade. This last point was a key part of Roddick's way of doing business. She **went out of her way** to support poor communities by buying products and ingredients from them. These include massagers from India and sesame-seed oil from Nicaragua (see map).

Led by Roddick, The Body Shop also supported a number of causes. Back in 1986, it **contributed** to Greenpeace's Save the Whales campaign. Also, using the power of its customer base, the company has **carried out** large petition drives. In 1996, it collected four million signatures for the Against Animal Testing campaign. The effort was successful, leading to a total ban on animal testing in the U.K.

In March 2006, The Body Shop was bought by L'Oréal. Some people were worried that the new owners would change the way The Body Shop was run. But Roddick, who died the next year, remained confident that the "green" company she created would stay true to its values.

Some of The Body Shop's Community Trade Partners	
AUSTRALIA: Tea-tree oil	**IRELAND:** Seaweed
BRAZIL: Soya oil	**NICARAGUA:** Sesame-seed oil
GHANA: Shea butter	**ZAMBIA:** Beeswax
INDIA: Massagers	**ITALY:** Bergamot oil

COMPREHENSION CHECK

1. ( ) How did Roddick learn about products like aloe vera?
   A. By buying them from a special shop
   B. By helping people in rural areas grow them
   C. By introducing The Body Shop to many people in England
   D. By traveling to many parts of the world

2. ( ) What was the benefit of selling The Body Shop franchises?
   A. It helped the company grow at a fast rate.
   B. Franchises became an important part of the community trade program.
   C. Without franchises, The Body Shop would not be able to sell ingredients like cocoa butter.
   D. With many franchises, the range of products sold can grow very quickly.

3. ( ) According to the article, a poor group of people might earn money by ________.
   A. growing a product that they can sell to The Body Shop
   B. buying products through the community trade program
   C. supporting one of The Body Shop's causes
   D. opening a franchise store

4. ( ) What does the article imply about The Body Shop's customer base?
   A. If it had not been so large, the Greenpeace campaign would have failed.
   B. It was the main point of attraction for L'Oréal.
   C. It contains a total of 4 million people.
   D. Its size is helpful during petition drives.

5. ( ) What concern did people have about the future of The Body Shop?
   A. It would stop selling products with interesting ingredients.
   B. Its new parent company would take The Body Shop in a different direction.
   C. Without Roddick, it would no longer be able to deliver excellent profits.
   D. L'Oréal would keep things exactly the way they had always been.

VOCABULARY BUILDING

ethical *(adj)* — moral

✦ Several organizations work to encourage companies to adopt more ethical business practices.

native *(adj)* — born in a certain place

✦ These trees aren't native to our country. They were brought here by overseas visitors many years ago.

rural *(adj)* — in the countryside, away from cities

✦ One of the best things about living in a rural area is the clean air.

ingredient *(n)* — one item in a group of items (such as a part of a recipe)

✦ Salt is a common ingredient in many dishes.

franchise *(n)* — a business (such as a restaurant or retail store) opened by acquiring rights from the company owner

✦ To open a restaurant franchise, you usually pay an "up-front" fee; after opening it, you pay a percentage of your monthly profits.

eventually *(adv)* — finally; ultimately

✦ I know it doesn't seem likely now, but we'll eventually come to an agreement.

core *(adj)* — central; very important

✦ Excellent customer service is a core part of our company's mission statement.

oppose *(v)* — be against

✦ Residents spoke out in the thousands to oppose the building of the new highway.

community *(n)* — a group of people living together or spending a lot of time together

✦ In farming communities, people regularly help one another.

contribute *(v)* — add to; give

✦ Once in a while, I contribute an article to a local newspaper.

PHRASE BUILDING

deal with — handle; manage

✦ Which of our lawyers should take on the McGregor case?

go out of one's way — make a special effort to do something

✦ Jackie went out of her way to buy those cookies for you. Remember to thank her.

carry out — do something; implement

✦ Mr. Morris gets angry when people don't immediately carry out his orders.

WHY DO WE SAY THAT?

go out of one's way — When you go from one place to another, you go along a certain route, or way. The same goes for our daily lives: Each of us has a certain way of doing things. So when you go out of your way, you do something that isn't part of your routine. We usually use the phrase to talk about making an extra-special effort to do something, often as a favor to someone.

SENTENCE PATTERNS

She	*was also introduced to*	many interesting locally grown products.
	came into contact with	
	was exposed to	

This last point is	*a key part*	of Roddick's way of doing business.
	an important component	
	at the heart	

WHAT PEOPLE ARE SAYING ABOUT ANITA RODDICK

Margaret Anita Roddick was one of my heroes. I think it's brilliant that no matter how rich and successful she was, she still gave so much time to good causes. It made me even prouder to see her succeed, like with the animal testing ban. That was a happy day.

Sherrie I like a lot of the things sold at The Body Shop, but I can't afford to shop there often. I don't understand why they have to put such expensive price tags on everything. Other than that, it's a cool store.

Dilip I admire the way Roddick looked in uncommon places for new products and business partners. Few people would have thought to look in jungles and mountain areas for new ingredients. But she did, and quite successfully. Plus, in the end, her company won, and the local people won. The world needs more stories like that.

chapter 15

AZIM PREMJI: THE BILLIONAIRE OF BANGALORE

READING PASSAGE

Bangalore, India, is one of the world's **booming** cities. Companies around the world are **scrambling** to set up telephone call centers, product development centers, and offices for their information technology (IT) activities in Bangalore. One of the city's key service providers is Wipro Technologies, an Indian company that is now one of the world's largest IT firms. **At the helm** is Azim Premji, the man who turned the company from a million-dollar business into a multibillion-dollar powerhouse.

Premji, born in 1945, took over his father's company at the early age of 21. At the time, Wipro **had nothing to do with** technology. In fact, it sold vegetable oils. Premji had not even graduated from university yet, but he had to win the confidence of the company's **shareholders**. He did this by **diversifying** the types of food products sold by the company. Later, seeing that IT was the way of the future, Premji **steered** the company to **focus** on computer software.

Under Premji's leadership, Wipro grew into a global IT leader, with some of the world's largest companies as its clients. For instance, Wipro is a big player in the cell-phone market, developing software for clients such as Nokia and NEC. The company has **put up** very impressive numbers, with 32 percent revenue growth in the 2007-8 **fiscal year** (see table) and about 80,000 employees.

Besides his business **ingenuity**, Premji is known for his charity work. In 2001, he started the Azim Premji Foundation. This organization supports the improvement of schools in India. Its mission is to make a quality education available for all of India's children. It has already helped more than 10,000 schools.

Azim Premji is proud not only of his company's achievements but also of India's economic growth. He encourages companies to reduce costs by looking to Indian firms for IT and BPO (Business Process **Outsourcing**) services. Premji may be one of the world's richest men (no. 60 in 2008, according to *Forbes* magazine), but he is **concerned** for the future of his country. That future, in Premji's eyes, starts with India's children.

Wipro 2007-8 Revenue & Growth (Rs. = Rupees)		
DEPARTMENT	FISCAL YEAR 2007-8 REVENUES	GROWTH OVER 2006-7
Wipro Global IT Services and Products	Rs. 136.28 billion (US$3.41 billion)	23%
Wipro India and AsiaPac IT Services and Products	Rs. 34.60 billion (US$865 million)	45%
Wipro Consumer Care and Lighting	Rs. 14.62 billion (US$365 million)	93%

COMPREHENSION CHECK

1. ( ) What was Premji's first challenge at Wipro?
   A. Attracting foreign companies to find partners in India
   B. Running the company while finishing his university studies
   C. Deciding on the best way to expand into computer software
   D. Convincing shareholders that he could handle the job

2. ( ) Why did Premji decide to go into the software business?
   A. He knew the industry was going to become very important.
   B. He was under pressure from shareholders to move into IT.
   C. The market for vegetable oils was getting too crowded.
   D. He didn't think there was a future in the food-products business.

3. ( ) The Azim Premji Foundation focuses on _________.
   A. building schools in India
   B. helping schools in India find more students
   C. making schools in India better
   D. setting up missions throughout India

4. ( ) What does "looking to" in the final paragraph mean?
   A. watching
   B. exchanging
   C. using
   D. servicing

5. ( ) What can be concluded about Wipro's 2007-8 revenues?
   A. Every department grew by at least 25 percent over the previous year.
   B. Wipro India and AsiaPac IT made up the smallest percentage of Wipro's total revenues.
   C. Revenues for Wipro Global IT were almost ten times the size of the revenues for Wipro Consumer Care and Lighting.
   D. Total revenues for the company were just over US$5 billion.

VOCABULARY BUILDING

booming *(adj)* — growing very quickly
- ✦ The market for portable MP3 players is booming.

scramble *(v)* — do something in a hurry
- ✦ When the pipe broke and water started pouring out, everyone in the office scrambled to save what they could.

shareholder *(n)* — a person who holds stock or a stake in a company
- ✦ Next Tuesday, shareholders will meet to vote on several important matters.

steer *(v)* — direct
- ✦ Steve is a good manager, but is he ready to steer the entire company?

focus *(v)* — concentrate one's attention and efforts in a certain area
- ✦ We should focus on the products that we know the most about.

fiscal year *(n)* — a 12-month period used for a company's financial calculations (may be from January to December, from March to February, etc.)
- ✦ Our fiscal year ends in May. At that time I'll give you a full report on our financial situation.

diversify *(v)* — increase the variety of products or investments
- ✦ Companies often diversify by buying other companies in different fields.

ingenuity *(n)* — unusual cleverness
- ✦ No one can match his ingenuity at keeping a large department running smoothly.

outsource *(v)* — have work done by someone outside the company, usually to save money
- ✦ As the global economy has grown, outsourcing has become more and more common.

concerned *(adj)* — worried
- ✦ Are you concerned that the high price of oil might increase your production costs?

PHRASE BUILDING

at the helm — in control
- ✦ With Warren at the helm, the company is in a great position to keep growing.

have nothing to do with — be unrelated to; not be involved with
- ✦ I had nothing to do with those rumors. They were started by someone else.

put up — post; report

✦ Investors are expecting the construction firm to put up solid fourth-quarter results.

WHY DO WE SAY THAT?

at the helm — The helm of the boat is used for steering. The person who stands at the helm can control the boat's direction. So, when we say a person is "at the helm" of a company, the idea is the same: The person is steering the company in some direction.

SENTENCE PATTERNS

This	*organization*	supports the improvement of schools in India.
	charity	
	group	

That future,	*in Premji's eyes,*	starts with India's children.
	according to Premji,	
	in his opinion,	

WHAT PEOPLE ARE SAYING ABOUT AZIM PREMJI

Ajit It would be hard to find someone in India who hasn't heard of Mr. Premji. He has created quite a lot of jobs for people here. Of course, he is very wealthy, but he is also concerned about our country.

Regina Our goal this year is to cut costs by 15 percent, and we need to find a way to do that without lowering the quality of our product or the strength of our research. We've heard many good things about Wipro. Perhaps Mr. Premji's firm can help us set up operations in India.

Wolfgang I recently watched an interview with Azim Premji. He made a lot of good points about the direction the global economy is heading in. He really made me wonder if, in the future, jobs will just flow from country to country, depending on what's best for the company. That means we all need to be flexible and ready to learn new skills, and perhaps even be ready to move abroad.

VOCABULARY AND PHRASE REVIEW

A. Complete each sentence, using the best word(s) from the box.

numerous	**venture**	**track record**
diversify	**core**	**achieve**
elegant	**focus**	**ethical**

1. It's like my father always says: To ____________________ your goals, you need to work hard, year after year.
2. We like to buy products from companies with ____________________ business practices.
3. If we try to ____________________ by creating a new product line now, we'll just go deeper into debt.
4. There are ____________________ hotels in the city to choose from. Why do you want to stay at this one?
5. Don't waste any more time trying to help Mike solve his problems. ____________________ on your own work and let me deal with him.
6. Your educational background looks good, and you seem to have an excellent ____________________ at the companies you've worked for. I'll be glad to offer you a position here.
7. Our shoes are ____________________, so you can wear them to a fancy restaurant, but they're also comfortable, so you can walk in them for hours.
8. Warren is a conservative person. I don't think he'd be interested in investing in a high-risk ____________________.

B. Choose the best word to complete each sentence.

1. I love living in this _________. Everybody helps each other out, and it's very safe.

   A. opportunity B. community C. franchise D. trademark

2. Employees are encouraged to turn off the lights when they leave a room. We're trying to _________ our electricity costs.

   A. launch B. bear C. reduce D. steer

3. Sure, _________ areas are peaceful and quiet, but I'd go crazy if I didn't live near a shopping mall!

   A. rural B. affluent C. native D. diverse

4. What a(n) ________ piece of property! It would take an entire day to walk from one end to the other.

   A. ambitious B. efficient C. enormous D. significant

5. When I was traveling in China, I had tea at some traditional teahouses. That gave me the ________ to open a similar type of place in San Francisco.

   A. mission B. inspiration C. charity D. accomplishment

C. Match the beginning and ending of each sentence.

1. Why do you oppose his research	the most important ingredient in the cake.
2. I'll contribute to your project	when you've never actually studied it?
3. You should be more concerned	about the money missing from the cash register.
4. We'll get under way as soon as	in any way I can.
5. My mom says brown sugar is	all the passengers are on board.

D. Choose the best response to what the first person says.

1. **Elizabeth:** If you like, I can look for the Gucci bag you want when I'm in Paris.
   A. Karen: Sure, we can set up something like that when you get back.
   B. Karen: I think you should jump at the chance!
   C. Karen: No, I don't want you to go out of your way to look for it.
2. **Mario:** After only two years, my brother is already a vice president.
   A. Coralie: He must be ambitious. He's really rising through the ranks!
   B. Coralie: At the helm of the company after two years? Incredible.
   C. Coralie: His division must be putting up some terrible sales figures.
3. **Raul:** We've had a string of excellent releases this month. In fact, one line completely sold out.
   A. Bai-rong: Well, at least you're trying. Is there anything else you can do to get a foothold in the market?
   B. Bai-rong: That's surprising. I expected your products to appeal to more people.
   C. Bai-rong: Congratulations! Have you found someone to help you deal with all the new business?

section 4
✦ FIVE INTERNET BUSINESSES

TARGET VOCABULARY

aggressive *(adj)* Chap. 19: Amazon
annual *(adj)* Chap. 20: Skype
appetite *(n)* Chap. 16: Yahoo!
array *(n)* Chap. 20: Skype
balloon *(v)* Chap. 19: Amazon
brainchild *(n)* Chap. 16: Yahoo!
brilliant *(adj)* Chap. 20: Skype!
bumpy *(adj)* Chap. 19: Amazon
bust *(n)* Chap. 19: Amazon
category *(n)* Chap. 16: Yahoo!
citizen *(n)* Chap. 20: Skype
combat *(v)* Chap. 17: EBay
combine *(v)* Chap. 16: Yahoo!
communicate *(v)* Chap. 20: Skype
continuously *(adv)* Chap. 18: Google
convince *(v)* Chap. 18: Google
countless *(adj)* Chap. 19: Amazon
critical *(adj)* Chap. 18: Google
criticism *(n)* Chap. 18: Google
crooked *(adj)* Chap. 17: EBay
destination *(n)* Chap. 16: Yahoo!
diligently *(adv)* Chap. 16: Yahoo!
discount *(n)* Chap. 19: Amazon
endeavor *(n)* Chap. 20: Skype
enhance *(v)* Chap. 20: Skype
envied *(adj)* Chap. 17: EBay
e-tailer *(n)* Chap. 19: Amazon
ever-growing *(adj)* Chap. 16: Yahoo!
fortune *(n)* Chap. 18: Google
fraud *(n)* Chap. 17: EBay
garage *(n)* Chap. 19: Amazon
high-end *(adj)* Chap. 17: EBay
humble *(adj)* Chap. 16: Yahoo!
initial *(adj)* Chap. 17: EBay
mature *(v)* Chap. 17: EBay
novice *(n)* Chap. 20: Skype

opposite *(adj)*	Chap. 20: Skype
outlook *(n)*	Chap. 16: Yahoo!
partnership *(n)*	Chap. 19: Amazon
premium *(adj)*	Chap. 20: Skype
provided *(conj)*	Chap. 17: EBay
resilient *(adj)*	Chap. 19: Amazon
revenue stream *(n)*	Chap. 18: Google
roam *(v)*	Chap. 18: Google
sensitive *(adj)*	Chap. 18: Google
stock split *(n)*	Chap. 17: EBay
subdivide *(v)*	Chap. 16: Yahoo!
suspicion *(n)*	Chap. 18: Google
track *(v)*	Chap. 18: Google
virtually *(adv)*	Chap. 17: EBay

TARGET PHRASES

at any given time	Chap. 17: EBay
at last	Chap. 20: Skype
easier said than done	Chap. 17: EBay
everything under the sun	Chap. 16: Yahoo!
fall into the wrong hands	Chap. 18: Google
tall order	Chap. 18: Google
fly the flag	Chap. 19: Amazon
go under	Chap. 19: Amazon
hand in hand	Chap. 18: Google
judging by	Chap. 16: Yahoo!
no wonder	Chap. 20: Skype
pay an arm and a leg	Chap. 20: Skype
pay off	Chap. 19: Amazon
peaches and cream	Chap. 17: EBay
up for	Chap. 16: Yahoo!

chapter 16

YAHOO! A NEW ONLINE WORLD

READING PASSAGE

As the Internet has grown, people have turned to it for more and more services. From business to entertainment to personal services, we've come to expect more from the online world. Yahoo.com, the world's most visited Web site, continues to expand to meet this **ever-growing appetite**. The Internet leader offers **everything under the sun**, from e-mail accounts to photo sharing to Web-site hosting.

Yahoo! was the **brainchild** of two Stanford University PhD students—Jerry Yang and David Filo—in 1994. Its beginnings were **humble**. The two friends created a list of their favorite Web sites and put it on the Internet. As the list grew, Yang and Filo **subdivided** the Web sites into **categories** to make it easier for people to use. The list became very popular, attracting 100,000 visitors within four months!

The following year, the two students founded a company, Yahoo! In April 1996 the company went public, and it immediately started expanding. One of its first moves was to open a site for Japanese users. Always forward-looking, Yahoo! has maintained its international **outlook** and now has sites in over 20 languages and over 30 countries.

In its early years, Yahoo! was mostly known for its search engine. However, the company has worked **diligently** to become much more. Its goal has been to create a **destination** where people can handle almost all their online tasks in one place. It has added dozens of features, including shopping (1998), auctions (1998), maps (2002), and social networking (2005). Users can create a My Yahoo! page to **combine** much of their favorite content on a single page.

Besides being popular among Net users, Yahoo! was also popular among investors—at least for its first ten years. But in 2006 its fortunes began to fade. Its aggressive rival Google had established itself as the most-used of all search engines, and the search engine became the entry point to Google's other features.

In 2008 Yahoo! remained the most-visited site in the world. But to keep its top spot on the Internet, Yahoo! will need to continue improving its search engine and other services. **Judging by** its impressive history, this Internet giant may well be **up to** the challenge.

Yahoo! Revenues and Earnings per Share		
YEAR	REVENUES (in millions)	EARNINGS PER SHARE
2001	$717.4	–$.08
2002	$953.1	$.09
2003	$1,625	$.18
2004	$3,575	$.58
2005	$5,258	$1.28
2006	$6,426	$.52
2007	$6,969	$.47

COMPREHENSION CHECK

1. ( ) According to the article, Internet users __________.
   A. want Web sites to continue adding services
   B. are happy enough with what's already available online
   C. don't have time to use all the features of their favorite Web sites
   D. mostly go online for business and entertainment services

2. ( ) Why did Yang and Filo divide their list of Web sites into categories?
   A. Because of the large number of people using the list.
   B. It was the only way to expand the list.
   C. At that time, there was limited space on the Internet for such a long list.
   D. They wanted to make their list less difficult to use.

3. ( ) Which of these Yahoo! services is not mentioned in the article?
   A. Online business development
   B. A page that lets people bring together different types of content
   C. Online shopping
   D. Instant messaging

4. ( ) From 2001 to 2007, for how many years did Yahoo! have revenues of more than one billion dollars?
   A. Zero
   B. Two
   C. Five
   D. Four

5. ( ) What does the article suggest Yahoo! needs to do to stay on top?
   A. Cooperate more with Google and Microsoft.
   B. Focus 100 percent of its efforts on improving its search engine.
   C. Make all its services better and better.
   D. Challenge other companies to improve their services.

VOCABULARY BUILDING

ever-growing *(adj)* — constantly getting bigger
✦ Our debt is an ever-growing problem. It's time we did something about it.

appetite *(n)* — hunger; interest; desire
✦ Carla has a huge appetite for books. She reads at least one book per week.

brainchild *(n)* — a creation or invention
✦ This motor was the brainchild of my grandfather. He spent his whole life developing it.

humble *(adj)* — modest
✦ A humble man, Anthony rarely talks about his past successes.

subdivide *(v)* — separate into smaller groups
✦ To get things done more quickly, we need to subdivide this project into smaller tasks.

category *(n)* — a division or group
✦ In a budget for a business trip, movies generally fall into the Entertainment category.

outlook *(n)* — a way of seeing things; attitude
✦ Maureen's current outlook on the stock market is more negative than mine.

diligently *(adv)* — done through hard work
✦ A repair crew is working diligently to fill the cracks in the wall.

destination *(n)* — a place or point someone is trying to reach
✦ I'm taking a flight to Rome, but my final destination is London.

combine *(v)* — put together
✦ If we combine these two departments, we can save thousands of dollars per year.

PHRASE BUILDING

everything under the sun — including many different things
✦ I love this store. It sells everything under the sun!

judging by — considering; based on
✦ Judging by the amount of rust on the bike, I'd say it's been sitting in the rain for months.

up to — prepared for; ready to face a challenge
✦ I know it won't be an easy hike, but I'm up to it.

WHY DO WE SAY THAT?

everything under the sun — Everything on the earth is beneath the sun. That includes a huge number of different things (the mountains, oceans, etc.). So, when we say a store, person, business, etc., includes or sells everything under the sun, we mean it has a very large range of things.

SENTENCE PATTERNS

The two friends	*created*	a list of their favorite Web sites.
	put together	
	came up with	

However, the company worked diligently to	*become much more.*
	increase its range of services.
	expand its selection.

WHAT PEOPLE ARE SAYING ABOUT YAHOO!

Maurice Yahoo! is my home page. Actually, I have a My Yahoo! page. It makes it really easy for me to see all my "must see" info as soon as I go online. If I only have five minutes to surf the Net, I can go to that one page and check out a lot of different things very quickly.

Mitsuko I like Yahoo!, but sometimes I feel it's just too much. I know there are a million different things to do on the Internet, but it can be overwhelming. I only want to check my e-mail and chat with friends, but even doing that is complicated. Maybe they'll come up with a "Yahoo! lite" that makes it easier for people who just want to use the basic services.

Patrick I used to be a huge Yahoo! fan when they were the only big search engine out there. Now I use Google. It's faster, and its toolbar makes it easy to perform searches any time. But if Yahoo! makes some changes for the better, I won't have a problem using them again. I'll go wherever the services are better and faster, as long as they stay free!

chapter 17

EBAY: SOMETHING FOR EVERYONE

READING PASSAGE

At any given time, most people have something they want to buy or sell. What they usually don't have is a storefront. That's where eBay.com, the Internet's largest auction site, can help. EBay makes it easy for people to sell **virtually** anything (**provided** it's legal), from $10 cookie jars to million-dollar beachfront houses.

The San Jose, California-based company started operations in 1995. At first, most auctions were for small, inexpensive items like household goods, CDs, and collectibles. Over the years, eBay has **matured** into a marketplace for cars, fine art, and other **high-end** products as well.

The business model is simple. EBay earns money by charging sellers to list items on its Web site. The owner may offer an item for a fixed price, or may instead sell it by auction—that is, sell it to the person who offers the most money. There are **initial** listing fees, fees for special features, and final selling fees. EBay also earns money from PayPal, a Web site owned by eBay that allows people to send money over the Internet.

With millions of items listed on the site every day, eBay has grown into a multibillion-dollar business. For several years, eBay was one of the Internet's most **envied** companies, and its success led to four **stock splits** in six years (see table). If you had bought just a single share of eBay stock in 1998, you would have had 24 shares by 2006!

But it hasn't all been **peaches and cream** for this Internet giant. **Fraud** has become a major issue. Though most sellers are honest, there are more than a few **crooked** dealers. For instance, in 2006 a woman paid $2,400 for a wedding gown that she never received, and another woman was charged with cheating people out of more than $50,000. EBay says it's working hard to **combat** fraud, but with over a billion items sold on the site in 2007, that's **easier said than done**.

There have also been complaints over eBay's fee structure. In response to eBay's increasing fees, some sellers have turned to other sites like Overstock.com and Amazon.com.

Still, it is estimated that 1.3 million people worldwide make all or part of their income by selling products on the site. And with over 15,000 employees and 100 million members, eBay remains a major company by any estimate. But its future performance, unlike its past, will probably be more solid than remarkable.

EBay's Stock Splits (1999–2005)

March 2, 1999	3-for-1 split
May 25, 2000	2-for-1 split
August 29, 2003	2-for-1 split
February 17, 2005	2-for-1 split

COMPREHENSION CHECK

1. ( ) How has eBay changed since it started operations?
   A. The number of fraud cases is lower than in 1995.
   B. Buyers are no longer charged a fee when they win an auction.
   C. The range of items up for auction is much greater than it once was.
   D. Auctions for household goods are not as popular as they used to be.

2. ( ) What type of item would not be allowed on eBay?
   A. An original Van Gogh painting
   B. A sports car
   C. A stolen CD player
   D. A rare baseball card

3. ( ) Every year the FBI receives many complaints from eBay buyers who didn't receive their items. This is an example of the _________.
   A. competition that eBay faces from other Web sites
   B. large number of items sold on eBay every day
   C. problems with fraud on eBay
   D. issues related to eBay's fee structure

4. ( ) What does "solid" in the third paragraph mean?
   A. Hard and tough
   B. Heavy
   C. Reliable and consistent
   D. Well made

5. ( ) Which of the following is *not* true?
   A. EBay's stock went through four different splits from 2000 to 2005.
   B. EBay says it is trying to fight fraud on the site.
   C. Other auction sites are benefiting from eBay's higher fees.
   D. It costs more money to add special features to an auction listing.

VOCABULARY BUILDING

virtually *(adv)* — nearly
- ✦ Virtually all of our profits go back into growing the business.

provided *(conj)* — if, as long as
- ✦ Provided there are enough interested people, we will be holding another charity auction this year.

mature *(v)* — grow into a stable and established company, industry, etc.
- ✦ Now that the video-game market has matured, it's harder to make a profit in the industry.

high-end *(adj)* — toward the top of a product's price range
- ✦ Since the economy is not in the best shape, high-end luxury cars are not selling well.

initial *(adj)* — beginning
- ✦ Our initial order is for 5,000 units.

stock split *(n)* — a situation in which each share of stock turns into more than one share (for example, in a "two-for-one split," each share becomes two shares)
- ✦ Shortly after the stock rose to $100, it underwent a two-for-one split.

fraud *(n)* — a crime in which somebody cheats somebody else
- ✦ Because online fraud has become so common, you have to be careful not to trust what you read in e-mails.

crooked *(adj)* — dishonest
- ✦ The crooked mayor was found guilty of taking bribes and was sentenced to five years in jail.

combat *(v)* — fight; work against
- ✦ Police in the area are doing their best to combat gang activity.

envied *(adj)* — being the object of jealousy
- ✦ As the owner of a beautiful collection of paintings, Barbara is envied by all her friends.

PHRASE BUILDING

at any given time — at any particular time
- ✦ At any given time, this old house nearly always needs some work done on it.

peaches and cream — a pleasant, enjoyable, and generally excellent situation
- ✦ Once we retired to Hawaii, life was peaches and cream again.

easier said than done — easy to suggest but difficult to do
- ✦ Keeping stray dogs out of our neighborhood is easier said than done.

WHY DO WE SAY THAT?

peaches and cream — Imagine eating peaches with cream on them. To many people, it represents the good life: comfortable, enjoyable, and luxurious. So when we say something is "peaches and cream," we mean it's a nice situation that is problem-free and pleasant. On the other hand, if something *isn't* all peaches and cream, that means there are some problems.

SENTENCE PATTERNS

What they usually don't have is a storefront.
Something they're often lacking is
Millions of people earn a living online without

The business model is *simple.*
somewhat complex.
based on other successful businesses.

WHAT PEOPLE ARE SAYING ABOUT EBAY

Eileen I live in a rural area, and there aren't a lot of stores around here, so I do a lot of shopping online. I used to get this and that from different Web sites, but nowadays I can get just about anything off of eBay, usually for really good prices.

Christopher I've been buying and selling things on eBay for more than five years. The site has really changed. In the beginning, it was more friendly. Buyers and sellers sent lots of e-mails to each other, and it felt like a small community. These days, it's still a nice site, but it's colder and a lot less friendly. You sell something; you get paid; you send the thing; you leave feedback. That's it. Anyway, that's been my experience.

Alexis I was recently cheated out of $150 by an eBay seller. I bought a used digital camera from the guy. The auction description looked fine, and it didn't say the camera had any problems. Well, the guy didn't send it for two weeks. He finally sent it by a really slow method, so I didn't receive it until 10 days after that. Then when I got the camera, it didn't work! We exchanged a few e-mails, and by the time I decided to file a claim with PayPal, the filing deadline had passed! What a nightmare.

chapter 18
GOOGLE POWER!

READING PASSAGE

Google.com is one of the world's most frequently visited Web sites. It was founded by Larry Page and Sergey Brin, two Stanford University graduate students, in 1998. Since then, Google has gone on to become the Internet's most popular search engine. However, **hand in hand with** this success has come a fair amount of **suspicion** and distrust.

Internet users love Google. It's fast (often delivering search results in less than a second), and it organizes search results clearly. Over the years, Google has grown to add services such as image searches, video searches, and Gmail, Google's version of e-mail (see table). You can even download a toolbar that lets you perform a Google search without visiting the Web site. The best part is, all of these services are free!

Web-site owners also love Google. The company's "Googlebots" **roam** the Internet **continuously**, cataloging the sites they visit. That means even the smallest of Web sites has a chance to appear in a Google search result. For e-commerce sites, Google is often **critical** to their business, and appearing high on a list of search results can help a company make a **fortune**. Appearing low on a list (or even worse, not appearing at all) can cause serious damage to a company's profits.

Clearly, Google is a very powerful Web site, and its business practices have attracted a lot of **criticism**. One of the company's main **revenue streams** is paid advertising. Critics charge that Google gives its advertisers suggestions so that they can make changes to help their Web sites appear higher up on a search.

People are also worried about privacy. For example, a copy of every user e-mail sent on Gmail is kept on a Google server. Also, when you install the Google toolbar, it lets Google **track** every Web site you visit. Google says it is simply trying to help you perform searches, but critics fear that this **sensitive** information could **fall into the wrong hands**.

As Google expands, it has to be careful to maintain the public's trust. It also must work hard to **convince** people that it treats all Web sites fairly. For an old, established company, that would be a **tall order**. For a young company like Google, it's a huge challenge.

Free Google Services			
SERVICE	DATE ADDED	SERVICE	DATE ADDED
Google searches in multiple languages	2000	Gmail	2004
Google toolbar for Internet browsers	2000	Google Maps	2004
Google Images (image search)	2001	Google Talk (instant messaging, etc.)	2005
Google News (news search)	2002	YouTube (video sharing)	2006
Blogger (blog creation)	2003	Google Docs (office applications)	2006

COMPREHENSION CHECK

1. ( ) What is the main idea?
   A. Google's search engine is the most popular one on the Internet.
   B. Though a popular site, Google has many people concerned about it.
   C. Google collects a lot of information about its users.
   D. Maintaining the public's trust is never easy.

2. ( ) How can new Web sites appear in a Google search?
   A. They must pay money to Google.
   B. They have to be one of the biggest sites on the Internet.
   C. They need to contact an e-commerce site for help.
   D. They need to be visited by the company's Googlebots.

3. ( ) What does "fair" in the first paragraph mean?
   A. Somewhat large
   B. Even
   C. Pale
   D. Attractive

4. ( ) What criticism are people making about the way Google treats its advertisers?
   A. Google is tracking the Web sites they visit.
   B. Google is storing all their information on a server.
   C. Google charges them too much to advertise on the site.
   D. Google is giving them advice so they can better benefit from searches.

5. ( ) Which of the following is *not* true about the Google toolbar?
   A. Some people are concerned that it sends too much information to Google.
   B. It costs a small fee.
   C. You can download it from the Internet.
   D. It was introduced by Google before Google Maps was released.

VOCABULARY BUILDING

suspicion *(n)* — the feeling that something is wrong or can't be trusted
- ✦ I understand that she doesn't trust you, but what's the reason for her suspicion?

continuously *(adv)* — constantly; without stopping
- ✦ The machine makes ice continuously, so don't worry that there won't be enough.

roam *(v)* — wander
- ✦ When I visit a new city, I like to roam around different areas.

critical *(adj)* — very important
- ✦ It is critical that you lock all the doors and windows before leaving at night.

fortune *(n)* — a large amount of money
- ✦ This advertising campaign is costing a fortune—it had better be successful.

criticism *(n)* — identifying the faults in something or someone
- ✦ Bob doesn't mind criticism, as long as it's helpful and not hurtful.

revenue stream *(n)* — an income source
- ✦ We receive monthly rent payments from the office building we own. It's our most important revenue stream.

track *(v)* — watch over a period of time
- ✦ Companies spend a fortune tracking the spending habits of young people.

sensitive *(adj)* — requiring care in handling because of importance or personal feelings
- ✦ This is sensitive data, so keep it locked in the safe and don't make any copies.

convince *(v)* — make someone agree with you
- ✦ How can I convince you that I had nothing to do with the accident?

PHRASE BUILDING

hand in hand with — along with
- ✦ Higher taxes go hand in hand with a higher salary.

fall into the wrong hands — be obtained by someone who should not have it
- ✦ Never send your credit-card information in an e-mail; you don't want it to fall into the wrong hands.

tall order — a very difficult or challenging request
- ✦ I understand you need the report soon, but asking for it by this afternoon is a tall order.

WHY DO WE SAY THAT?

tall order — When you buy a large number of things from someone, or you ask about purchasing something that is difficult to get, that is a "tall order." The same is said about a request that is difficult to fill. So, for example, asking someone to finish a week's work of paperwork in 10 minutes would be a very tall order.

SENTENCE PATTERNS

People are also worried about *privacy.*
their personal data.
being cheated.

For *a young company like Google,* it's a huge challenge.
a company in our position,
a firm that size,

WHAT PEOPLE ARE SAYING ABOUT GOOGLE

Tom My Web connection is very slow (I still use a dial-up modem), so I appreciate Google's speed and simplicity. There are no fancy graphics, so the page loads quickly. And searches are superfast—much faster than other search engines.

Lawrence I've read some disturbing things about Google. I'm not saying the company is out to do no good, but it's just too powerful, and it has way too much of our personal information as it is. We hear about people stealing from so-called "secure" servers all the time. How do I know my Gmail messages aren't going to be stolen next week? For now, I'm not comfortable about leaving e-mail messages on a server somewhere. I'll keep them on my home PC, where I know they're safe.

Guo-yi I like Google's style. It's still a fresh young company with a new way of doing things. Some of the things Google is doing will change the way we share information and access data at home and online. I think that's pretty exciting. Bring on the future!

chapter 19

AMAZON: MORE THAN JUST A BOOKSELLER

READING PASSAGE

It's hard to imagine the Internet without Amazon.com. One of the Web's first major **e-tailers**, Amazon has become almost synonymous with online shopping. Since its early days of just selling books, Amazon has **ballooned** into a multi-product, multibillion-dollar company. Along the way, it has survived the ups and downs of the Internet's growth, which has seen many competitors come and go.

Amazon opened its doors online in 1995. It was truly a "**garage business**"; the company's founder, Jeff Bezos, started by packaging and shipping books from his home garage. The concept of shopping for books online was very exciting to people. At last, they could locate almost any book without having to make phone calls to several bookstores. People could also save money by shopping on Amazon, which offered **discount** prices that traditional bookstores couldn't match.

As Amazon's reputation grew, it made many **aggressive** moves. The company grew its market by launching international Web sites, starting with sites for England and Germany in 1998. With a goal of becoming a one-stop shopping site, Amazon expanded its product lines to include DVDs, CDs, and **countless** other items. And the company formed **partnerships** with many e-tailers and individuals to help sell their products using Amazon's technology and services.

Despite all the hard work, the road to success has been a **bumpy** one. For years, Amazon lost huge amounts of money. Some of its partnerships, such as its relationship with Toys "R" Us, have not worked out. After the dot-com **bust** of 2000, when many Internet businesses **went under**, Amazon's future was not at all clear.

During the long storm, Amazon kept flying the flag and pushing on, investing millions each year to improve its technology (see table). The hard work has paid off. From 2001 to 2007, the resilient company grew by an average of almost 30 percent per year. In 2003 Amazon achieved its first profit, and it continued to deliver impressive sales figures and profits in the years that followed. Not bad for a company that started in someone's garage.

Amazon's Road to Profitability

	2001	2002	2003	2004	2005	2006	2007
Revenues (in millions)	$3,122	$3,932	$5,263	$6,921	$8,490	$10,711	$14,835
Net Income (in millions)	-$567	-$149	$35	$588	$359	$190	$476
Research and Development Spending (in millions)	$241	$215	$207	$251	$451	$662	$818

COMPREHENSION CHECK

1. ( ) When Amazon first started selling books, ________.
   A. many people worked in their home garages to help pack the books
   B. they had partners in England and Germany helping out
   C. they also aggressively sold other products like CDs and DVDs
   D. the owner of the company did a lot of the work by hand

2. ( ) What is suggested about Amazon's competitors?
   A. They have all gone bankrupt.
   B. They always survive for a long time.
   C. Many have come, but even more have disappeared.
   D. They often have trouble staying in business.

3. ( ) What can we assume about Amazon's partnerships with other companies?
   A. Unsuccessful partnerships have been one of Amazon's key problems.
   B. Most of them have been failures.
   C. In 2000, Amazon ended them all.
   D. They're the main reason why Amazon lost huge amounts of money.

4. ( ) After starting operations, how long did it take Amazon to make a profit?
   A. Two years
   B. Three years
   C. Eight years
   D. Ten years

5. ( ) Which of the following is true about Amazon from 2001 to 2007?
   A. Every year, spending on research and development was greater than net income.
   B. Net income was negative for two out of seven years.
   C. Revenues increased by at least one billion dollars every year.
   D. Net income increased every year.

VOCABULARY BUILDING

e-tailer *(n)* — a store that sells things on the Internet
✦ More and more e-tailers are accepting PayPal as a form of payment.

balloon *(v)* — quickly expand
✦ Gas prices have ballooned in the last few years.

garage *(n)* — a building where a car is parked
✦ I keep all my tools in the garage.

aggressive *(adj)* — forceful and active in trying to achieve something
✦ The supervisors in every division are ready to lead our new aggressive sales push.

countless *(adj)* — very many
✦ Countless people have held this position. It seems nobody wants to stay on as manager.

partnership *(n)* — two or more businesses or people working together
✦ Setting up partnerships overseas can be rewarding, but it takes time and patience.

discount *(n)* — an amount of money taken off a product or service's usual price
✦ The store offers large discounts, which attract thousands of customers.

bumpy *(adj)* — not smooth; difficult
✦ The next 12 months will be a bumpy time as we restructure our operations.

bust *(n)* — a failure or serious downturn
✦ The plan was a bust because we didn't consider all the problems we might face.

resilient *(adj)* — tough; not easily quitting or failing
✦ Jeff will make it through these hard times. He's a resilient guy.

PHRASE BUILDING

go under — go out of business
✦ If we don't make a profit this month, we'll definitely go under.

fly the flag — show support for one's organization
✦ After all the negative media reports, the drug company is still flying the flag as if nothing had happened.

pay off — prove worthwhile
✦ This new computer is really paying off. I can get my work done faster than ever.

WHY DO WE SAY THAT?

fly the flag — Government buildings, navy ships, and other official and private places usually display the country's flag on a pole. That's called "flying" a flag, because the flag blows in the wind. When people "fly the flag," they are claiming or showing that their business or organization is alive and healthy. It's not necessary for there to be an actual flag, though many groups do have their own flags.

SENTENCE PATTERNS

It's hard to imagine	*the Internet*	without	*Amazon.com.*
	this town		*the old movie theater.*
	visiting Italy		*eating pasta.*

As Amazon's reputation grew, it made many	*aggressive*	moves.
	bold	
	questionable	

WHAT PEOPLE ARE SAYING ABOUT AMAZON

J.T. Amazon has pretty much ended the trips I used to make to bookstores. No, I take that back: I still go to bookstores to look at new titles, but I don't usually buy anything. It's cheaper to order online since Amazon has discounts on most titles, and I don't have to pay sales tax. Plus, the site often has free shipping if you order a certain amount.

Omar Amazon is a good company, but it's just too big. It takes away business from the smaller Web sites. It's almost impossible to avoid Amazon on the Internet, since its ads pop up all over the place when I search for information or visit other Web sites.

Henri I like Amazon's selection, but not its international shipping rates. I understand that shipping overseas costs more, but they also add a handling charge for each type of item you buy. That adds up to a lot of money. There are also restrictions on the types of things I can order, since I'm not in the States.

chapter 20

SKYPE: LET'S TALK!

READING PASSAGE

Since the mid-1990s, one of the greatest online challenges has been setting up voice chat over the Internet. Many early **endeavors** were criticized for their poor quality. Then along came Skype, a company started by two Europeans looking to change the way we **communicate**.

Skype was founded by Niklas Zennström (a Swedish **citizen**) and Janus Friis (a Danish citizen) in 2003. Neither of these **brilliant** young men were **novices** in the field. Together they had formed several software and Internet companies, including KaZaA, a program that lets people share files over the Internet.

To use Skype, two computers need to install the free program. Then, using a microphone and speaker (or headset), people can talk to each other for free over the Internet. It's as simple as that. **No wonder** the software has been downloaded nearly 300 million times (see table).

Aside from voice chat, Skype has an **array** of other features, such as text-chat, video-chat, and file-sharing functions. The program is used by individuals, companies, and even English teachers, who hold conversation classes through Skype. **At last**, people can talk across long distances without **paying an arm and a leg**.

But Skype is not a charity. It earns money by charging for **premium** services. With SkypeIn, you pay an **annual** fee for a local phone number in the U.S., Japan, or one of many other countries. When someone calls that number from a regular telephone, you receive the phone call on your computer. SkypeOut works the **opposite** way. You pay a fee to use your computer to call a regular telephone. Skype also charges a fee for its Skype Voicemail service. Still, these services are generally much cheaper than those offered by traditional telephone companies.

In October 2005, the fast-rising company was bought by eBay for $2.1 billion. Skype continues to **enhance** its software while adding new ways for people to use its services—on cell phones and PDAs, for example. As more people say "I'll Skype you" instead of "I'll call you," the way we communicate may never be the same again.

Skype by the Numbers (as of 2008)

Number of times Skype has been downloaded	over 700 million
Number of different languages Skype software is made in	28
Number of people registered with Skype	over 300 million
Average number of people logged onto Skype at the same time	12 million

COMPREHENSION CHECK

1. ( ) The founders of Skype _________.
   A. were new to setting up Internet companies
   B. had previously set up other companies, but they weren't well known
   C. had experience establishing online companies
   D. were both from Sweden

2. ( ) The article does *not* suggest that _________ are frequent Skype users.
   A. teachers
   B. charity workers
   C. businesspeople
   D. people who want to chat with faraway friends

3. ( ) Which of the following does not cost any money?
   A. Signing up to use SkypeIn for a year
   B. Making a call from your computer to a telephone using SkypeOut
   C. Using your computer to talk to another Skype user who is also using a computer
   D. Receiving Skype Voicemails

4. ( ) In the fifth paragraph, what does "But Skype is not a charity" mean?
   A. The company does not believe in giving its software away.
   B. Skype is in business to make a profit.
   C. The founders of Skype have never given anything to charity.
   D. Not all businesses can earn money.

5. ( ) Which of the following is true?
   A. Skype plans to make it easier for people to use its software on cell phones.
   B. SkypeIn costs money, but SkypeOut is free.
   C. There are always at least three million people logged onto Skype.
   D. To use SkypeOut, the person you are calling needs to be using a computer.

VOCABULARY BUILDING

endeavor *(n)* — an attempt
✦ Not every business endeavor will succeed. That's just a fact of life.

communicate *(v)* — talk; interact
✦ E-mail is a great way to communicate with distant friends.

citizen *(n)* — a passport holder of a country
✦ Dan lives in Japan, but he's an Australian citizen.

brilliant *(adj)* — very smart
✦ Elise is brilliant. She never gets a math problem wrong.

novice *(n)* — a newcomer; inexperienced person
✦ Even a novice can learn to use that program in 10 minutes.

array *(n)* — a large number
✦ Supermarkets sell an incredible array of things to eat.

opposite *(adj)* — completely different
✦ His brother had the opposite personality—warm, happy, and fun-loving.

premium *(adj)* — top-quality
✦ Our premium hotel packages include breakfast in bed and free use of our spa.

annual *(adj)* — yearly
✦ With an annual research budget in the billions, IBM regularly invents new technologies.

enhance *(v)* — improve
✦ Some people say that listening to classical music can enhance a child's intelligence.

PHRASE BUILDING

no wonder — the reason is obvious why
✦ Housing prices are terribly high. It's no wonder so many people rent instead of buying.

at last — finally
✦ At last, we have a few moments alone, away from the children!

pay an arm and a leg — pay a lot of money
✦ Don't shop at that store unless you want to pay an arm and a leg.

WHY DO WE SAY THAT?

pay an arm and a leg — If something is very expensive, you may have to use all your money to pay for it. When all of your money is gone, what's left to use as payment? To say that something is so expensive that we would need to sell our body parts to pay for it (which no one would actually do), we say you would have to "pay an arm and a leg" for it.

SENTENCE PATTERNS

Together	they had formed several software and Internet companies.
Working as a team,	
Joining forces,	

Skype also	*charges a fee for*	its Skype Voicemail service.
	makes you pay to use	
	earns income from	

WHAT PEOPLE ARE SAYING ABOUT SKYPE

Yu-zhen I just started using Skype last month. At first I wasn't used to talking into a microphone, but I got used to it pretty quickly. Sometimes there's a delay of a second or two if the connection is bad. That happens a lot when I talk to a friend in Thailand. I think she has a slow Internet connection.

Dominique For my business, I make a lot of phone calls, both within my country and overseas. I used to purchase calling cards on the Internet to save money on long-distance charges. That was good, but not nearly as cheap and easy as SkypeOut. Now I make probably a dozen calls around the world every day, and the quality is generally very good.

Tristan I've heard that Skype relies on a number of computers with super-fast connections to support slower computers. But they don't really tell you that, or at least they don't announce it loudly. So if you use Skype and you have a fast connection, there's a chance that your Internet speed may slow down. I'm not sure if that affects a lot of people or if they've changed the way traffic is directed. But it's something that has affected my use of the software.

VOCABULARY AND PHRASE REVIEW

A. Complete each sentence, using the best word(s) from the box.

convince	**aggressive**	**partnership**
destination	**communicate**	**combat**
sensitive	**enhance**	**revenue stream**

1. I've tried to talk to Stephen about how loud he plays his music, but he doesn't seem to understand. It's very hard to ________________ with him sometimes.

2. Adding cameras would ________________ security, but it would be expensive.

3. There's ________________ information about our employees in those files, so only three people are allowed to look at them.

4. Ladies and gentlemen, we'll reach our ________________ in 3½ hours. Just sit back, relax, and enjoy the flight.

5. Those pants are in last year's style, so their sales don't provide much of a(n) ________________ anymore.

6. Everyone in the neighborhood needs to work together to ________________ crime. If you see anything unusual, report it to the police.

7. We all agree we need to redo our Web site. The question is, how can I ________________ Ms. Lin to approve the project?

8. Rick is a(n) ________________ salesperson. He never quits, and he sometimes spends months trying to win a new client.

B. Choose the best word to complete each sentence.

1. Oil is selling for $140 a barrel. Prices sure have _________ recently.

   A. combined B. matured C. ballooned D. tracked

2. Our _________ order will be for 5,000 pieces. We'll order more when that lot sells out.

   A. initial B. bumpy C. resilient D. critical

3. There are two _________ of customers. One type will keep buying from us if our prices rise slightly; the other type will switch to a competitor.

   A. fortunes B. categories C. suspicions D. outlooks

4. You don't need to be so _________. Tell everyone how you were responsible for most of your firm's profits last year.

A. brilliant B. humble C. premium D. envied

5. There's a(n) _________ of paper types to choose from. It depends on the level of quality and style that you're looking for.

   A. array B. discount C. endeavor D. bust

C. Match the beginning and ending of each sentence.

1. Virtually everybody here	knows one another.
2. I wouldn't say I'm an expert,	we shouldn't start investing in metals.
3. There are countless reasons why	will be held at the convention center.
4. In the 1990s, Ryan made a fortune	but I'm not a novice either.
5. This summer, our annual party	buying and selling stocks.

D. Choose the best response to what the first person says.

1. **Olivia:** Our stock is up, and every employee will be receiving a $1,000 bonus and 10 shares of stock at the end of the year.

   A. Albert: Why should employees have to pay an arm and a leg for the stock?

   B. Albert: Your revenue stream must have improved a lot.

   C. Albert: Gosh, it sure hasn't been all peaches and cream for you guys.

2. **Gene:** I don't know how we're going to keep from going under.

   A. Walter: Gene, you know the risk of failing goes hand in hand with running a business. You did your best.

   B. Walter: No wonder Antoine is in such a great mood. You chose a good partner.

   C. Walter: All the hard work is finally paying off.

3. **Florence:** If you reduced these items to half their current size, would it increase the battery's life by 25 percent?

   A. Mac: Doubling the battery's life is easier said than done.

   B. Mac: Judging by what our customers are saying, I don't think we should increase the size.

   C. Mac: That's quite a tall order. I'm not sure it's possible.

section 5

✦ FIVE BUSINESS LEGENDS

TARGET VOCABULARY

abroad *(adv)*	Chap. 21: Sony	**icon** *(n)*	Chap. 23: Gucci
assemble *(v)*	Chap. 25: IKEA	**immigrate** *(v)*	Chap. 24: A. Carnegie
classic *(adj)*	Chap. 22: Sam Walton	**innovate** *(v)*	Chap. 21: Sony
complex *(adj)*	Chap. 23: Gucci	**intentionally** *(adv)*	Chap. 25: IKEA
convict *(v)*	Chap. 23: Gucci	**inventory** *(n)*	Chap. 22: Sam Walton
craftsperson *(n)*	Chap. 25: IKEA	**involvement** *(n)*	Chap. 22: Sam Walton
creative *(adj)*	Chap. 23: Gucci	**labor** *(n)*	Chap. 25: IKEA
developing country *(n)*	Chap. 25: IKEA	**legendary** *(adj)*	Chap. 21: Sony
donate *(v)*	Chap. 24: A. Carnegie	**luxury** *(n)*	Chap. 23: Gucci
eliminate *(v)*	Chap. 25: IKEA	**massive** *(adj)*	Chap. 24: A. Carnegie
emphasis *(n)*	Chap. 21: Sony	**mercy** *(n)*	Chap. 22: Sam Walton
entrepreneur *(n)*	Chap. 25: IKEA	**miserable** *(adj)*	Chap. 24: A. Carnegie
evidence *(n)*	Chap. 21: Sony	**momentous** *(adj)*	Chap. 25: IKEA
evolve *(v)*	Chap. 21: Sony	**multiply** *(v)*	Chap. 24: A. Carnegie
generosity *(n)*	Chap. 24: A. Carnegie	**notable** *(adj)*	Chap. 21: Sony

odd job *(n)*	Chap. 22: Sam Walton	**roots** *(n)*	Chap. 25: IKEA
option *(n)*	Chap. 24: A. Carnegie	**scholarship** *(n)*	Chap. 22: Sam Walton
philanthropist *(n)*	Chap. 24: A. Carnegie	**setback** *(n)*	Chap. 21: Sony
pocket-sized *(adj)*	Chap. 21: Sony	**shrewd** *(adj)*	Chap. 22: Sam Walton
reality *(n)*	Chap. 22: Sam Walton	**specifically** *(adv)*	Chap. 25: IKEA
remainder *(n)*	Chap. 23: Gucci	**stake** *(n)*	Chap. 23: Gucci
research *(n)*	Chap. 24: A. Carnegie	**stock exchange** *(n)*	Chap. 21: Sony
revival *(n)*	Chap. 23: Gucci	**tale** *(n)*	Chap. 22: Sam Walton
roaring *(adj)*	Chap. 23: Gucci	**triumph** *(n)*	Chap. 23: Gucci
rock-bottom *(adj)*	Chap. 22: Sam Walton	**working-class** *(adj)*	Chap. 24: A. Carnegie

TARGET PHRASES

at one time or another	Chap. 21: Sony	**lay off**	Chap. 24: A. Carnegie
buy out	Chap. 22: Sam Walton	**make ends meet**	Chap. 22: Sam Walton
climb the corporate ladder	Chap. 24: A. Carnegie	**odds and ends**	Chap. 25: IKEA
firing on all cylinders	Chap. 25: IKEA	**on the plus side**	Chap. 23: Gucci
by leaps and bounds	Chap. 22: Sam Walton	**push the envelope**	Chap. 21: Sony
ins and outs	Chap. 25: IKEA	**see eye to eye**	Chap. 23: Gucci
keep one's nose to the grindstone	Chap. 21: Sony	**take the reins**	Chap. 23: Gucci
		without question	Chap. 24: A. Carnegie

Chapter 21

SONY

READING PASSAGE

At one time or another, most of us have either owned or used a Sony product. For more than 60 years, the company has filled the world with millions of radios, cameras, and other electronic wonders. It also owns some of the world's largest movie, music, and television businesses.

Founded in Japan in 1946 by Akio Morita (a physicist) and Masaru Ibuka (an engineer), the company was originally called Tokyo Telecommunications Engineering Corporation. (The name was changed to Sony Corporation in 1958.) The two businessmen led a team of 20 people in designing and building electric products. The first of these, a simple rice cooker, was a failure. But the team members **kept their noses to the grindstone**, looking for the right product that they could sell locally and **abroad**.

The hard work paid off in the 1950s with a very popular line of **pocket-sized** radios. Millions of units were sold, and Sony went on to become a household name in Asia, Europe, North America, and beyond.

As **evidence** of its international outlook, Sony started selling shares on the New York **Stock Exchange** in 1970 (see chart). That made it the first Japanese company to sell its stock on the exchange. And believing that local manufacturing would be best for overseas markets, it opened factories in the U.S. in 1972 and England in 1974.

Over the decades, Sony continued **innovating**, filling store shelves with many new and exciting products. These included the Trinitron TV (1968), the Walkman (1979), the CD player (1982), the 3½-inch floppy disk (1982), the PlayStation video-game system (1994), and the Blu-Ray Disc (2006). A key reason for this unending stream of new products has been an **emphasis** on research and design. Indeed, Sony gives bonuses to engineers whose designs are made into products.

Yet not every Sony product has been a success. Its most **notable** failure was the Betamax video-recording format. Launched in 1975, it eventually lost out in the home consumer market to the more popular VHS format. And Sony suffered badly when its stock price, which had increased rapidly in the high-tech bubble, burst in 2000. Still, **setbacks** like these only challenge Sony to work harder and continue **pushing the envelope**. With more than 180,000 employees and revenues topping US$85 billion in 2007, this **legendary** company continues to **evolve** and amaze.

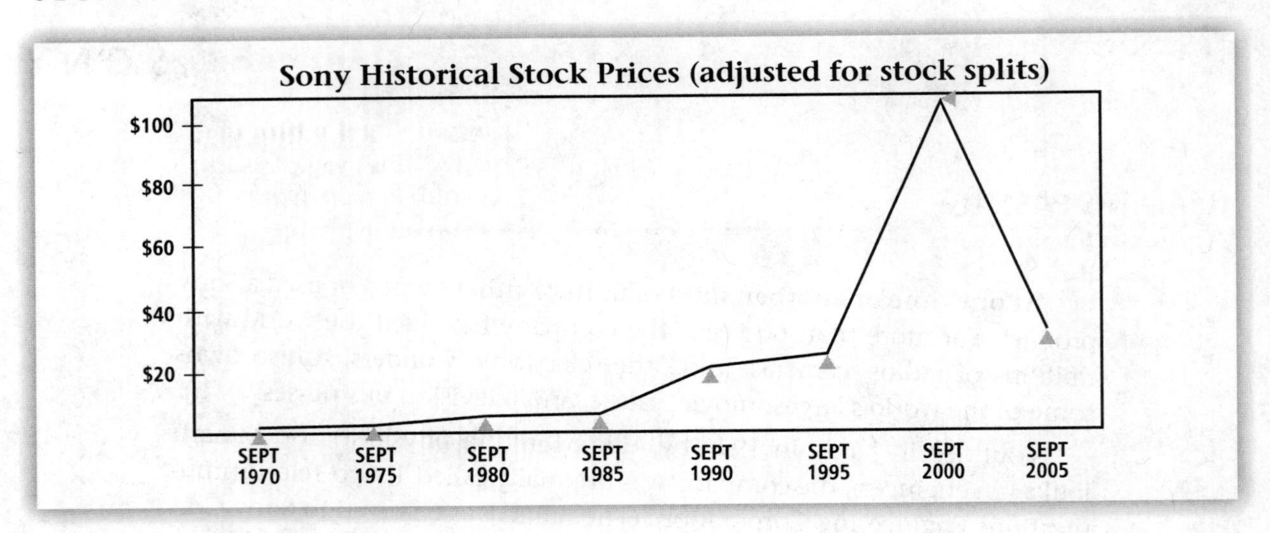

COMPREHENSION CHECK

1. ( ) How did the Sony team react to the performance of their first product?
   A. They were extremely happy.
   B. They hired 20 engineers and physicists to improve their research strength.
   C. They went abroad to look for a better product.
   D. They kept working hard to develop a successful product.

2. ( ) Which product helped Sony win international fame early in its history?
   A. The PlayStation
   B. The Betamax video format
   C. A rice cooker
   D. A small radio

3. ( ) The article suggests that Sony ________.
   A. has a history of only producing successful electronic goods
   B. has relied on selling the same products for 40 years
   C. is careful not to spend a lot of money on research and development
   D. sometimes releases products that don't succeed

4. ( ) What does "wonders" in the first paragraph mean?
   A. serious questions
   B. amazing things
   C. big doubts
   D. fantastic imaginations

5. ( ) What would happen if a Sony engineer designed a TV that was later produced?
   A. The engineer would be promoted.
   B. The engineer would receive extra pay.
   C. The marketing campaign for the TV would be led by the engineer.
   D. Sony would name the TV after the engineer.

VOCABULARY BUILDING

abroad *(adv)* — overseas
✦ Each year, millions of people travel abroad to study, do business, or take a tour of another country.

pocket-sized *(adj)* — small enough to fit in your pocket
✦ I love this MP3 player. It's pocket-sized, so I can carry it anywhere.

evidence *(n)* — proof
✦ Do we have any evidence that Sam is the thief?

stock exchange *(n)* — a place where stocks are bought and sold
✦ Being allowed to trade on the floor of a stock exchange costs a lot.

innovate *(v)* — develop new methods, styles, or techniques
✦ Research is very expensive, so the cost of innovating keeps going up and up.

emphasis *(n)* — special importance
✦ Here at Brockman & Laird Corp., we place a strong emphasis on honesty and loyalty.

notable *(adj)* — significant; important
✦ Several notable painters went to school here.

setback *(n)* — something that causes a delay or loss
✦ Losing the Smith account was a setback, but we have plenty of other clients to keep us going.

legendary *(adj)* — very famous, usually for many years
✦ Warren Buffett is a legendary investor, with assets worth billions of dollars.

evolve *(v)* — change, grow, and develop
✦ At first we only made ice cream, but we've evolved into one of the country's largest sellers of cookies and cakes.

PHRASE BUILDING

at one time or another — at some time in the past
✦ We've all been treated badly at one time or another.

keep one's nose to the grindstone — keep working hard
✦ I'm afraid I'll be keeping my nose to the grindstone all week. I can't go anywhere until I'm finished.

push the envelope — refuse to accept limits that most people accept
✦ For many years, his research has pushed the envelope in astronomical theory.

WHY DO WE SAY THAT?

keep one's nose to the grindstone — A grindstone is a stone wheel that is used to sharpen knives and other metal objects. When you are working hard to sharpen something, you may bend over the grindstone, with your face (and nose) getting very close to it. So when you are working hard at something, we say you are keeping your nose to the grindstone.

SENTENCE PATTERNS

The first of these, a simple rice cooker, was a failure.
One of their offerings,
Their initial product,

Yet not every Sony product *is a success.*
works out.
meets expectations.

WHAT PEOPLE ARE SAYING ABOUT SONY

Roger I've been using the same Sony Trinitron TV for more than 15 years. It's not as fancy as some of the newer TVs, but it still works fine. I wish more companies would make products that were built to last.

Hideki I've got a Sony cell phone and digital camera. My son has the new PlayStation, which he plays all the time. And my wife wants us to get a new Sony flat-screen TV. It seems Sony makes just about every type of electronic product we need, plus the quality is excellent. Why buy from another company?

Doreen One of my friends says the best things from Sony are the ones made in Japan, and the quality isn't as good when they're made in other countries. I'm not sure if that's true, but I've noticed that the products made in Japan tend to be more expensive.

SAM WALTON: FOUNDER OF THE WAL-MART EMPIRE

chapter 22

READING PASSAGE

Sam Walton's story reads like a **classic tale** of the American dream come true. From humble beginnings on a Midwestern farm, Walton eventually built an empire that made him the richest man in America. Along the way, he helped change the way the world does business.

Sam Walton was born on March 29, 1916, in Oklahoma, a rural state. His family lived on a farm until he was five. During that time, and through the Great Depression, Walton worked at **odd jobs** to help **make ends meet**. He learned the necessity of hard work and the importance of saving.

In 1945, Walton started his career in retail sales. He bought one of the franchise stores of a company called Ben Franklin, which sold household items. It became very successful, and Walton opened several more franchise stores for Ben Franklin, though he was allowed to use the name Walton 5&10. Eventually, in 1962, he felt it was time to start his own chain of stores. Wal-Mart was born.

Walton's business philosophy was an important part of his rapid success. He made sure that the shelves were always well-stocked and clean, while emphasizing high-volume sales, **rock-bottom** prices, and excellent customer service. Walton also made a number of innovations, like moving the checkout counters to the front of the stores and sharing profits with his employees. Later he added an advanced **inventory** system, to keep the shelves full and the customers happy.

As these methods were perfected, Wal-Mart expanded. The company grew from 24 stores in 1967 to 276 by 1979 (see chart). Walton also **bought out** many competitors, while forcing others out of business by selling goods so cheaply that nobody could match the price.

Yet Walton was more than a **shrewd** businessman. He started college **scholarship** programs for local students. He also established Wal-Mart's long **involvement** in local charity events.

After Sam Walton died on April 16, 1992, the empire he founded continued to grow **by leaps and bounds**. Indeed, Wal-Mart is now the world's largest retailer and largest private employer, with more than two million employees. But it all started as a dream on an Oklahoma farm—a dream that became **reality** through hard work, vision, and a total lack of **mercy** for the competition.

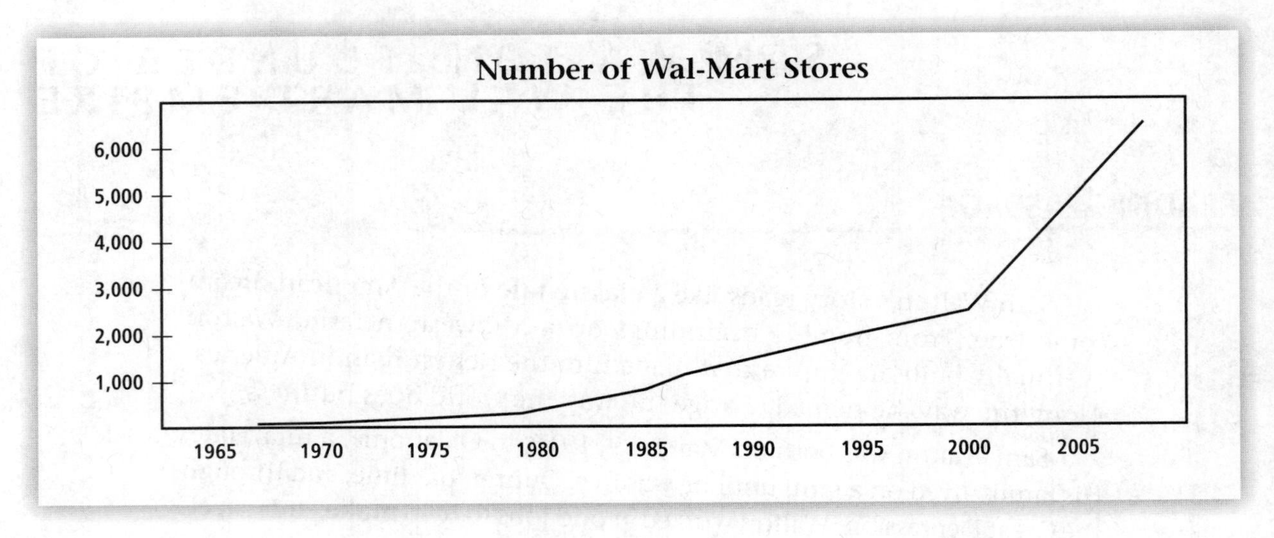

COMPREHENSION CHECK

1. ( ) Sam Walton was very careful with money. What does the article suggest is the source of this habit?
   A. Walton grew up poor.
   B. Walton had to fight with competitors year after year.
   C. Walton spent his life working in retail.
   D. Walton wanted to save all he could to support local charities.

2. ( ) Walton's idea of moving checkout counters to the front of the store is an example of ______.
   A. something Walton learned from the Ben Franklin store owners
   B. a business technique Walton learned from his father
   C. a new idea Walton put to work in his stores
   D. Wal-Mart's competitors' business practices

3. ( ) What does the article imply about Wal-Mart's attitude toward competitors?
   A. The company is happy to allow local competitors to share its market.
   B. Wal-Mart always uses the same method to deal with competitors.
   C. Wal-Mart believes in buying every competitor it can.
   D. The company does not ignore its competitors.

4. ( ) The article does *not* state that Sam Walton was concerned with __________.
   A. his stores' treatment of customers
   B. selling large quantities of goods
   C. making large profits through the sale of luxury goods
   D. keeping the store shelves filled with products

5. ( ) Which of the following is true?
   A. When Sam Walton died, Wal-Mart had more than 1,000 stores.
   B. The number of Wal-Mart stores doubled from 1987 to 1995.
   C. The greatest period of growth in Wal-Mart stores was from 1985 to 1987.
   D. In its first decade in business, Wal-Mart opened more than 200 stores.

VOCABULARY BUILDING

classic *(adj)* — standard, typical
✦ That guy was trying to pressure you into buying something. It's a classic sales technique.

tale *(n)* — a story
✦ When I was young, I loved to listen to my father's tales of his overseas travels.

odd job *(n)* — a short and temporary job
✦ In college, I had a few odd jobs to make some spending money.

rock-bottom *(adj)* — lowest
✦ Fifty dollars is my rock-bottom price. I can't go any lower than that.

inventory *(n)* — a stock or supply, usually of goods for sale
✦ We've got to move at least half of this inventory out of here before the end of the month.

shrewd *(adj)* — clever
✦ Your mother is a shrewd businesswoman. Nobody would try to cheat her.

scholarship *(n)* — a sum of money awarded to someone to pay for school costs
✦ Because of his good grades in high school, Barry won a scholarship to a top university.

involvement *(n)* — participation
✦ Lucy doesn't want anyone to know about her involvement in our business.

reality *(n)* — truth; existence
✦ In reality, almost everyone enjoys eating junk food.

mercy *(n)* — kindness toward someone who could be punished
✦ The thief asked for mercy, saying he only stole the money to feed his family.

PHRASE BUILDING

make ends meet — have enough money to pay one's bills and daily living costs
✦ Now that I'm the only one in the family with a job, it's harder to make ends meet.

buy out — purchase someone's share in a company
✦ There are two other partners in the firm, but I plan to buy them out.

by leaps and bounds — with large increases in growth, size, amount, etc.
✦ This city is growing by leaps and bounds. I remember when the area was mostly farmland.

WHY DO WE SAY THAT?

by leaps and bounds — Leaps and bounds are especially big jumps. If you leap from place to place, you can quickly cover large distances. So, when something happens "by leaps and bounds," it means there are large changes in growth, amount, etc.

SENTENCE PATTERNS

As these	*methods were perfected,*	Wal-Mart expanded.
	problems were figured out,	
	issues were resolved,	

Yet Walton was more than a	*shrewd*	businessman.
	clever	
	hardworking	

WHAT PEOPLE ARE SAYING ABOUT SAM WALTON

Michael Sam Walton's story reminds me of my father's. He also started with nothing, but went on to build a successful business. Of course, my father wasn't nearly as wealthy (I wish!), but there are some similarities, like the way they were both careful with money, and how they both focused on customer service.

Adriana I can see how every business wants to grow, but I wonder if Wal-Mart has gotten too big. Every time they open a new store, the smaller stores in the area seem to start losing customers and may even go out of business. But I can see how that isn't all Wal-Mart's fault. People are deciding themselves to shop there to save money. I just wish there was a way that both large and small businesses could exist side by side.

Jacques The way the world works, I think it's natural that someone like Sam Walton came along to build his giant chain of stores. The most efficient businesses are rewarded, and the best of those get bigger and bigger. Then eventually they've got a ton of power—even enough to affect how companies design and make things.

chapter 23
GUCCI: A FAMILY STORY

READING PASSAGE

Drama. Murder. Father against son. Brother against brother. Gucci's story is like an Italian opera, full of **complex** and violent relationships. But after hard times and horror stories, the name stands today as an **icon** in the world of **luxury** goods.

Guccio Gucci founded the company in Florence in 1921. He soon earned a reputation for high-quality handbags and other leather goods. He himself designed some of the firm's best-known products.

Following Guccio's death in 1953, his two sons, Aldo and his movie-star brother Rodolfo, **took the reins**. Aldo took Gucci global, opening stores in New York (1953), London (1961), and Tokyo (1972). In just a short period of time, the company had risen to the summit of the fashion world, with film stars proudly wearing Gucci styles.

The Gucci brothers didn't always **see eye to eye**. In fact, they fought constantly over every aspect of the business. Their children joined in the battle, and Aldo's son managed to send his 81-year-old father to prison. By the late 1980s, the company was in financial trouble, and something had to be done. Rodolfo's son Maurizio sold the **remainder** of his **stake** to a foreign group in 1993, taking the company completely out of the Gucci family's hands. But its **revival** was about to begin.

1995 was a year of **triumph** and tragedy for Gucci Group (its new name). **On the plus side**, Tom Ford, a young American designer, became the **creative** director. His first clothing line was a **roaring** success, making Gucci hip and hot again. 1995 was also the year the company went public. That very same year, Maurizio Gucci was murdered outside the Gucci office in Milan. His ambitious ex-wife, intensely angered by his decision to remarry, was later **convicted** of hiring a professional killer to do the job. Now that's drama!

The company grew with a series of purchases, including Yves Saint Laurent (1999) and Balenciaga (2001) (see table). In 2004, Gucci Group was bought by PPR, one of Europe's largest companies. Tom Ford also left Gucci that year, a decade after leading the company back to glory.

The Gucci brand continues to shine bright, with sales of US$7.7 billion in 2007. Over 400 Gucci stores and other dealers sell the label's watches, handbags, clothing, and other fine goods. Through all the drama, the luxury legend lives on.

Sampling of Gucci Group Acquisitions	
November 1999	70% stake in Sergio Rossi (increased to 100% in 2004)
December 1999	100% stake in Yves Saint Laurent
May 2000	100% stake in Boucheron
February 2001	78.5% stake in Bottega Veneta
March 2001	100% stake in Di Modolo
July 2001	91% stake in Balenciaga

COMPREHENSION CHECK

1. ( ) What is the main idea?
   A. Guccio Gucci created one of the world's most famous fashion labels.
   B. It's hard for family members to run a successful company.
   C. Gucci has had to work hard to keep its place in the fashion world.
   D. In the late 1980s, Gucci faced some of its biggest challenges ever.

2. ( ) How long were members of the Gucci family involved in running the company?
   A. 21 years
   B. 40 years
   C. 72 years
   D. 83 years

3. ( ) How did Tom Ford help Gucci?
   A. He designed very popular clothes for the company.
   B. He took the company public.
   C. He served as the CEO of the company for 10 years.
   D. He renamed the company.

4. ( ) What did *not* happen in 1995?
   A. A member of the Gucci family was killed.
   B. Shares of Gucci were publicly sold.
   C. Gucci hired a new creative director.
   D. A Gucci executive was accused of murdering Maurizio Gucci.

5. ( ) Which of the following is true about Gucci Group acquisitions?
   A. The group always purchases a 100 percent stake in other companies.
   B. The Boucheron and Bottega Veneta purchases occurred three months apart.
   C. It took over four years for the group to completely acquire Sergio Rossi.
   D. The group made four purchases per year from 1999 to 2001 on average.

VOCABULARY BUILDING

complex *(adj)* — complicated
✦ These reports are complex. You'd need to be a specialist to understand them.

icon *(n)* — a symbol of something
✦ Bill Gates is an icon of the PC business.

luxury *(n)* — an expensive item that is purely for comfort or enjoyment
✦ For a lot of people, owning a car is a luxury that they can't afford. They rely instead on public transportation to get around.

creative *(adj)* — having a strong imagination
✦ As a product designer, she was able to use her creative energies almost every day.

remainder *(n)* — the quantity that is left
✦ We gave away most of the umbrellas. What should we do with the remainder?

stake *(n)* — an ownership share in a business or other activity
✦ Since oil prices are so high, this might be a good time to buy a stake in a gas station.

revival *(n)* — a return to a better state; a recovery
✦ Companies in trouble often hire a new CEO to lead their revival.

triumph *(n)* — a victory or great success
✦ Winning the highway construction contract was a triumph. It's just what we needed.

roaring *(adj)* — huge; amazing
✦ The studio expects the new Daniel Craig movie to be a roaring hit.

convict *(v)* — find somebody guilty of a crime
✦ The evidence against him isn't strong. I don't think the jury will convict him.

PHRASE BUILDING

take the reins — take control; start directing something
✦ While I'm in South America, I need someone to take the reins at the head office.

see eye to eye — agree
✦ We may not always see eye to eye, but I consider you a dear friend.

on the plus side — referring to something positive

✦ On the plus side, our customers love us. But that customer base isn't large enough to keep us in business.

WHY DO WE SAY THAT?

take the reins — Reins are ropes or straps used to control a horse. When you take a horse's reins, you take control of the horse. We also use the phrase to refer to other situations in life. When you "take the reins," you take charge of a situation.

SENTENCE PATTERNS

The Gucci brand continues to shine bright, with *sales of US$7.7 billion in 2007.*
a huge increase in turnover last year.
a 21% year-on-year increase in profits.

Through *all the drama,* the luxury legend lives on.
some very hard times,
all kinds of trouble,

WHAT PEOPLE ARE SAYING ABOUT GUCCI

Lisa There's something about Gucci bags that's hard to explain. It's not just one thing. It's the quality, the look, the style . . . all those things together. I think it's my mother's fault. She bought me my first Gucci bag when I was in high school. Since then, they're almost the only bags I'll buy. It's like drinking good wine. Once you've had the best, you don't want anything else!

Joon-Seung Gucci items are very big status symbols in Korea. If you wear Gucci sunglasses, clothes, or anything else, you're telling people that you're fashionable and you can afford the best.

Katya I only buy what I like, and only if it suits me. Some Gucci clothes are nice. They go well with my jewelry. But others . . . I don't know, you don't always get what you pay for. Do you know what I mean? With designer clothes, you're paying a lot for the label. Sometimes it's worth it and sometimes it isn't.

chapter 24 ANDREW CARNEGIE

READING PASSAGE

The legend of Andrew Carnegie is complex. On the one hand, the steel king is remembered as a powerful businessman—at one time the world's richest man. On the other hand, he gave away 90 percent of his fortune, making him one of history's greatest **philanthropists**.

Carnegie was born in Scotland in 1835 into a **working-class** family. As machines replaced workers in the textile business, his father was **laid off**. Poor, yet hopeful for a better future, the family **immigrated** to America when Andrew was 13. It was a 50-day trip in **miserable** conditions.

In America, a classroom education was not an **option** for Andrew. He had to work to help pay the bills. But he was smart and hardworking, and he moved on to better and better jobs, from factory worker to factory master.

At the Pennsylvania Railroad, where Carnegie worked for 12 years, he quickly **climbed the corporate ladder**. He then opened his own business in 1865, building iron bridges. Later, he turned to making steel, and his riches **multiplied** even faster. Eventually, in 1901, Carnegie sold his steel company to J.P. Morgan for a **massive** profit (see table).

But Carnegie was not only concerned with money. From his parents, he had learned to believe in the equality of all people. He also believed in the power of education. As a boy, Carnegie had a chance to use a small library, and as an adult he continued to educate himself through reading.

One might say that Carnegie wanted the world to read. During his lifetime, he **donated** money to open more than 2,800 public libraries, including one in his hometown in Scotland. He also gave to universities and supported peace-building efforts. His largest gift, of $125 million, formed the Carnegie Corporation, which supported schools and scientific **research**.

Without question, Carnegie was a complex man. His fortune was made from modern factories and industries—the type that had put his father out of work. History does not look kindly on the way Carnegie treated his workers. And yet he gave and gave, supporting the common person through his **generosity**. For that, history remembers Andrew Carnegie fondly.

Highlights of Andrew Carnegie's Career

YEAR	EVENT
1853	Starts working at Pennsylvania Railroad
1859	Becomes superintendent at Pennsylvania Railroad
1865	Leaves Pennsylvania Railroad and opens Keystone Bridge Company
1875	Opens the first of many steel factories
1889	Publishes *The Gospel of Wealth,* encouraging the rich to use their money for good causes
1901	Sells Carnegie Steel to J. P. Morgan for a $250 million personal profit (valued at more than $4 billion in today's money)

COMPREHENSION CHECK

1. ( ) Why did Carnegie's family move to America?
   A. Andrew's father was offered a good job in the U.S.
   B. To allow Andrew to get a good education.
   C. The family wasn't doing well in Scotland.
   D. To invest in an American textile business.

2. ( ) A decade after Carnegie left his job at the railroad, __________.
   A. he opened a bridge-building business
   B. his first steel factory started operating
   C. he finished climbing the corporate ladder
   D. he wrote a book about the importance of charity

3. ( ) According to the article, how was Carnegie a complicated person?
   A. In some ways he was very kind, and in other ways unkind.
   B. He had more money than he could spend.
   C. He gave away 90 percent of his money, but he didn't understand why.
   D. He helped found many libraries, yet he didn't know how to read.

4. ( ) Which type of charity work is not mentioned?
   A. Giving to libraries
   B. Donating bridges
   C. Helping schools
   D. Supporting research

5. ( ) What does "that" in the final sentence refer to?
   A. Carnegie's fortune
   B. The people who worked for Carnegie
   C. Carnegie's work as a philanthropist
   D. The generosity of the common person

VOCABULARY BUILDING

philanthropist *(n)* — a person who makes great efforts to help others, especially by giving a lot of money to charity

✦ Some businesspeople become great philanthropists after they retire. Others start giving away their money during their working years.

working-class *(adj)* — of an economic class of people working at factories and other manual jobs

✦ This is a working-class bar. Most people who come here work at the nearby mill.

immigrate *(v)* — permanently move to another country

✦ Many people immigrate to another country to give their children a chance at a better education.

miserable *(adj)* — very unpleasant

✦ This cold weather makes me miserable. I wish the sun would come out!

option *(n)* — a choice

✦ If your boss won't give you a raise, I suppose quitting is an option.

massive *(adj)* — huge

✦ The new downtown shopping center is massive. It has 300 stores inside.

research *(n)* — serious study in order to discover new information, especially for practical uses

✦ The company had spent almost a billion dollars on research over five years.

donate *(v)* — give away

✦ I don't need these clothes. I'm going to donate them so someone else can wear them.

multiply *(v)* — increase by a very large amount

✦ After their largest factory burned down, the company's problems multiplied.

generosity *(n)* — the quality of giving without needing to be asked

✦ Ms. Franklin is known for her generosity. She recently gave the school $10,000 to repair its basketball courts.

PHRASE BUILDING

lay off — fire

✦ When this factory closes, more than 100 people will be laid off.

climb the corporate ladder — rise to higher and higher positions in a company

✦ Johnny is impatient. He doesn't want to spend 10 years climbing the corporate ladder. He thinks he can become the CEO this year.

without question — definitely
✦ Ralph, this is without question the best chocolate cake I have ever eaten.

WHY DO WE SAY THAT?

climb the corporate ladder — A ladder is a simple structure for climbing. As you go up a ladder, you climb up to higher and higher steps, or rungs. Likewise, a corporate ladder includes many positions, with the boss or CEO at the top rung. Someone who "climbs the corporate ladder" works hard to rise to higher and higher positions in a company.

SENTENCE PATTERNS

In America, a classroom education was *not an option* for Andrew.
out of reach
just a dream

He also believed in the power of *education.*
friendship.
positive thinking.

WHAT PEOPLE ARE SAYING ABOUT ANDREW CARNEGIE

Melvin I live in New York City, and I love music, so I go to performances at Carnegie Hall several times a year. It's a gorgeous building, and the sound carries fabulously. Though I'm not related or connected in any way to Andrew Carnegie, I feel like I know him. I mean, he donated so much money to the arts. When you go to a place like Carnegie Hall, you can really see and feel his generosity.

Lourdes It's interesting how Carnegie grew up poor but then worked hard to become so rich later on. It's like he saw life as a competition to make more money than anyone else. Since he had so little as a child, he wanted to have everything as an adult.

Collin Andrew Carnegie was like any one of us. We've each got the potential for good and bad, selfishness and giving. He just happened to have both of these qualities on a large scale. Or maybe it was because he was so rich that it seemed that way. Carnegie had more money than he could ever spend on his own needs. I just wish more modern businesspeople would exercise more of their giving side.

chapter 25 IKEA

READING PASSAGE

If you recently went shopping at IKEA for a Billy (a bookshelf) or a Detolf (a glass cabinet), you had a lot of company. Over the last 60 years, the retail legend with unique product names has probably sold more furniture than any other company. Millions of customers worldwide have filled their homes with IKEA products, turning the Swedish chain into a multibillion-dollar giant.

IKEA's **roots** were far more humble. Founded in 1943 by Ingvar Kamprad, a 17-year-old Swede, the company started as a mail-order business. One might expect such a young **entrepreneur** to grow tired of the **ins and outs** of a daily business, but not Ingvar. Within four years, he went from selling pens, watches, and other **odds and ends** to hiring local **craftspeople** to build furniture for IKEA.

The 1950s were a **momentous** period for the company. Kamprad opened his first showroom in 1953. Two years later, the company started designing its own furniture. Shortly after that, IKEA began selling items in "flat packages." That is, the products came in several pieces, packed in a box, and customers **assembled** the items at home. According to the company, this idea came from an IKEA employee who had to take apart a table to make it fit into a car.

Besides do-it-yourself furniture and "one-way" store layouts (IKEA stores are **intentionally** designed to make you walk through every section before arriving at the cash register), IKEA is known for its emphasis on children. It sells many products designed **specifically** for use by boys and girls. The company is also a big supporter of children's rights, helping in efforts to **eliminate** child **labor** in **developing countries**.

With sales of $28.9 billion in 2007, IKEA is **firing on all cylinders**. It now has more than 250 stores in over 30 countries (see table). As the world buys Billys and Detolfs by the thousands, Ingvar Kamprad (already one of the world's richest people) will continue to have a reason to smile. If there isn't an IKEA near you yet, that could change soon, as the retail legend grows and grows.

IKEA By the Numbers (2007)

Number of stores	278
Number of countries with IKEA stores	36
Number of employees	118,000
Number of products sold by IKEA	over 9,500
Number of customers	522 million

COMPREHENSION CHECK

1. ( ) What does the article suggest is unique about Kamprad as a young man?
   A. Despite his age, he stayed focused on growing the company.
   B. He was able to sell odds and ends in the mail.
   C. Local craftspeople were willing to work for him, although he was young.
   D. He opened a business at a very young age.

2. ( ) When did IKEA start selling "flat packages"?
   A. 1943
   B. 1950
   C. 1953
   D. around 1955

3. ( ) What does the article imply about "one-way" layouts?
   A. They make it easier for children to walk through stores.
   B. The layouts make room for cash registers in every section of the store.
   C. Their intention is to allow customers to exercise by walking a lot.
   D. Their purpose is to have customers look at many different products before leaving the store.

4. ( ) Which of the following is true?
   A. IKEA sells close to 100,000 different products.
   B. More than half a billion people shopped at IKEA in 2007.
   C. IKEA had sales of $28.9 million in 2007.
   D. The number of different products IKEA sells is nearly 10 times larger than the number of IKEA employees.

5. ( ) What does the article suggest about IKEA's future?
   A. The company is happy with its current size.
   B. As IKEA already has stores in 200 countries, opening more will be hard.
   C. The company plans to keep expanding.
   D. Kamprad hopes to become the world's richest person.

VOCABULARY BUILDING

roots *(n)* — beginnings

✦ This music has its roots in New Orleans jazz.

entrepreneur *(n)* — a businessperson willing to take risks on new moneymaking opportunities

✦ Of course there's risk in being an entrepreneur. But there's also the chance to make a lot of money.

craftsperson *(n)* — a person who makes things using traditional methods

✦ These bowls were made by a local craftsperson.

momentous *(adj)* — extremely important

✦ The meeting this afternoon is a momentous occasion. We're going to sign the contract for our biggest deal ever.

assemble *(v)* — put together

✦ Can you help me assemble this bicycle? I'm terrible with instructions.

intentionally *(adv)* — on purpose

✦ Those stones were put there intentionally to prevent people from parking motorcycles in front of the school.

specifically *(adv)* — in an exact way

✦ My supervisor didn't specifically mention Claire's name, but I know he was talking about her.

eliminate *(v)* — make something disappear completely

✦ If you want to eliminate all risk, don't invest your money. Just leave it in the bank.

labor *(n)* — work done by a person

✦ The parts needed to fix your car won't be expensive, but the labor cost will be very high.

developing country *(n)* — a country that is still modernizing

✦ In parts of some developing countries, clean water is hard to find.

PHRASE BUILDING

ins and outs — all the details, both small and large

✦ You should speak with Salvador. He knows all the ins and outs of the refrigerator business.

odds and ends — various items

✦ I packed my clothes, camera, towels, and a few other odds and ends.

firing on all cylinders — working successfully with full energy

✦ Now that our stores in Asia and Europe are open, we're firing on all cylinders. Business has never been better.

WHY DO WE SAY THAT?

firing on all cylinders — When the spark plug on a car engine's cylinder fires, the piston inside the cylinder moves. This is part of a process that provides energy and movement to the car. So, when we say something or someone is "firing on all cylinders," we mean they are moving forward with great energy.

SENTENCE PATTERNS

IKEA's roots *were far more humble.*

were not nearly as interesting.

are deep in this town.

The 1950s were a momentous period for the company.

The first few years

The years after the merger

WHAT PEOPLE ARE SAYING ABOUT IKEA

Li-wen IKEA has a few shops in Taiwan. They're always very busy on the weekend. Young people especially like to shop there, since they want to make their houses more modern-looking.

Nate To be honest, I'm not such a big IKEA fan. As an artist, I'm into more unique furniture with interesting colors and designs. At IKEA, it seems to me that almost everything is either creamy white, brown, or black. I guess they're trying to make it easier for people to match colors.

Heidi A lot of my furniture is from IKEA. I just graduated from college, so I'm living in my own apartment for the first time. It was nice to go to IKEA and get almost everything I needed in one place. And most of it was cheap—an important point when you've got a budget like mine!

VOCABULARY AND PHRASE REVIEW

A. Complete each sentence, using the best word(s) from the box.

notable	**setback**	**immigrate**
eliminate	**abroad**	**remainder**
odd jobs	**convict**	**roaring**

1. I don't feel like traveling ________________ this year. I'd rather not deal with all the airports, packing, and everything else.
2. When I was young, I made extra money from ________________ like washing cars and mowing grass.
3. I'll spend $300 on a new DVD player, and spend the ________________ of my bonus on some DVDs.
4. Our children are still young. We want to wait until they're older before we ________________ to Canada.
5. This is just a minor ________________. The factory will be running again in less than a week.
6. A subway system would ________________ most of the city's traffic problems.
7. The storewide sale was a(n) ________________ success. We made over $35,000.
8. Building a new zoo was one of the mayor's most ________________ achievements.

B. Choose the best word to complete each sentence.

1. We do some product design, but our ________ is on Web design.

   A. emphasis B. reality C. evidence D. mercy

2. If you can __________ just $5 or $10, it would help us raise money to build a new community center.

   A. assemble B. innovate C. donate D. evolve

3. The launch of the new car model was a __________, and it's enjoying record sales.

   A. revival B. option C. roots D. triumph

4. Your dog looks __________ sitting there all alone. Why don't you take him out for a walk?

   A. massive B. classic C. miserable D. legendary

5. I've finished going over the ________ in our warehouse. We've got enough stock to last another three months.

   A. inventory B. luxury C. icon D. generosity

C. Match the beginning and ending of each sentence.

1. I'm hoping to win a scholarship	design a strong advertising message in just 24 hours.
2. The creative challenge was to	so I need to find a way to deal with the problem.
3. It's a complex account,	why did he hire a manager with no experience?
4. Quitting is not an option for me,	which is why three partners are working on it.
5. If Mr. Lewis is so shrewd,	to help cover my school costs next year.

D. Choose the best response to what the first person says.

1. **Marianne:** If Tim loses his job, we're going to have trouble paying the bills.

   A. Yvonne: He's always pushing the envelope with his work.

   B. Yvonne: In this economy, a lot of people are having trouble making ends meet.

   C. Yvonne: I'm sorry to hear you might be laid off.

2. **Igor:** I don't want to work at a big company. I prefer being self-employed.

   A. Martina: I'm not surprised. I never expected you to climb the corporate ladder.

   B. Martina: Then we see eye to eye. I plan to be a CEO one day.

   C. Martina: So it's true. You do plan to take the reins once your father retires.

3. **Bret:** Natasha's English is improving by leaps and bounds. In fact, she's one of our best employees.

   A. Sal: Maybe she just needs a new tutor.

   B. Sal: It's not easy, but I'm keeping my nose to the grindstone.

   C. Sal: She's a smart woman. Before long, she'll know all the ins and outs of your company.

answer key

SECTION 1

1: Starbucks: Comprehension Check

1. C
2. B
3. D
4. B
5. D

2: Lenovo: Comprehension Check

1. C
2. D
3. C
4. A
5. B

3: Apple: Comprehension Check

1. B
2. A
3. D
4. B
5. C

4: MTN: Comprehension Check

1. C
2. A
3. C
4. C
5. B

5: BHP Billiton: Comprehension Check

1. D
2. B
3. A
4. A
5. C

Section 1 Vocabulary and Phrase Review

A

1. costly
2. decade
3. revenue
4. based
5. unique
6. know-how
7. bottom line
8. asset

B

1. A
2. C
3. A
4. D
5. A

C

1. We've been trying for years to push our market share past 8 percent.
2. The TV's best feature is that it lets you watch two shows at the same time.
3. If the oil news is true, it will certainly affect our business.
4. How were you able to afford such a huge house?
5. After those record losses, how can they keep from going out of business?

D

1. B
2. C
3. C

SECTION 2

6: New Coke: Comprehension Check

1. C
2. D
3. A
4. B
5. C

7: Big Airlines: Comprehension Check

1. C
2. D
3. A
4. B
5. A

8: Barings Bank: Comprehension Check

1. A
2. B
3. C
4. C
5. B

9: Enron: Comprehension Check

1. C
2. B
3. A
4. B
5. B

10: Arthur Andersen: Comprehension Check

1. A
2. D
3. D
4. A
5. C

Section 2 Vocabulary and Phrase Review

A

1. interfere
2. handful
3. portfolio
4. tragedy
5. accurate
6. appoint
7. account
8. dramatic

B

1. C
2. C
3. D
4. B
5. A

C

1. We have to work here for 30 years to qualify for the pension plan.
2. I'm sorry, but visitors are forbidden to enter this area.
3. Maybe we should hire a consultant to advise us what to do.
4. I've been told the police are investigating the fire.
5. We're all so thrilled that you decided to come work with us.

D

1. C
2. A
3. B

SECTION 3

11: Richard Branson: Comprehension Check

1. C
2. B
3. D
4. B
5. A

12: Donna Karan: Comprehension Check

1. B
2. C
3. D
4. C
5. D

13: Wang Yung-ching: Comprehension Check

1. A
2. C
3. D
4. B
5. A

14: Anita Roddick: Comprehension Check

1. D
2. A
3. A
4. D
5. B

15: Azim Premji: Comprehension Check

1. D
2. A
3. C
4. C
5. C

Section 3 Vocabulary and Phrase Review

A

1. achieve
2. ethical
3. diversify
4. numerous
5. focus
6. track record
7. elegant
8. venture

B

1. B
2. C
3. A
4. C
5. B

C

1. Why do you oppose his research when you've never actually studied it?
2. I'll contribute to your project in any way I can.
3. You should be more concerned about the money missing from the cash register.
4. We'll get under way as soon as all the passengers are on board.
5. My mom says brown sugar is the most important ingredient in the cake.

D

1. C
2. A
3. C

SECTION 4

16: Yahoo!: Comprehension Check

1. A
2. D
3. A
4. C
5. C

17: EBay: Comprehension Check

1. C
2. C
3. C
4. C
5. A

18: Google: Comprehension Check

1. B
2. D
3. A
4. D
5. B

19: Amazon: Comprehension Check

1. D
2. D
3. A
4. C
5. B

20: Skype: Comprehension Check

1. C
2. B
3. C
4. B
5. A

Section 4 Vocabulary and Phrase Review

A

1. communicate
2. enhance
3. sensitive
4. destination
5. revenue stream
6. combat
7. convince
8. aggressive

B

1. C
2. A
3. B
4. B
5. A

C

1. Virtually everybody here knows one another.
2. I wouldn't say I'm an expert, but I'm not a novice either.
3. There are countless reasons why we shouldn't start investing in metals.
4. In the 1990s, Ryan made a fortune buying and selling stocks.
5. This summer, our annual party will be held at the convention center.

D

1. B
2. A
3. C

SECTION 5

21: Sony: Comprehension Check

1. D
2. D
3. D
4. B
5. B

22: Sam Walton: Comprehension Check

1. A
2. C
3. D
4. C
5. A

23: Gucci: Comprehension Check

1. C
2. C
3. A
4. D
5. C

24: Andrew Carnegie: Comprehension Check

1. C
2. B
3. A
4. B
5. C

25: IKEA: Comprehension Check

1. A
2. D
3. D
4. B
5. C

Section 5 Vocabulary and Phrase Review

A

1. abroad
2. odd jobs
3. remainder
4. immigrate
5. setback
6. eliminate
7. roaring
8. notable

B

1. A
2. C
3. D
4. C
5. A

C

1. I'm hoping to win a scholarship to help cover my school costs next year.
2. The creative challenge was to design a strong advertising message in just 24 hours.
3. It's a complex account, which is why three partners are working on it.
4. Quitting is not an option for me, so I need to find a way to deal with the problem.
5. If Mr. Lewis is so shrewd, why did he hire a manager with no experience?

D

1. B
2. A
3. C

index

VOCABULARY INDEX

PHRASE INDEX

Andrew E. Bennett holds an EdM (Master of Education) degree from Harvard University and a BA degree from UC—Santa Cruz. He has studied seven languages and has traveled in more than 50 countries. He has been involved in English education since 1993, both as a teacher and a writer. He has taught a variety of subjects, including English composition, business writing, English literature, and TOEFL preparation. He is the author of more than 40 English learning books, including classroom texts, supplementary books, self-study books, and preparation books for the TOEIC, GEPT, and other tests.

DIABETIC DIET COOKBOOK FOR BEGINNERS AFTER 50:

Low-Carb, Low-Fat, Low-Sugar and Vegetarian Senior's Diabetic Recipes.

By
Jessica Williams

CONTENTS

SNACKS RECIPES / 37

POULTRY RECIPES / 47

MEAT RECIPES / 53

Introduction

Hey there, fabulous over-50 foodies! Welcome to a kitchen adventure tailored just for you. If there's one thing life's taught us, it's that hitting the big 5-0 comes with its own set of superpowers – wisdom, experience, and a whole lot of sass. But along with those perks, there's something else that demands our attention: our health, especially when it comes to what's cooking in our kitchens.

Let's talk turkey (or tofu, if that's your vibe) – as we age, our bodies deserve some extra TLC, and that starts with what we put on our plates. Our fifties are like the golden ticket to the health rollercoaster – we want to ride the highs without getting derailed by the lows. That's where a balanced, nutritious diet swoops in to save the day.

Now, let's address the elephant in the room – diabetes. It's like that uninvited guest crashing the party, but with a little know-how and a dash of culinary creativity, we can show it the door. Managing diabetes isn't just about watching sugar levels; it's about crafting meals that nourish our bodies, boost our energy, and keep us kicking butt well into our golden years.

This book is your new kitchen BFF – the Diabetic Diet Cookbook After 50. This isn't your grandma's dusty old cookbook; this is a game-changer, specially designed to satisfy your taste buds. Inside, you'll find a treasure trove of recipes that are not only delicious but also crafted with your health needs in mind.

Why It's Important To Manage Diabetes After 50?

Managing diabetes after the age of 50 becomes increasingly crucial as individuals navigate the unique challenges that come with aging. Diabetes, a chronic condition characterized by increased blood sugar levels, requires vigilant management to prevent complications and maintain overall health and well-being.

Preventing Complications Through Blood Sugar Management:

As individuals cross the threshold of 50, the importance of managing diabetes escalates, primarily to stave off the complications that can arise from uncontrolled blood sugar levels. Diabetes, a chronic condition characterized by elevated blood sugar, demands a vigilant approach to prevent its cascade of potential health issues. With age, the body becomes more susceptible to various health challenges, and diabetes can exacerbate these risks. High blood sugar levels over time can lead to an array of complications, including heart disease, stroke, kidney disease, nerve damage, and vision problems. Therefore, actively managing diabetes becomes paramount to reduce the likelihood of developing these serious health complications and maintain an optimal quality of life.

Sustaining Vitality and Energy Levels:
Another critical aspect of managing diabetes after 50 is the maintenance of energy levels and vitality. With aging, natural declines in energy levels and metabolic function can occur. However, diabetes can further impact energy levels by hindering the body's ability to utilize glucose for fuel efficiently. Through the proactive management of blood sugar levels via diet, medication, and lifestyle adjustments, individuals can help sustain their energy levels. This prevention of fatigue and lethargy enables them to remain active and engaged in their daily activities, fostering a fulfilling lifestyle in their later years.

Preserving Physical and Mental Health:
Effective diabetes management also plays a pivotal role in preserving overall physical and mental health. Diabetes often intertwines with other health conditions, such as obesity, high blood pressure, and high cholesterol, amplifying the risk of heart disease and stroke. By managing diabetes through a blend of healthy eating, regular physical activity, and medication, individuals can better control these associated risk factors. Moreover, maintaining stable blood sugar levels supports cognitive function and reduces the risk of cognitive decline and dementia in older adults with diabetes, safeguarding both physical and mental well-being.

Enhancing Emotional Well-Being and Quality of Life:
Beyond physical health, managing diabetes after 50 can enhance emotional well-being and quality of life. Living with a chronic condition like diabetes can induce stress, anxiety, or depression, especially amid life changes and responsibilities associated with aging. However, taking an active role in diabetes management empowers individuals to regain control over their health and make positive choices to promote their overall well-being. Additionally, the support of healthcare professionals, peer groups, and educational resources can aid individuals in navigating the emotional challenges of living with diabetes, fostering a sense of community and connection.

Tools and Resources for Successful Diabetes Management:
To support successful diabetes management after 50, an array of tools, resources, and support systems are available. These include access to healthcare professionals for personalized guidance, engagement with peer support groups for communal encouragement, and utilization of educational materials for comprehensive understanding. By leveraging these tools and resources, individuals can navigate the complexities of diabetes management with confidence, empowering them to lead fulfilling lives while effectively managing their condition in their golden years.

Foods to Eat

Whole grains & whole pulses

Nutrient rich and full of fibre

Nuts & seeds

Packed with nutrients, especially Vitamin E and Omega-3 fatty acids

Fruits & vegetables

Loaded with fibre, antioxidants, vitamins and minerals and easy to find!

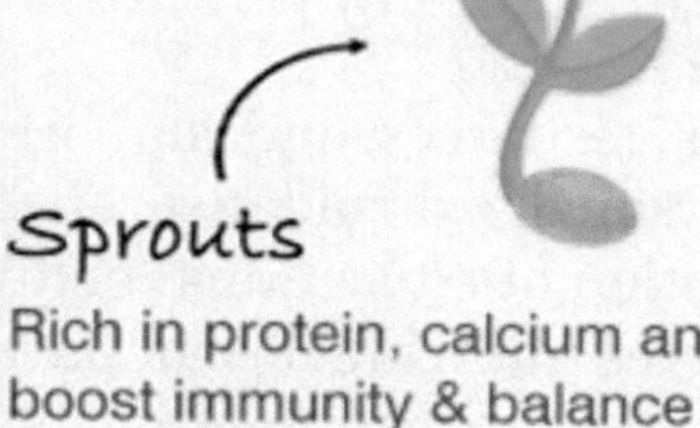

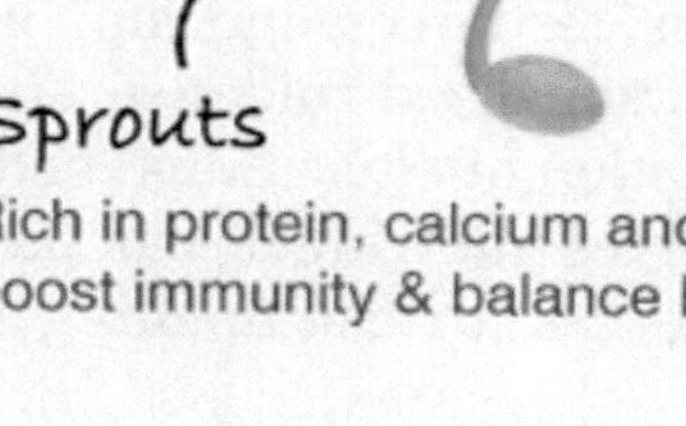

Sprouts

Rich in protein, calcium and nutrients that boost immunity & balance blood sugar

Isabgol

Take it daily to increase fibre intake

Vitamins A, C & E

Protect the body from premature aging

Fish like salmon & mackerel

Eat fish twice a week or more for Omega-3 fatty acids

Essential Foods for Diabetes Management

Navigating a diabetes diagnosis can feel daunting, especially when it comes to making dietary choices. However, with proper knowledge and guidance, managing diabetes through diet can become not only manageable but also enjoyable. Below, we'll explore a variety of foods suitable for individuals with diabetes, along with their importance in supporting overall health and blood sugar management.

Non-Starchy Vegetables: Non-starchy vegetables such as leafy greens, broccoli, cauliflower, peppers, and cucumbers are low in carbohydrates and calories while being rich in essential nutrients like vitamins, minerals, and antioxidants. Incorporating these vegetables into meals adds bulk and fiber, which can help regulate blood sugar levels, improve digestion, and promote satiety, making them an excellent choice for individuals with diabetes.

Whole Grains: Whole grains like oats, quinoa, brown rice, and barley are packed with fiber, which slows down the absorption of sugar into the bloodstream, preventing spikes in blood sugar levels. Additionally, whole grains provide essential nutrients like B vitamins, iron, and magnesium, supporting overall health and reducing the risk of heart disease, a common complication of diabetes.

Lean Proteins: Lean protein sources such as poultry, fish, tofu, beans, and legumes are essential for individuals with diabetes as they provide a steady source of energy without causing significant fluctuations in blood sugar levels. Protein also helps promote fullness and muscle health, making it crucial for maintaining a healthy weight and managing blood sugar levels effectively.

Healthy Fats: Healthy fats found in foods like avocados, nuts, seeds, and olive oil play a vital role in diabetes management by improving insulin sensitivity and reducing inflammation. Including sources of healthy fats in meals can help stabilize blood sugar levels, promote heart health, and enhance overall well-being.

Fruits: While fruits contain natural sugars, they also provide essential vitamins, minerals, and antioxidants that are beneficial for individuals with diabetes. Choosing whole fruits over fruit juices and dried fruits can help regulate blood sugar levels due to their fiber content. Berries, apples, citrus fruits, and stone fruits are excellent options for individuals with diabetes due to their lower glycemic index and high fiber content.

Low-Fat Dairy: Low-fat dairy products such as Greek yogurt, skim milk, and cottage cheese are rich in protein and calcium, making them valuable additions to a diabetes-friendly diet. Calcium is essential for bone health, while protein helps promote satiety and stabilize blood sugar levels, making low-fat dairy an excellent choice for individuals with diabetes.

Herbs and Spices: Herbs and spices not only add flavor to meals but also offer potential health benefits for individuals with diabetes. Certain herbs and spices like cinnamon, turmeric, and ginger have been shown to improve insulin sensitivity, reduce inflammation, and lower blood sugar levels, making them valuable additions to a diabetes-friendly diet.

Water: Staying hydrated is essential for everyone, but particularly for individuals with diabetes. Drinking an adequate amount of water helps regulate blood sugar levels, prevent dehydration, support kidney function, and promote overall health. Opting for water over sugary beverages like soda and fruit juices can also help prevent unnecessary spikes in blood sugar levels.

Foods to avoid

White rice & 'maida' (white flour)
Contain starch & high on carbohydrates

Caffeine
Raises blood sugar & insulin levels

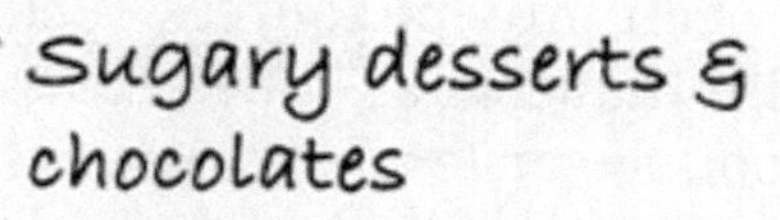

Sugary desserts & chocolates
Lead to dangerous spikes in blood sugar levels

Deep-fried foods
Do you really want weight gain in addition to diabetes

Soft drinks & sweetened fruit juices
Raise blood sugar levels and lead to weight gain

Frozen meals
Loaded with sodium again!

Salt
Reduce your sodium intake to keep your blood pressure in check

Foods to Avoid for Effective Diabetes Management

Certain foods can significantly impact blood sugar levels and overall health, making it essential to understand their potential risks and implications. Below, we'll explore a variety of foods that individuals with diabetes should limit or avoid, along with the reasons behind their exclusion.

Sugary Beverages: Sugary beverages such as soda, fruit juice, sweetened tea, and sports drinks are loaded with added sugars and provide little to no nutritional value. Consuming these beverages can cause rapid spikes in blood sugar levels, increasing the risk of insulin resistance and diabetes complications like heart disease, weight gain, and dental problems.

Processed and Packaged Foods: Processed and packaged foods like cookies, cakes, pastries, chips, and ready-to-eat meals are often high in refined carbohydrates, unhealthy fats, and added sugars. These foods can lead to sharp increases in blood sugar levels and contribute to weight gain, inflammation, and insulin resistance, making them detrimental to diabetes management.

White Bread and Refined Grains: White bread, white rice, pasta, and other refined grains are stripped of their fiber and nutrients during processing, resulting in quick spikes in blood sugar levels when consumed. These foods also lack satiety, leading to overeating and potential weight gain. Opting for whole grains like whole wheat bread, brown rice, and quinoa is a healthier choice for individuals with diabetes as they provide more fiber and nutrients and have a lower impact on blood sugar levels.

Sugary Snacks and Desserts: Sugary snacks and desserts like candy, chocolate, ice cream, and pastries are high in refined sugars and carbohydrates, making them unsuitable for individuals with diabetes. Consuming these foods can lead to rapid increases in blood sugar levels, insulin resistance, and weight gain. Instead, individuals with diabetes can satisfy their sweet cravings with healthier alternatives like fresh fruit, Greek yogurt with berries, or dark chocolate in moderation.

Fried Foods: Fried foods like French fries, fried chicken, and battered fish are typically high in unhealthy fats, calories, and refined carbohydrates. Consuming fried foods regularly can contribute to weight gain, insulin resistance, and inflammation, increasing the risk of diabetes complications like heart disease and stroke. Opting for healthier cooking methods like baking, grilling, steaming, or sautéing can help reduce the intake of unhealthy fats and promote better blood sugar control.

High-Sodium Foods: High-sodium foods like processed meats, canned soups, salty snacks, and fast food items can negatively impact blood pressure and cardiovascular health, increasing the risk of heart disease and stroke, which are common complications of diabetes. Individuals with diabetes should aim to limit their sodium intake and choose fresh, whole foods whenever possible to support overall health and well-being.

Alcohol: While moderate alcohol consumption may be acceptable for some individuals with diabetes, excessive alcohol intake can disrupt blood sugar levels, increase the risk of hypoglycemia, and contribute to weight gain. Additionally, alcoholic beverages like beer, sweet wines, and mixed drinks are high in carbohydrates and calories, further complicating blood sugar management. Individuals with diabetes need to consume alcohol in moderation and monitor their blood sugar levels closely when drinking.

Highly Processed and Trans Fat-Rich Foods: Highly processed foods like margarine, shortening, and certain packaged snacks often contain trans fats, which are known to raise LDL (bad) cholesterol levels and increase the risk of heart disease. Trans fats can also promote inflammation and insulin resistance, making them particularly harmful for individuals with diabetes. Opting for healthier fat sources like olive oil, avocado, nuts, and seeds can support better blood sugar control and overall health.

Now that you have learned about the essential foods to include and avoid for effective diabetes management, it's time to start cooking! This book is filled with delicious recipes for hearty breakfasts, satisfying main courses, and indulgent desserts. Each recipe is designed to excite your taste buds while supporting your health goals. So, put on your apron, sharpen your knives, and start your journey to create flavorful, nourishing, and healthy meals. Let's make every meal a celebration of good food and good health!

Breakfast Recipes

Red Smoothie Bowl

Prep period: 0
Cooking Period: 15 mins.

Ingredients Required:
Serving: 2

- Beet – ½ C. (75 g), peel removed and cut up
- Fresh strawberries – ½ C. (60 g)
- Unsweetened almond milk – ½ C. (120 ml)
- Ice cubes – 4-6

Procedure of Cooking:

1. Put the beet and remnant ingredients into a high-power blender and process to form a creamy anc smooth mixture.
2. Enjoy right away.

Per Person: Calories 40, Fat 1.1g, Carbs 7.5g, Protein 1.2g

Berries & Almond Yogurt Bowl

Prep period: 0
Cooking Period: 10 mins.

Ingredients Required:
Serving: 4

- Fresh strawberries – ¼ C. (30 g), hulled and slivere
- Fresh blueberries – ¼ C. (30 g)
- Fresh raspberries – ¼ C. (30 g)
- Fresh blackberries – ¼ C. (30 g)
- Fat-free plain Greek yogurt – 1 C. (250 g)
- Almonds – 2 tbsp., cut up

Procedure of Cooking:

1. Put the berries into a large-sized basin and stir.
2. Divide yogurt into serving bowls and top with berries and almonds.
3. Enjoy right away.

Per Person: Calories 172, Fat 6.6g, Carbs 15.2g, Protein 10.9g

Vanilla Chia Pudding

Prep period: 0
Cooking Period: 10 mins.

Procedure of Cooking:

1. Put almond milk and remnant ingredients into a basin and whisk to incorporate thoroughly.
2. Place the mixture in your refrigerator for at least 10 minutes before eating.
3. Top the mixture with strawberry slivers and enjoy.

Ingredients Required:
Serving: 2

- Unsweetened almond milk – 1 C. (240 ml)
- Organic vanilla extract – 1 tsp.
- Sea salt – 1 pinch
- Chia seeds – 1/3 C. (60 g)
- Liquid stevia – 3-4 drops

Per Person: Calories 130, Fat 10g, Carbs 10g, Protein 5.5g

Nuts & Seeds Porridge

Prep period: 10 mins.
Cooking Period: 35 mins.

Procedure of Cooking:

1. Put the pecans, walnuts, and sunflower seeds into a clean food processor and process them to form a crumbly mixture.
2. Put the nut mixture, chia seeds, coconut flakes, almond milk, spices, and stevia powder into a large pot on a burner at around medium heat.
3. Cook the mixture until boiling, stirring frequently.
4. Turn the heat to low.
5. Cook for around 20-30 minutes, stirring frequently.
6. Enjoy right away.

Ingredients Required:
Serving: 5

- Pecans – ½ C. (60 g)
- Walnuts – ½ C. (50 g)
- Sunflower seeds – ¼ C. (35 g)
- Chia seeds – ¼ C. (40 g)
- Low-fat unsweetened coconut flakes – ¼ C. (25 g)
- Unsweetened almond milk – 4 C. (960 ml)
- Powdered cinnamon – ½ tsp.
- Powdered ginger – ¼ tsp.
- Liquid stevia – 5-6 drops

Per Person: Calories 188, Fat 17.9g, Carbs 7.6g, Protein 4.5g

Yogurt Waffles

Prep period: 15 mins.
Cooking Period: 50 mins.

Procedure of Cooking:

1. Put the flour, Erythritol, protein powder, baking soda, baking powder, xanthan gum, and salt into a large-sized basin and blend thoroughly.
2. Put the egg whites into a second small-sized basin and whisk to form stiff peaks.
3. Put 2 egg yolks, whole eggs, almond milk, coconut oil, and yogurt into a third basin and whisk to incorporate thoroughly.
4. Put the egg mixture into the basin of flour mixture and blend to incorporate thoroughly.
5. Lightly blend in whipped egg whites.
6. Preheat the waffle iron and then spray it with baking spray.
7. Place the desired amount of the mixture into a preheated waffle iron.
8. Cook for around 4-5 minutes.
9. Cook the remnant waffles in the same manner.
10. Enjoy moderately hot.

Ingredients Required:
Serving: 2

- Almond flour – 1 1/3 C. (140 g)
- Erythritol – 2 tbsp.
- Unsweetened vanilla whey protein powder – 2 tbsp.
- Baking soda – ½ tsp.
- Baking powder – 1 tsp.
- Xanthan gum – ½ tsp.
- Sea salt – 1 pinch
- Large-sized eggs – 2 (whites and yolks separated)
- Whole eggs – 2
- Unsweetened almond milk – ¼ C. (60 ml)
- Coconut oil – 3 tbsp.
- Fat-free plain Greek yogurt – 6 oz. (150 g)
- Olive oil baking spray

Per Person: Calories 160, Fat 13.1g, Carbs 5.2g, Protein 7.6g

Blueberry Pancakes

Prep period: 10
Cooking Period: 16 mins.

Procedure of Cooking:

1. Put the cottage cheese, oatmeal, powdered peanuts, and egg whites into a small-sized blender and process to form a smoot mixture. (The mixture should be like a pancake batter).
2. Shift the mixture into a basin.
3. Lightly blend in blueberries.
4. Lightly spray an anti-sticking wok with baking spray and sizzle on a burner at around medium heat.
5. Put ¼ of the mixture and, with a spoon, spread it into an even layer.
6. Cook for around 2 minutes from both sides.
7. Cook the remnant pancakes in the same manner.
8. Enjoy moderately hot.

Ingredients Required:
Serving: 4

- Low-fat cottage cheese – ½ C. (110 g)
- Gluten-free instant oatmeal – ½ C. (50 g)
- Powdered peanuts – 2 tbsp.
- Large-sized egg whites – 4
- Frozen blueberries – ½ C. (75 g)
- Olive oil baking spray

Per Person: Calories 111, Fat 3.6g, Carbs 11.6g, Protein 10.2g

Spinach Muffins

Prep period: 10 mins.
Cooking Period: 25 mins.

Procedure of Cooking:

1. For preheating, set your oven at 350 °F (175 °C).
2. Spray 10 holes of a muffin tin with baking spray.
3. Put the spinach and remnant ingredients into a basin and blend to incorporate thoroughly.
4. Place the mixture into the muffin holes.
5. Bake in your oven for around 20-25 minutes.
6. Take out the muffin tin from the oven and place it onto a cooling wire rack to cool for around 10 minutes.
7. Take out the muffins from the holes and place them onto a platter.
8. Enjoy moderately hot.

Ingredients Required:
Serving: 10

- Olive oil baking spray
- Frozen chopped spinach – 1 (10-oz.) (280-g) package, thawed and liquid removed
- Liquid egg whites – 2 (4-oz.) (110-g) cartons
- Low-fat sharp cheddar cheese – 6 oz. (150 g), shredded
- Hot sauce – 1 tsp.
- Sea salt – 1 tsp.
- Powdered black pepper – ½ tsp.

Per Person: Calories 88, Fat 5.8g, Carbs 1.3g, Protein 7.5g

Sesame Seed Bread

Prep period: 10 mins.
Cooking Period: 1 hr. 10 mins.

Procedure of Cooking:

1. For preheating, set your oven at 350 °F (175 °C).
2. Place a bakery paper into a 9x5-inch bread loaf pan and then spray it with baking spray.
3. Put the flour and remnant ingredients into a large-sized basin and stir to incorporate thoroughly.
4. Place the mixture into the bread loaf pan.
5. Bake in your oven for around 70 minutes.
6. Take out of the oven and place the loaf pan onto a cooling wire rack to cool for at least 10 minutes.
7. Take out the bread from the pan and place onto the rack to cool thoroughly.
8. Cut the bread loaf into serving portions and enjoy.

Ingredients Required:
Serving: 15

- Olive oil baking spray
- Spelt flour – 4 C. (430 g)
- Sesame seeds – ¼ C. (40 g)
- Baking soda – 1 tsp.
- Sea salt – ¼ tsp.
- Liquid stevia – 10-12 drops
- Unsweetened almond milk – 2 C. plus 2 tbsp. (510 ml)

Per Person: Calories 239, Fat 4.2g, Carbs 45.1g, Fiber: 8.1g, Protein 9.3g

Tuna Omelet

Prep period: 10 mins.
Cooking Period: 5 mins.

Ingredients Required:
Serving: 2

- Eggs – 4
- Unsweetened almond milk – ¼ C. (60 ml)
- Scallion – ½, cut up
- Garlic clove – 1, finely cut up
- Jalapeño pepper – ½, finely cut up
- Sea salt and powdered black pepper – as desired
- Water-packed tuna – 1 (5-oz.) (140 g) can, liquid removed and flaked
- Olive oil – 1 tbsp.
- Bell pepper – 3 tbsp. (30 g), seeded and cut up
- Tomato, cut up – 3 tbsp. (50 g)
- Low-fat cheddar cheese – ¼ C. (30 g), shredded

Procedure of Cooking:

1. Put the eggs, almond milk, scallions, garlic jalapeño pepper, salt, and pepper into a large-sized basin and whisk thoroughly.
2. Add the tuna and stir to incorporate.
3. Sizzle oil into a large-sized anti-sticking wok on a burner at around medium heat.
4. Pour in the egg mixture and spread in an even layer.
5. Cook for around 1-2 minutes, without stirring.
6. Carefully lift the edges to run the uncooked portion flow underneath.
7. Put the veggies over the egg mixture and spread them.
8. Sprinkle with the cheese and immediately cover the wok.
9. Cook for around 30-60 seconds.
10. Take off the lid and fold the omelet in half.
11. Take it off the burner and place it on a platter.
12. Cut the omelet into 2 portions and enjoy right away.

Per Person: Calories 322, Fat 20.4g, Carbs 3.1g, Protein 31.4g

Eggs in Bell Pepper Rings

Prep period: 15 mins.
Cooking Period: 6 mins.

Procedure of Cooking:

1. Lightly spray a large-sized anti-sticking wok with baking spray and sizzle on a burner at around medium heat.
2. Lay out the bell pepper rings in the wok.
3. Cook for around 2 minutes.
4. Flip the rings and then crack an egg in the middle of each.
5. Sprinkle each egg with salt and pepper.
6. Cook for around 2-4 minutes.
7. Enjoy with the decoration of parsley.

Ingredients Required:
Serving: 2

- Olive oil baking spray
- Bell pepper – 1, cut into 4 (¼-inch) rings and seeded
- Eggs – 4
- Sea salt and powdered black pepper – as desired
- Fresh parsley – 2 tbsp., cut up

Per Person: Calories 149, Carbs 2.1g, Fat 9.4g, Protein 11.8g

Lunch Recipes

Cucumber & Onion Salad

Prep period: 15 mins.
Cooking Period: 0
Procedure of Cooking:

1. For the salad, put the cucumbers, onion, and dill into a large salad dish and stir them.
2. For the dressing, put the oil and remnant ingredients into a small basin and whisk to incorporate thoroughly.
3. Place the dressing over the salad and toss it all to mingle nicely.
4. Enjoy right away.

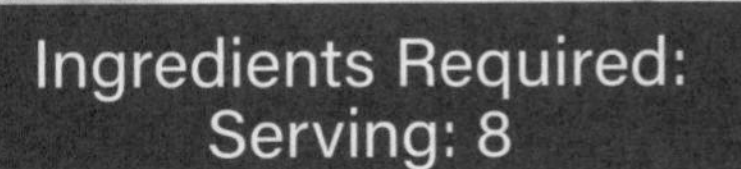

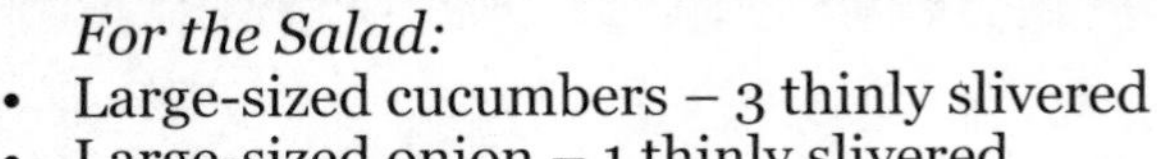

Ingredients Required:
Serving: 8

For the Salad:

- Large-sized cucumbers – 3 thinly slivered
- Large-sized onion – 1 thinly slivered
- Fresh dill – ½ C. (10 g)

For the Dressing:

- Olive oil – ¼ C. (60 ml)
- Balsamic vinegar – 2 tbsp.
- Fresh lemon juice – 1 tbsp.
- Dried oregano – 1 tsp.
- Sea salt and powdered black pepper – as desired

Per Person: Calories 105, Fat 1.6g, Carbs 5.2g, Protein 17g

Mixed Berries Salad

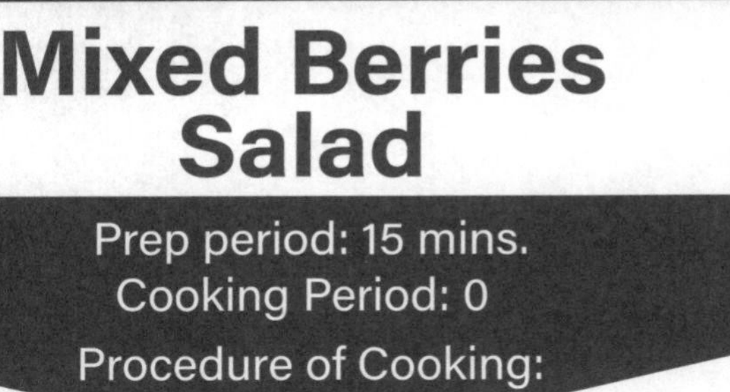

Prep period: 15 mins.
Cooking Period: 0
Procedure of Cooking:

1. Put the berries and remnant ingredients into a salad dish and toss it all to mingle nicely.
2. Enjoy right away.

Ingredients Required:
Serving: 4

- Fresh strawberries – 1 C. (125 g), hulled and slivered
- Fresh blackberries – ½ C. (75 g)
- Fresh blueberries – ½ C. (75 g)
- Fresh raspberries – ½ C. (60 g)
- Fresh arugula – 6 C. (120 g)
- Fresh lemon juice – 1 tbsp.
- Olive oil – 2 tbsp.
- Sea salt and powdered black pepper – as desired

Per Person: Calories 105, Fat 7.6g, Carbs 10.1g, Protein 1.6g

Shrimp Lettuce Wraps

Prep period: 15 mins.
Cooking Period: 5 mins.

Ingredients Required:
Serving: 2

- Olive oil – 1 tsp.
- Garlic clove – 1, finely cut up
- Shrimp – 1½ lb. (680 g), peel removed, deveined and cut up
- Sea salt – as desired
- Large-sized lettuce leaves – 8
- Carrot – 1 C. (150 g), peel removed and julienned
- Cucumber – 1 C. (120 g), julienned
- Fresh chives – 2 tbsp., finely cut up

Procedure of Cooking:

1. Sizzle oil into a large-sized wok on a burner at around medium heat.
2. Sauté the garlic for around 1 minute.
3. Add the shrimp and stir.
4. Cook for around 3-4 minutes.
5. Take off the wok of shrimp from the burner.
6. Set it aside to cool slightly.
7. Lay out the lettuce leaves onto serving plates.
8. Put the shrimp, carrot, and cucumber over the leaves.
9. Decorate with chives and enjoy right away.

Per Person: Calories 230, Fat 4.1g, Carbs 6.8g, Protein 39.3g

Chicken & Tomato Kabobs

Prep period: 15 mins.
Cooking Period: 7 mins.

Ingredients Required:
Serving: 6

- Olive oil baking spray
- Low-fat Parmesan cheese – ¼ C. (30 g), shredded
- Olive oil – 1 tbsp. (45 ml)
- Garlic cloves – 2, finely cut up
- Fresh basil leaves – 1 C. (20 g), cut up
- Sea salt and powdered black pepper – as desired
- Boneless chicken breasts – 1¼ lb. (570 g), cut into 1-inch cubes
- Cherry tomatoes – 24

Procedure of Cooking:

1. Put the cheese, oil, garlic, basil, salt, and pepper into a clean food processor and process to form a smooth mixture.
2. Transfer the basil mixture to a large bowl.
3. Add in the chicken cubes and stir thoroughly.
4. Cover the basin and place into your refrigerator to marinate for at least 4-5 hours.
5. For preheating, set your grill to medium-high heat.
6. Generously spray the grill grate with baking spray.
7. Thread the chicken cubes and tomatoes onto presoaked wooden skewers.
8. Lay out the skewers onto the grill.
9. Cook for around 3-4 minutes.
10. Flip and cook for around 2-3 minutes.
11. Take off from the grill and place onto a platter for around 5 minutes before enjoying.

Per Person: Calories 183, Fat 10.4g, Carbs 0.4g, Protein 21.6g

Buckwheat Burgers

Prep period: 15 mins.
Cooking Period: 1¼ hrs.

Ingredients Required:

Serving: 4

- Dry buckwheat – ¾ C. (125 g)
- Water – 1½ C. (360 ml)
- Sea salt – as desired
- Olive oil – 2 tbsp. (30 ml), divided
- Large-sized onion – ½, finely cut up
- Large-sized carrot – ½, peel removed and grated
- Celery stalk – ½, finely cut up
- Fresh kale leaf – 1, tough ribs removed and finely cut up
- Large-sized cooked sweet potato – 1, peel removed and mashed
- Almond butter – 2 tbsp.
- Low-sodium soy sauce – 2 tbsp.
- Fresh salad greens – 4 C. (300 g)

Procedure of Cooking:

1. For preheating, set your oven at 350 °F (175 °C).
2. Place a bakery paper onto a baking tray.
3. For patties: sizzle an anti-sticking wok on a burner at around medium heat.
4. Toast the buckwheat for around 5 minutes, stirring all the time.
5. Put in water and salt and immediately turn the heat to high.
6. Cook the mixture until boiling.
7. Turn the heat to low.
8. Cook with the cover on for around 15 minutes.
9. In the meantime, sizzle half of the oil into a wok on a burner at medium heat.
10. Sauté the onion for around 4-5 minutes.
11. Put in the carrot and celery and stir.
12. Cook for around 5 minutes.
13. Stir in the remaining ingredients and take off the heat.
14. Put the mixture into a basin with the buckwheat and stir to incorporate.
15. Set aside to cool thoroughly.
16. Shape the mixture into 4 patties.
17. Lay out the patties onto the baking tray.
18. Bake in your oven for around 20 minutes on both sides.
19. Enjoy right away alongside the greens.

Per Person: Calories 287, Fat 12.7g, Carbs 40.2g, Protein 8.3g

NOTES

Zucchini Soup

Prep period: 15 mins.
Cooking Period: 45 mins.

Ingredients Required:
Serving: 4

- Zucchini – 2 C. (230 g), cut up
- Dried onion – 2 tbsp. (10 g), finely crushed
- Homemade boiling vegetable broth – 1 C. (240 ml)
- Low-fat cheddar cheese – ½ C. (60 g), shredded
- Olive oil – 1 tbsp.
- Dried thyme – ¼ tsp.
- Sea salt and powdered black pepper – as desired

Procedure of Cooking:

1. Put the zucchini and dried onion into a microwave-safe basin and microwave on high setting for around 4 minutes.
2. Place the zucchini in a high-power blender and process to cut it finely.
3. Put the broth, half of the cheese, oil, thyme, salt, and pepper in the blender and process to form a smooth mixture.
4. Enjoy right away with the decoration of remnant cheese.

Per Person: Calories 204, Fat 16.8g, Carbs 6.2g, Protein 9g

Pumpkin Soup

Prep period: 15 mins.
Cooking Period: 25 mins.

Ingredients Required:
Serving: 4

- Olive oil – 2 tsp.
- Onion – 1, cut up
- Fresh ginger – 1 tsp., cut up
- Garlic cloves – 2, cut up
- Fresh cilantro – 2 tbsp., cut up
- Pumpkin – 3 C. (735 g), peel removed and cubed
- Homemade vegetable broth – 4¼ C. (1250 ml)
- Sea salt and powdered black pepper – as desired
- Coconut cream – ½ C. (120 g)
- Fresh lime juice – 2 tbsp.

Procedure of Cooking:

1. Sizzle oil in a large soup pan on the burner at medium heat.
2. Sauté the onion, turmeric, ginger, garlic, and cilantro for around 3-4 minutes.
3. Put in pumpkin and broth.
4. Cook the mixture until boiling.
5. Turn the heat to low.
6. Cook with the cover for around 15 minutes.
7. Take off the burner and set it aside to cool slightly.
8. Place the mixture in a high-power blender in batches with avocado and process to form a smooth mixture.
9. Return the soup to the same pot on the burner at medium heat.
10. Cook for around 3 minutes.
11. Enjoy right away.

Per Person: Calories 208, Fat 11.5g, Carbs 21g, Protein 8.3g

Tofu with Spinach

Prep period: 15 mins.
Cooking Period: 10 mins.

Procedure of Cooking:

1. Sizzle the oil into a large anti-sticking wok on a burner at around medium-high heat.
2. Stir-fry the tofu for around 2-3 minutes.
3. Put in ginger, garlic, and red pepper flakes and blend.
4. Cook for around 1 minute, stirring all the time.
5. Stir in spinach and soy sauce.
6. Stir-fry for around 4-5 minutes.
7. Enjoy right away.

Ingredients Required:
Serving: 2

- Olive oil – 1 tbsp.
- Tofu – ½ lb. (225 g), pressed, liquid removed and cubed
- Fresh ginger – 1 tsp., finely cut up
- Garlic clove – 1, finely cut up
- Red pepper flakes – ¼ tsp.
- Fresh spinach – 6 oz. (150 g), cut up
- Low-sodium soy sauce – 1 tbsp.

Per Person: Calories 190, Fat 11.8g, Carbs 12.6g, Protein 12.5g

Scallops with Broccoli

Prep period: 15 mins.
Cooking Period: 9 mins.

Procedure of Cooking:

1. Sizzle oil in a large cast-iron wok on a burner at around medium heat.
2. Cook the broccoli and garlic for around 3-4 minutes, stirring from time to time.
3. Put in the scallops and stir.
4. Cook for around 3-4 minutes, flipping them occasionally.
5. Stir in lemon juice and take off the burner.
6. Enjoy right away.

Ingredients Required:
Serving: 2

- Fresh strawberries – 1 C. (125 g), hulled and slivered
- Olive oil – 2 tbsp.
- Broccoli – 1 C. (90 g), cut into small-sized pieces
- Garlic clove – 1, finely cut up
- Sea scallops ½ lb. – (230 g), side muscle removed
- Fresh lemon juice – 1 tsp.
- Sea salt – as desired

Per Person: Calories 220, Fat 12.6g, Carbs 6.3g, Protein 20.5g

Turkey Meatloaf

Prep period: 15 mins.
Cooking Period: 45 mins.

Ingredients Required:

Serving: 4

- Olive oil – 2 tsp.
- Onion – ½ C. (120 g), cut up
- Garlic cloves – 2, minced
- Lean ground turkey – 1 lb. (455 g)
- Low-fat feta cheese – 1/3 C. (40 g), crumbled
- Whole-wheat breadcrumbs – ¼ C. (40 g)
- Roasted red peppers – ½ C. (75 g), cut up
- Green olives – ¼ C. (45 g), pitted and cut up
- Fresh parsley – 2 tbsp., cut up
- Fresh dill – 1 tbsp., cut up
- Dried oregano – 2 tsp.
- Salt and powdered black pepper – as desired
- Egg – 1
- Fat-free milk – 1 tbsp.

Procedure of Cooking:

1. For preheating, set your oven to 400 °F (205 °C).
2. Place a bakery paper onto a baking tray.
3. Sizzle oil in an anti-sticking wok on the burner at medium heat.
4. Sauté the onion for around 2 minutes.
5. Put in garlic and blend.
6. Sauté for around 1 minute.
7. Take off the burner and place the mixture in a large bowl.
8. Put the remnant ingredients into the basin, and with your hands, blend to incorporate thoroughly.
9. Lay out the mixture onto the baking tray and, with your hands, shape it into a loaf.
10. Bake in your oven for around 30-40 minutes.
11. Take out of the oven and set the meatloaf aside for around 10 minutes.
12. Cut the meatloaf into serving portions and enjoy.

Per Person: Calories 283, Fat 14.8g, Carbs: 6.4g, Protein 26.5g

NOTES

This page is for your notes

Dinner Recipes

Tuna Salad

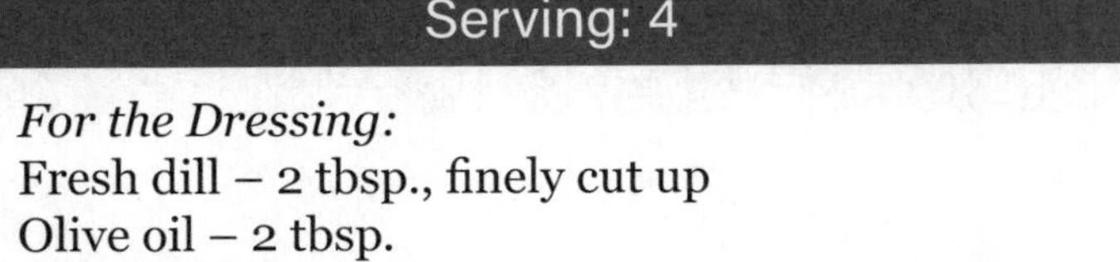

Prep period: 15 mins.
Cooking Period: 0

Ingredients Required:
Serving: 4

For the Dressing:
- Fresh dill – 2 tbsp., finely cut up
- Olive oil – 2 tbsp.
- Fresh lime juice – 1 tbsp.
- Sea salt and powdered black pepper – as desired

For the Salad:
- Fresh spinach – 4 C. (120 g), torn
- Water-packed tuna – 2 (6-oz.) (150-g) cans, liquid removed and flaked
- Hard-boiled eggs – 6, peel removed and slivered
- Tomato – 1 C. (200 g), cut up
- Large-sized cucumber – 1, slivered

Procedure of Cooking:

1. For the dressing, put dill, oil, lime juice, salt, and pepper into a small-sized basin and whisk to incorporate thoroughly.
2. Lay out the spinach onto serving plates and top each with tuna, egg, cucumber, and tomato.
3. Drizzle with dressing and enjoy.

Per Person: Calories 274, Fat 14.7g, Carbs 7g, Protein 29.8g

Chicken Salad

Prep period: 15 mins.
Cooking Period: : 16 mins.

Ingredients Required:
Serving: 8

For the Chicken:
- Boneless chicken breasts – 2 lb. (900 g)
- Olive oil – ½ C. (120 ml)
- Fresh lemon juice – ¼ C. (60 ml)

For the Salad:
- Large-sized apples – 4, cored and slivered
- Cucumber – 2 C. (240 g), slivered
- Romaine lettuce – 12 C. (560 g), torn

Procedure of Cooking:

1. For the marinade, put the oil, lemon juice, sugar, garlic, salt, and pepper into a large basin and whisk to incorporate thoroughly.
2. Put the chicken and ¾ C. (225 g) of marinade into a large-sized, resealable plastic bag.
3. Seal the bag and shake to coat thoroughly.
4. Place in your refrigerator overnight.
5. Cover the basin of the remnant marinade and place it in your refrigerator before enjoying it.
6. For preheating, set your grill to medium heat.
7. Spray the grill grate with baking spray.
8. Take out the chicken from the bag and discard the marinade.
9. Lay out the chicken breasts on the grill.
10. Cook with the cover for around 5-8 minutes on both sides.
11. Take out the chicken from the grill and cut it into strips.
12. Divide the chicken strips, apple slivers, cranberries, pecans, and lettuce into serving bowls.
13. Drizzle with reserved marinade and enjoy.

Per Person: Calories 436, Fat 25.7g, Carbs 25.9g, Protein 28.8g

Beef & Mushroom Soup

Prep period: 15 mins.
Cooking Period: 1 hr. 20 mins..

Ingredients Required:
Serving: 6

- Olive oil – ¼ C. (60 ml)
- Beef tenderloin – 2 lb. (910 g), fat removed and cut into ½-inch chunks
- Onion – ½ C. (60 g), cut up
- Garlic cloves – 2, finely cut up
- Dried thyme – 1 tsp.
- Fresh mushrooms – 12 oz. (340 g), slivered
- Tomatoes – 2 C. (400 g), finely cut up
- Homemade chicken broth – 6 C. (1440 ml)
- Fresh lemon juice – 3 tbsp.
- Fresh cilantro – ¼ C. (5 g), cut up
- Sea salt and powdered black pepper – as desired

Procedure of Cooking:

1. Sizzle 2 tbsp. of oil into a large-sized pot on a burner at medium heat.
2. Sear the beef cubes in 2 batches for around 3-4 minutes.
3. With a frying ladle, move the beef cubes into a basin.
4. Sizzle remnant oil in the same pot on the burner at medium heat.
5. Sauté the onion and garlic for around 2-3 minutes.
6. Put in mushrooms and blend.
7. Cook for around 5-6 minutes, stirring from time to time.
8. Stir in cooked beef cubes, tomatoes, and broth.
9. Cook the mixture until boiling.
10. Turn the heat to low.
11. Cook for around 1 hour.
12. Stir in lemon juice, cilantro, salt, and pepper, and take off from the burner.
13. Enjoy right away.

Per Person: Calories 422, Fat 19.6g, Carbs 6.6g, Protein 53.3g

NOTES

Beans & Barley Soup

Prep period: 15 mins.
Cooking Period: 40 mins.

Procedure of Cooking:

1. Sizzle oil into a large-sized soup pan on a burner a medium heat.
2. Sauté the onion, celery, and carrot for around 4-: minutes.
3. Put in garlic and rosemary and stir.
4. Sauté for around 1 minute.
5. Add the tomatoes and stir.
6. Cook for around 3-4 minutes, crushing with th back of a spoon.
7. Add the barley and broth mixture.
8. Cook the mixture until boiling.
9. Turn the heat to low.
10. Cook with the cover for around 20-25 minutes.
11. Stir in beans and lemon juice.
12. Cook for around 5 minutes.
13. Decorate with parsley and enjoy right away.

Ingredients Required:
Serving: 4

- Dry buckwheat – ¾ C. (125 g)
- Olive oil – 1 tbsp.
- Onion – 1, cut up
- Celery stalks – 2, cut up
- Large-sized carrot – 1, peel removed and cut up
- Fresh rosemary – 2 tbsp., cut up
- Garlic cloves – 2, finely cut up
- Tomatoes – 4 C. (400 g), cut up
- Homemade vegetable broth – 4 C. (960 ml)
- Pearl barley – 1 C. (200 g)
- Cooked white beans – 2 C. (280 g)
- Fresh lemon juice – 2 tbsp.
- Fresh parsley leaves – ¼ C. (5 g), cut up

Per Person: Calories 392, Fat 5.6g, Carbs 71g, Protein 16.1g

Turkey, Beans & Corn Chili

Prep period: 15 mins.
Cooking Period: 45 mins.

Procedure of Cooking:

1. Sizzle oil into a large-sized Dutch oven on a burner at around medium-low heat.
2. Sauté the bell pepper, onion, and garlic for around 5 minutes.
3. Put in turkey and stir.
4. Cook for around 5-6 minutes.
5. Put in water, tomatoes, and spices, and turn the heat to around high.
6. Cook the mixture until boiling.
7. Turn the heat to around medium-low and stir in beans and corn.
8. Cook with the cover for around 30 minutes, stirring from time to time.
9. Enjoy right away.

Ingredients Required:
Serving: 6

- Olive oil – 2 tbsp.
- Bell pepper – 1, seeded and cut up
- Onion – 1, cut up
- Garlic cloves – 2, cut up
- Lean ground turkey – 1 lb. (455 g)
- Water – 2 C. (480 ml)
- Tomatoes – 3 C. (600 g), finely cut up
- Powdered cumin – 1 tsp.
- Powdered cinnamon – ½ tsp.
- Red kidney beans – 1 (15-oz.) (425-g) can, liquid removed
- Frozen corn – 1½ C. (260 g), thawed

Per Person: Calories 270, Fat 10.9g, Carbs 27g, Protein 21.3g

Shrimp & Veggies Stir-Fry

Prep period: 20 mins.
Cooking Period: 10 mins.

Procedure of Cooking:

1. Sizzle 1 tbsp. (15 ml) of oil in a large anti-sticking wok on a burner at around medium heat.
2. Cook the shrimp for around 1 minute on both sides.
3. With a frying ladle, move the shrimp onto a plate.
4. Sizzle remnant oil in the same wok on a burner at around medium heat.
5. Sauté the onion and garlic for around 2-3 minutes.
6. Put in vegetables, soy sauce, and pepper, and stir.
7. Stir-fry for around 2-3 minutes.
8. Put in cooked shrimp and stir.
9. Stir-fry for around 1-2 minutes.
10. Enjoy right away.
11. Cook for around 5 minutes.
12. Decorate with parsley and enjoy right away.

Ingredients Required:
Serving: 4

- Olive oil – 2 tbsp. (30 ml), divided
- Large-sized shrimp – 1 lb. (455 g), peeled and deveined
- Medium-sized onion – ½, cut up
- Garlic cloves – 3, finely cut up
- Bell peppers – 2 C. (300 g), seeded and slivered
- Fresh snow peas – 1 C. (160 g)
- Carrot – 1 C. (150 g), peel removed and julienned
- Low-sodium soy sauce – 2 tbsp.
- Powdered black pepper – as desired
- Fresh parsley – 2 tbsp., cut up

Per Person: Calories 250, Fat 9.2g, Carbs 12.9g, Protein 29.5g

Shrimp & Scallops with Veggies

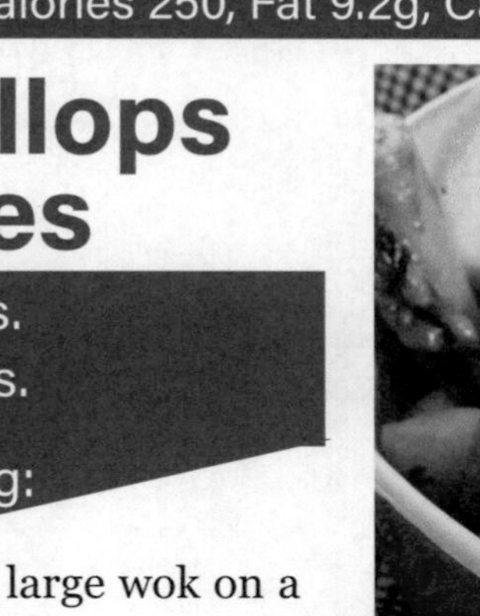

Prep period: 20 mins.
Cooking Period: 11 mins.

Procedure of Cooking:

1. Sizzle 1 tbsp. (15 ml) of oil into a large wok on a burner at around medium heat.
2. Stir-fry the asparagus and bell peppers for around 4-5 minutes.
3. With a frying ladle, shift the vegetables onto a plate.
4. Sizzle remnant oil in the same wok and stir-fry shrimp and scallops for around 2 minutes.
5. Put in parsley, garlic, salt and pepper and stir.
6. Cook for around 1 minute.
7. Put in the cooked vegetables and stir.
8. Cook for around 2-3 minutes.
9. Enjoy right away.

Ingredients Required:
Serving: 5

- Olive oil – 1 tbsp. (45 ml), divided
- Fresh asparagus – 1 lb. (455 g), cut into 2-inch pieces
- Bell peppers – 2, seeded and cut up
- Shrimp – ¾ lb. (340 g), peeled and deveined
- Scallops – ¾ lb. (340 g), side muscle removed
- Dried parsley – 2 tsp.
- Garlic cloves – 2, finely cut up
- Sea salt and powdered black pepper – as desired

Per Person: Calories 230, Fat 8.8g, Carbs 8.5g, Protein 29.4g

Chicken & Kale Stew

Prep period: 15 mins.
Cooking Period: 35 mins.

Ingredients Required:
Serving: 6

- Olive oil – 2 tbsp.
- Onion – 1, cut up
- Garlic cloves – 4, finely cut up
- Fresh ginger – 2 tsp., finely cut up
- Powdered turmeric – 1 tsp.
- Powdered cumin – 1 tsp.
- Powdered coriander – 1 tsp.
- Paprika – 1 tsp.
- Boneless chicken thighs – 4 (6-oz.) (150-g), cut into 1-inch pieces
- Tomatoes – 4, cut up
- Unsweetened coconut milk – 12 oz. (360 ml)
- Homemade chicken broth – 1/4 C. (60 ml)
- Sea salt and powdered black pepper – as desired
- Fresh kale – 6 C. (330 g), tough ribs removed and cut up
- Fresh lemon juice – 2 tbsp.

Procedure of Cooking:

1. Sizzle oil into a large-sized heavy-bottomed pot on a burner at medium heat.
2. Sauté the onion for around 3-4 minutes.
3. Put in ginger, garlic, and spices and stir.
4. Sauté for around 1 minute.
5. Put in chicken cubes and stir.
6. Cook for around 4-5 minutes.
7. Put in tomatoes, coconut milk, broth, salt, and pepper, and stir.
8. Cook the mixture until boiling.
9. Turn the heat to low.
10. Cook with the cover for around 10-15 minutes.
11. Put in kale and stir.
12. Cook for around 4-5 minutes.
13. Put in lemon juice and take off the burner.
14. Enjoy right away.

Per Person: Calories 300, Fat 7.3g, Carbs 46g, Protein 15.3g

NOTES

Chickpeas & Spinach Stew

Prep period: 15 mins.
Cooking Period: 30 mins.

Ingredients Required:
Serving: 4

- Olive oil – 1 tbsp.
- Medium-sized onion – 1, cut up
- Carrots – 2 C. (300 g), peel removed and cut up
- Garlic cloves – 2, finely cut up
- Red pepper flakes – 1 tsp.
- Large-sized tomatoes – 2, peel removed, seeded, and finely cut up
- Homemade vegetable broth – 2 C. (480 ml)
- Cooked chickpeas – 2 C. (330 g)
- Fresh spinach – 2 C. (60 g), cut up
- Fresh lemon juice – 1 tbsp.
- Sea salt and powdered black pepper – as desired

Procedure of Cooking:

1. Sizzle oil in a large-sized pot on the burner at medium heat.
2. Sauté the onion and carrot for around 6 minutes.
3. Put in garlic and red pepper flakes and stir.
4. Sauté for around 1 minute.
5. Put in tomatoes and stir.
6. Cook for around 2-3 minutes.
7. Put in broth and stir.
8. Cook the mixture until boiling.
9. Turn the heat to around low.
10. Cook for around 10 minutes.
11. Put in chickpeas and stir.
12. Cook for around 5 minutes.
13. Put in spinach and stir.
14. Cook for around 3-4 minutes.
15. Stir in lemon juice and seasoning and take off the burner.
16. Enjoy right away.

Per Person: Calories 217, Fat 6.6g, Carbs 31.4g, Protein 10.6g

NOTES

Ground Lamb with Green Peas

Prep period: 15 mins.
Cooking Period: 50 mins.

Ingredients Required:
Serving: 4

- Olive oil – 1 tbsp.
- Medium-sized onion – 1, cut up
- Fresh ginger – 2 tsp., finely cut up
- Garlic cloves – 4, finely cut up
- Powdered coriander – ½ tsp.
- Powdered cumin – ½ tsp.
- Powdered turmeric – ½ tsp.
- Lean ground lamb – 1 lb. (455 g)
- Tomato – ½ C. (100 g), cut up
- Water – 1½ C. (360 ml)
- Fresh green peas – 1 C. (160 g), shelled
- Fat-free plain Greek yogurt – 2 tbsp. (30 g), whipped
- Fresh cilantro – ¼ C. (5 g), cut up
- Sea salt and powdered black pepper – as desired

Procedure of Cooking:

1. Sizzle oil into a Dutch oven on the burner at around medium-high heat.
2. Sauté the onion for around 3-4 minutes.
3. Put in ginger, garlic, ground spices, and bay leaf and stir.
4. Sauté for around 1 minute.
5. Put in lamb and stir.
6. Cook for around 5 minutes.
7. Put in tomato and stir.
8. Cook for around 10 minutes, stirring from time to time.
9. Put in water and green peas and stir.
10. Cook the mixture until boiling.
11. Turn the heat to low.
12. Cook with the cover for around 25-30 minutes.
13. Put in yogurt, cilantro, salt, and pepper and stir.
14. Cook for around 4-5 minutes.
15. Enjoy right away.

Per Person: Calories 297, Fat 12.2g, Carbs 10.7g, Protein 35g

NOTES

Snacks Recipes

Cinnamon Almonds

Prep period: 5 mins.
Cooking Period: 10 mins.

Ingredients Required:
Serving: 4

- Whole almonds – 1 C. (140 g)
- Powdered cinnamon – ½ tsp.
- Powdered cumin – ¼ tsp.
- Sea salt and powdered black pepper – as desired
- Olive oil – 2 tbsp.

Procedure of Cooking:

1. For preheating, set your oven at 350 °F (175 °C).
2. Place bakery paper into a baking pan.
3. Put the almonds and remnant ingredients into a basin and toss it all to mingle nicely.
4. Spread the almonds into the baking pan.
5. Roast in your oven for around 10 minutes, flipping twice.
6. Take out of the oven and let the almonds cool thoroughly before enjoying.

Per Person: Calories 198, Fat 18.9g, Carbs 5.3g, Protein 4g

Glazed Cashews

Prep period: 10 mins.
Cooking Period: 12 mins.

Ingredients Required:
Serving: 8

- Maple syrup – 1 tbsp.
- Coconut oil – 1 tbsp., liquefied
- Erythritol – 2 tbsp.
- Sea salt – ½ tsp.
- Raw cashews – 2 C. (260 g)

Procedure of Cooking:

1. For preheating, set your oven at 325 °F (165 °C).
2. Place a bakery paper onto a baking tray.
3. Put the maple syrup, coconut oil, Erythritol, and salt into a large basin and stir until the Erythritol dissolves thoroughly.
4. Add the cashews and toss them all to mingle nicely.
5. Lay out the cashews onto the baking tray and spread them in an even layer.
6. Roast in your oven for around 10-12 minutes, tossing after every 5 minutes.
7. Take out of the oven and let the cashews cool for 10-12 minutes before enjoying.

Per Person: Calories 211, Fat 15.5g, Carbs 10.7g, Protein 5g

Salted Edamame

Prep period: 10 mins.
Cooking Period: 20 mins.

Ingredients Required:
Serving: 8

- Frozen shelled edamame – 2 C. (320 g), thawed
- Olive oil – 2 tsp.
- Sea salt – 1 tsp.

Procedure of Cooking:

1. For preheating, set your oven at 450 °F (230 °C).
2. Put the edamame, oil, and salt in a basin and toss it all to mingle nicely.
3. Lay out the edamame onto the baking tray and spread in an even layer.
4. Roast in your oven for around 15-20 minutes, stirring once halfway through.
5. Take out of the oven and let the edamame cool thoroughly before enjoying.

Per Person: Calories 104, Fat 5.5g, Carbs 7.1g, Protein 8.3g

Apple Chips

Prep period: 10 mins.
Cooking Period: 2 hrs.

Ingredients Required:
Serving: 5

- Powdered cinnamon – 2 tbsp.
- Powdered ginger – ½ tbsp.
- Powdered cloves – 1 tsp.
- Powdered nutmeg – 1 tsp.
- Fuji apples – 3, thinly slivered in rounds

Procedure of Cooking:

1. For preheating, set your oven at 200 °F (95 °C).
2. Place a bakery paper onto a baking tray.
3. Put all spices into a basin and stir thoroughly.
4. Lay out the apple slivers onto a baking tray in a single layer and sprinkle generously with spice mixture.
5. Bake in your oven for around 1 hour.
6. Flip the apple slices to the other side and sprinkle with the spice mixture again.
7. Bake in your oven for around 1 hour.
8. Enjoy moderately hot.

Per Person: Calories 71, Fat 0.6g, Carbs 18.5g, Protein 0.5g

Kale Chips

Prep period: 10 mins.
Cooking Period: 16 mins.

Procedure of Cooking:

1. For preheating, set your oven at 350 °F (175 °C).
2. Place bakery paper onto a large baking tray.
3. Lay out the kale pieces onto the baking tray.
4. Sprinkle the kale with cayenne pepper powder and salt and drizzle with oil.
5. Bake in your oven for around 10-15 minutes.
6. Take out the baking tray of kale chips from the oven and let them cool before enjoying.

Ingredients Required:
Serving: 6

- Fresh kale leaves – 1 lb. (455 g), stemmed and torn
- Cayenne pepper powder – ¼ tsp.
- Sea salt – 1 pinch
- Olive oil – 1 tbsp.

Per Person: Calories 57, Fat 2.3g, Carbs 8g, Protein 2.3g

Carrot & Walnut Cookies

Prep period: 15 mins.
Cooking Period: 14 mins.

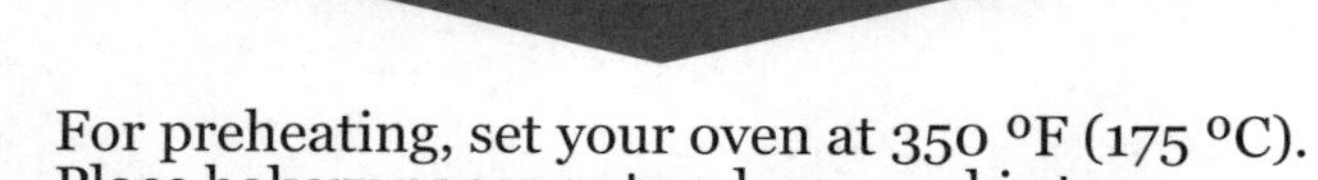

Procedure of Cooking:

1. For preheating, set your oven at 350 °F (175 °C).
2. Place bakery paper onto a large cookie tray.
3. Put the flours, baking soda, and salt into a basin and stir thoroughly.
4. Put the egg, Erythritol, coconut oil, and vanilla extract into another large basin and whisk to incorporate thoroughly.
5. Put in flour mixture and blend to form a dough.
6. Lightly stir in walnuts and carrots.
7. With a 1-inch cookie scooper, scoop 12 cookies onto the cookie sheet about 4 inches apart.
8. With your palm, flatten each cookie slightly.
9. Bake in your oven for around 12-14 minutes.
10. Take the tray out of the oven and place it onto a cooling wire rack to cool for about 5-10 minutes.
11. Remove the cookies from the baking tray and place the cookies themselves onto the rack to cool thoroughly before enjoying.

Ingredients Required12
Serving: 8

- Almond flour – ¾ C. (75 g)
- Coconut flour – ¼ C. (20 g)
- Baking soda – ¼ tsp.
- Sea salt – ¼ tsp.
- Large-sized organic egg – 1
- Erythritol – ¾ C. (140 g)
- Coconut oil – ¼ C. (50 g), liquefied
- Organic vanilla extract – 1 tsp.
- Walnuts – 1/3 C. (40 g), cut up
- Carrots – ¼ C. (40 g), peel removed, shredded and cut up

Per Person: Calories 105, Fat 9.8g, Carbs 2.1g, Protein 3g

Pecan Cookies

Prep period: 15 mins.
Cooking Period: 14 mins.

Procedure of Cooking:

1. For preheating, set your oven at 350 °F (175 °C).
2. Place bakery paper onto a large-sized cookie tray.
3. Put the eggs, almond butter, and coconut oil in a basin and whisk to incorporate them.
4. Add the flour and cinnamon and stir to incorporate thoroughly.
5. Lightly blend in coconut and pecans.
6. Spoon the mixture onto the cookie tray in a single layer.
7. With your hands, flatten each cookie slightly.
8. Bake in your oven for around 12-14 minutes.
9. Take out of the oven and move onto a cooling wire rack to cool on the tray for around 5 minutes.
10. Take the cookies off the baking tray and put the cookies themselves onto the rack to cool thoroughly before enjoying.

Ingredients Required:
Serving: 6

- Eggs – 2
- Almond butter – ½ C. (120 g)
- Coconut oil – 2 tsp., liquefied
- Organic vanilla extract – ½ tsp.
- Coconut flour – 1 tbsp.
- Powdered cinnamon – 1 tsp.
- Low-fat unsweetened coconut – 1 C. (100 g), shredded
- Pecans – ¼ C. (30 g), finely cut up

Per Person: Calories 131, Fat 11.9g, Carbs 4.3g, Protein 3.3g

Nut & Seed Bars

Prep period: 20 mins.
Cooking Period: 5 mins.

Procedure of Cooking:

1. Lay out bakery paper into a 13x9-inch baking pan.
2. Put the hazelnuts, walnuts, and almonds into a large basin and stir thoroughly.
3. Shift 1 C. of the nut mixture into another large basin and chop them roughly.
4. Put the remnant nut mixture in the food processor and process to grind finely.
5. Shift the ground nut mixture into the basin of the cut-up nuts.
6. Add the seeds, raisins, and coconut flakes and blend thoroughly.
7. Put the oil, maple syrup, and cinnamon into a small pot on a burner at around medium-low heat.
8. Cook for around 3-5 minutes, blending all the time.
9. Take off the burner and immediately pour over the nut mixture, blending all the time to incorporate thoroughly.
10. Set it aside to cool slightly.
11. Place the mixture into the baking pan, and with the back of a spoon, smooth the top surface by pressing it slightly.
12. Shift into your refrigerator for around 1 hour.
13. Cut into equal-sized bars and enjoy.

Ingredients Required: 30
Serving: 5

- Hazelnuts – ½ C. (120 g), toasted
- Walnuts – ½ C. (50 g), toasted
- Whole almonds – ½ C. (70 g), toasted
- Sesame seeds – ½ C. (75 g)
- Pumpkin seeds – ½ C. (65 g), shelled
- Dried unsweetened cherries – 1 C. (170 g)
- Low-fat unsweetened coconut flakes – 2 C. (200 g)
- Coconut oil – ¼ C. (50 g)
- Maple syrup – 1/3 C. (110 g)
- Powdered cinnamon – ½ tsp.
- Sea salt – ½ tsp.

Per Person: Calories 114, Fat 8.5g, Carbs 7.6g, Protein 2.6g

Cranberry Bars

Prep period: 20 mins.
Cooking Period: 35 mins.

Ingredients Required:
Serving: 16

- Olive oil baking spray
- Fresh cranberries – 1 C. (100 g), finely cut up
- Powdered Erythritol – 2 tsp.
- Almond flour – ¼ C. (25 g)
- Coconut flour – ¼ C. (23 g)
- Flaxseed meal – ¼ C. (40 g)
- Baking powder – 1 tsp. (4 g)
- Sea salt – 1 pinch
- Coconut oil – 1/3 C. (75 g), softened
- Granulated Erythritol – 1/3 C. (72 g)
- Eggs – 2
- Organic vanilla extract – 1 tsp.

Procedure of Cooking:

1. For preheating, set your oven at 350 °F (175 °C).
2. Spray an 8x8-inch baking pan with baking spray.
3. Put the cranberries and powdered Erythritol into a small basin and toss it all to mingle nicely.
4. Put the flours, flaxseed meal, baking powder, and salt into a second basin and stir thoroughly.
5. Put the almond butter and granulated Erythritol into a third large basin and mix thoroughly.
6. Add 1 egg and whisk thoroughly.
7. Repeat with the remnant egg.
8. Put in vanilla extract and stir thoroughly.
9. Slowly add the flour mixture and stir to incorporate.
10. Lightly stir in cranberries.
11. Place the bar mixture into the baking pan, and with the back of a spoon, smooth the top surface.
12. Bake in your oven for around 30-35 minutes.
13. Take the baking pan of bars out of the oven and place them onto a cooling wire rack to cool thoroughly.
14. Cut into equal-sized bars and enjoy.

Per Person: Calories 90, Fat 5.4g, Carbs 5.5g, Protein 1.7g

Hummus Bites

Prep period: 15 mins.
Cooking Period: 0

Procedure of Cooking:

1. For preheating, set your oven at 325 °F (165 °C).
2. Put the oats and remnant ingredients into a large basin and stir to incorporate thoroughly.
3. Make small-sized balls from the mixture.
4. Enjoy right away.

Ingredients Required:
Serving: 8

- Gluten-free old-fashioned oats – 2 C. (200 g)
- Hummus – 1 C. (250 g)
- Olive oil – 1 tbsp.
- Roasted chickpeas – ¼ C. (40 g)
- Pumpkin seeds – ¼ C. (30 g)
- Sunflower seeds – ¼ C. (30 g)
- Sea salt – ¼ tsp.
- Powdered black pepper – ¼ tsp.
- Red pepper flakes – ¼ tsp.
- Nutritional yeast – 1 tbsp.

Per Person: Calories 187, Fat 9.1g, Carbs 21.4g, Protein 7.3g

Blueberry Bites

Prep period: 20 mins.
Cooking Period: 0

Procedure of Cooking:

1. Place bakery paper onto a large-sized baking tray. Set aside.
2. Put the protein powder, flour, Erythritol, cinnamon, and salt into a large-sized basin and stir thoroughly.
3. Add the blueberries and stir to incorporate.
4. Gradually add the desired amount of almond milk and mix to form a dough.
5. Make desired-sized balls from the blueberry mixture.
6. Lay out the balls onto the baking tray in a single layer.
7. Move into your refrigerator to set for around 30 minutes before enjoying.

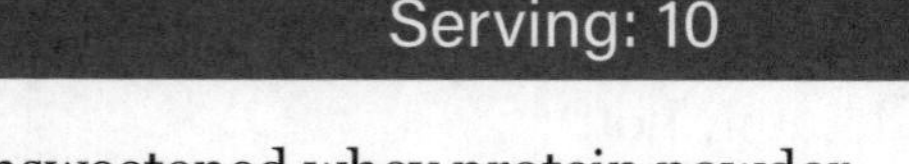

Ingredients Required:
Serving: 10

- Unsweetened whey protein powder – 1 scoop
- Coconut flour – ½ C. (45 g), sifted
- Erythritol – 2 tbsp.
- Powdered cinnamon – ¼ tsp.
- Sea salt – 1 pinch
- Unsweetened dried blueberries – ¼ C. (37 g)
- Unsweetened almond milk – ½-1 C. (120-240 ml)

Per Person: Calories 18, Fat 0.4g, Carbs 1.3g, Protein 2.4g

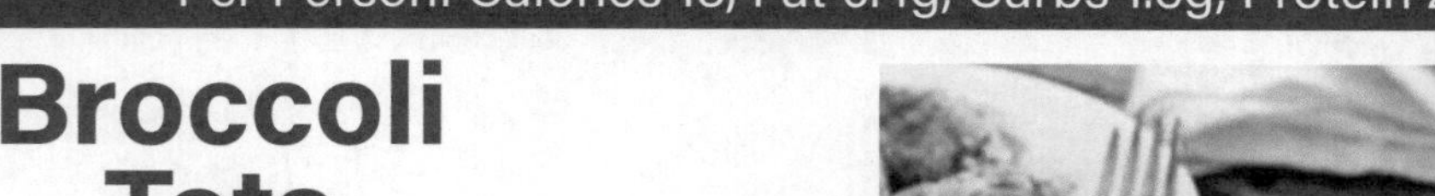

Broccoli Tots

Prep period: 15 mins.
Cooking Period: 35 mins.

Procedure of Cooking:

1. For preheating, set your oven at 400 °F (205 °C).
2. Place bakery paper onto two baking trays and then lightly spray each with baking spray.
3. Put the broccoli into a microwave-safe dish and microwave with the cover for around 5 minutes, stirring once halfway through.
4. Drain the broccoli thoroughly.
5. Put the eggs, oregano, garlic powder, cayenne pepper, red pepper flakes, salt, and white pepper into a large basin and whisk to incorporate thoroughly.
6. Add the cooked broccoli, cheddar cheese, and almond flour and stir to incorporate them thoroughly.
7. With slightly wet hands, make 24 equal-sized patties from the mixture.
8. Lay out the patties onto baking trays into a single layer about 2 inches apart.
9. Lightly spray each patty with baking spray.
10. Bake in your oven for around 15 minutes on both sides.
11. Take the trays out of the oven and enjoy them moderately hot.

Ingredients Required:
Serving: 12

- Frozen chopped broccoli – 1 (16-oz.) (455-g) package
- Large-sized eggs – 3
- Dried oregano – ½ tsp.
- Garlic powder – 1 pinch
- Cayenne pepper powder – ¼ tsp.
- Red pepper flakes – 1 pinch
- Salt and ground white pepper – as desired
- Low-fat cheddar cheese – 1 C. (120 g), grated
- Almond flour – 1 C. (100 g)
- Olive oil baking spray

Per Person: Calories 123, Fat 9.2g, Carbs 4.9g, Protein 7g

Cauliflower Poppers

Prep period: 15 mins.
Cooking Period: 30 mins.

Procedure of Cooking:

1. For preheating, set your oven at 450 ºF (230 ºC).
2. Spray a roasting pot with baking spray.
3. Put cauliflower and remnant ingredients into a basin and toss it all to mingle nicely.
4. Shift the cauliflower mixture into the roasting pot and spread it into an even layer.
5. Roast in your oven for around 25-30 minutes.
6. Enjoy moderately hot.

Ingredients Required:
Serving: 4

- Olive oil baking spray
- Cauliflower florets – 4 C. (420 g)
- Olive oil – 2 tsp.
- Red chili powder – 1/4 tsp.
- Sea salt and powdered black pepper – as desired

Per Person: Calories 46, Fat 2.5g, Carbs 5.4g, Protein 2g

Chicken Nuggets

Prep period: 15 mins.
Cooking Period: 30 mins.

Procedure of Cooking:

1. Cut each chicken breast into 2x1-inch chunks.
2. Put egg whites into a basin and whisk thoroughly.
3. Put flour, oregano, paprika, salt, and pepper into another shallow basin and stir to incorporate thoroughly.
4. Dip the chicken nuggets in whisked eggs and then evenly coat them with the flour mixture.
5. Lay out the chicken nuggets onto the baking tray.
6. Bake in your oven for around 30 minutes.
7. Enjoy moderately hot.

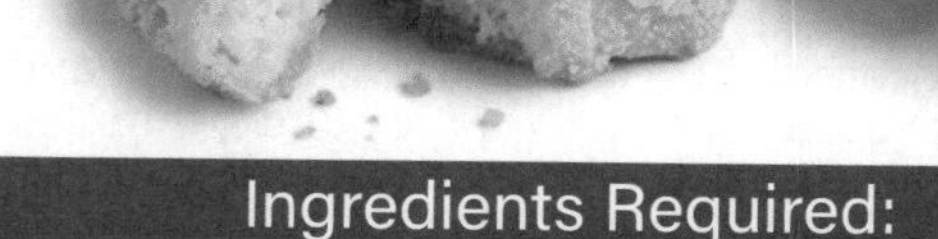

Ingredients Required:
Serving: 8

- Boneless chicken breasts – 2 (8-oz.) (220 g)
- Egg whites – 4
- Almond flour – 1 C. (100 g)
- Dried oregano – 1 tsp. (1 g)
- Paprika – 1/2 tsp.
- Sea salt and powdered black pepper – as desired

Per Person: Calories 201, Fat 10.9g, Carbs 3.3g, Protein 21.2g

Chickpea Fries

Prep period: 20 mins.
Cooking Period: 50 mins.

Ingredients Required:
Serving: 8

- Olive oil baking spray
- Water – 4 C. (960 ml)
- Chickpea flour – 2 C. (180 g)
- Bell pepper – ½ C. (75 g), seeded and cut up
- Onions – ½ C. (60 g), cut up
- Fresh oregano – 1 tbsp., cut up
- Onion powder – 1 tsp.
- Cayenne pepper powder – 1 tsp.
- Sea salt – as desired

Procedure of Cooking:

1. Spray 2 bakery papers with baking spray.
2. Place a bakery paper onto a baking tray and then spray it again with baking spray.
3. Put the water and flour into a large pot on a burner at medium heat and whisk to incorporate thoroughly.
4. Add the remnant ingredients and stir.
5. Cook for around 10 minutes, stirring frequently.
6. Take the pot off the burner and place the mixture onto the baking tray.
7. With a spatula, smooth the top surface.
8. With another greased bakery paper, cover the surface, and with another baking tray, press tightly.
9. Freeze for around 20 minutes.
10. For preheating, set your oven at 400 °F (205 °C).
11. Lightly spray a baking tray with baking spray.
12. Take off the bakery paper from the top and cut into desired-sized fries.
13. Lay out the fries onto the baking tray and put them into a single layer.
14. Bake in your oven for around 20 minutes.
15. Carefully flip the fries over and bake in your oven for around 10-15 minutes.
16. Enjoy moderately hot.

Per Person: Calories 98, Fat 1.7g, Carbs 15.3g, Protein 5.4g

NOTES

This page is for your notes

Poultry Recipes

Chicken Bruschetta

Prep period: 15 mins.
Cooking Period: 12 mins.

Ingredients Required:
Serving: 4

For the Chicken:

- Boneless chicken breasts – 2 (8-oz.) (220 g), halved horizontally
- Garlic cloves – 4, finely cut up
- Italian seasoning – 2 tsp.
- Sea salt – as desired
- Olive oil – 1 tbsp.

For the Topping:

- Roma tomatoes – 3, finely cut up
- Onion – ½ C. (60 g), cut up
- Garlic cloves – 3, finely cut up
- Fresh basil – ¼ C. (5 g), shredded
- Olive oil – 2 tbsp.
- Sea salt – as desired
- Low-fat Parmesan cheese – ½ C. (55 g), shredded

Procedure of Cooking:

1. Put the chicken, garlic, Italian seasoning, and sa into a basin and stir thoroughly.
2. Sizzle oil in a wok on a burner at medium-hig heat.
3. Sear the chicken breasts for around 6 minutes o both sides.
4. In the meantime, for the topping, put the tomatoe and remnant ingredients except the Parmesa cheese into a basin and stir.
5. Take off the wok from the burner.
6. Put the chicken breasts onto serving plates.
7. Enjoy right away with the decoration of the tomat mixture and Parmesan cheese.

Per Person: Calories 380, Fat 22.3g, Carbs 6.6g, Protein 38g

Parsley Chicken Breasts

Prep period: 10 mins.
Cooking Period: 14 mins.

Ingredients Required:
Serving: 4

- Chicken breast halves – 4 (5 oz.) (140 g)
- Sea salt and powdered black pepper – as desired
- Olive oil – 2 tbsp.
- Fresh parsley – 2 tbsp., cut up

Procedure of Cooking:

1. Rub each chicken breast half with salt and pepper.
2. Place chicken over a rack arranged onto a rimmed baking tray.
3. Place into your refrigerator for at least 30 minutes.
4. Take the baking tray from out of the refrigerator and pat dry with paper towels.
5. Sizzle oil in an anti-sticking wok on a burner at around medium-low heat.
6. Put chicken breast halves into the wok, smooth side down.
7. Cook for around 7-8 minutes without moving.
8. Flip the chicken breasts.
9. Cook for around 5-6 minutes.
10. Stir in parsley and take off the wok from the burner.
11. Let the chicken stand in the wok for around 3 minutes before enjoying.

Per Person: Calories 274, Fat 11.3g, Carbs 0g, Protein 41.1g

Herbed Chicken Thighs

Prep period: 10 mins.
Cooking Period: 16 mins.

Ingredients Required:
Serving: 4

- Olive oil – 2 tbsp. (30 ml), divided
- Fresh lemon juice – 1 tbsp.
- Lemon zest – 1 tbsp. , grated
- Dried oregano – 1 tsp.
- Dried thyme – 1 tsp.
- Dried rosemary – 1 tsp.
- Salt and powdered black pepper – as desired
- Bone-in chicken thighs – 1½ lb. (680 g)

Procedure of Cooking:

1. For preheating, set your oven at 420 °F (215 °C).
2. Put in 1 tbsp. (15 ml) of the oil, lemon juice, lemon zest, dried herbs, salt, and pepper into a large-sized basin and mix to incorporate thoroughly.
3. Put in chicken thighs and stir with the mixture.
4. Move into your refrigerator to marinate for at least 20 minutes.
5. Sizzle the remnant oil into an ovenproof wok on a burner at around medium-high heat.
6. Sear the chicken thighs for around 2-3 minutes on both sides.
7. Immediately shift the wok into your oven.
8. Bake in your oven for around 10 minutes.
9. Enjoy right away.

Per Serving: Calories 260, Fat 13.9g, Carbs 1g, Protein 33.3g

Chicken & Tomato Curry

Prep period: 15 mins.
Cooking Period: 35 mins.

Ingredients Required:
Serving: 8

- Olive oil – 2 tbsp.
- Onion – 1, cut up
- Garlic cloves – (4) finely cut up
- Fresh ginger – 2 tsp., finely cut up
- Powdered turmeric – 1 tsp.
- Powdered cumin – 1 tsp.
- Powdered coriander – 1 tsp.
- Paprika – 1 tsp.
- Cayenne pepper powder – 1 tsp.
- Boneless chicken thighs – 6 (4-oz.) (110-g), cut into 1-inch pieces
- Roma tomatoes – 4, cut up
- Unsweetened coconut milk – 1 (14-oz.) (400 ml)
- Sea salt and powdered black pepper – as desired
- Fresh cilantro – ¼ C. (5 g), cut up

Procedure of Cooking:

1. Sizzle oil in a large-sized pot on a burner at medium heat.
2. Sauté the onion for around 4-5 minutes.
3. Add the ginger, garlic, and spices and stir.
4. Sauté for around 1 minute.
5. Add the chicken and blend.
6. Cook for around 4-5 minutes.
7. Put in tomatoes, almond milk, salt, and pepper and blend.
8. Cook the mixture until boiling.
9. Turn the heat to low.
10. Cook with the cover for around 10-15 minutes.
11. Stir in cilantro and take off from the burner.
12. Enjoy right away.

Per Person: Calories 224, Fat 10.1g, Carbs 7.3g, Protein 26.9g

Turkey Chili

Prep period: 10 mins.

Cooking Period: 2¼ hrs.

Ingredients Required:

Serving: 8

- Olive oil – 2 tbsp.
- Small-sized onion – 1, cut up
- Bell pepper – 1, seeded and cut up
- Garlic cloves – 4, finely cut up
- Jalapeño pepper – 1, cut up
- Dried thyme – 1 tsp.
- Red chili powder – 2 tbsp.
- Powdered cumin – 1 tbsp.
- Lean ground turkey – 2 lb. (910 g)
- Tomatoes – 2 C. (400 g), finely cut up
- Tomato paste – 2 oz.
- Homemade chicken broth – 2 C. (480 ml)
- Water – 1 C. (240 ml)
- Sea salt and powdered black pepper – as desired

Procedure of Cooking:

1. Sizzle oil in a large-sized Dutch oven on a burner at medium heat.
2. Sauté the onion and bell pepper for around 5-7 minutes.
3. Put in garlic, jalapeño pepper, thyme, and spices and stir.
4. Sauté for around 1 minute.
5. Put in turkey and stir.
6. Cook for around 4-5 minutes.
7. Put in tomatoes, tomato paste and stir.
8. Cook for around 2 minutes.
9. Put in broth and water and stir.
10. Cook the mixture until boiling.
11. Turn the heat to low.
12. Cook with the cover for around 2 hours.
13. Stir in salt and pepper and take off from the burner.
14. Enjoy right away.

Per Person: Calories 234, Fat 12.6g, Carbs 6.9g, Protein 24.9g

Braised Chicken Thighs

Prep period: 10 mins.

Cooking Period: 55 mins.

Ingredients Required:

Serving: 6

- Bone-in chicken thighs – 6 (8-oz.) (220 g)
- Sea salt and powdered black pepper – as desired
- Olive oil – 2 tbsp.
- Medium-sized onion – ½, slivered
- Homemade chicken broth – 3 C. (720 ml)
- Powdered turmeric – ½ tsp.
- Fresh dill sprigs – 8
- Lemon – 1, cut into thin slivers
- Fresh dill – 1 tbsp., cut up

Procedure of Cooking:

1. Sprinkle the chicken thighs with salt and pepper.
2. Sizzle oil in a large anti-sticking wok on a burner at around high heat.
3. Lay out the chicken thighs into the wok, skin side down.
4. Cook for around 3-4 minutes.
5. With a frying ladle, move the thighs onto a plate.
6. Put the onion into the same wok on the burner at around medium heat.
7. Sauté for around 4-5 minutes.
8. Return the thighs into the wok, skin side up.
9. Put in broth, turmeric, salt and pepper.
10. Place the dill sprigs over the thighs.
11. Cook the mixture until boiling.
12. Turn the heat to around medium-low.
13. Cook with the cover for around 40 minutes, coating the thighs with cooking liquid.
14. Stir in lemon slivers.
15. Cook for around 5 minutes.
16. Discard the thyme sprigs and enjoy hot with the decoration of cut-up dill.

Per Person: Calories 499, Fat 22.3g, Carbs 2.3g, Protein 68.4g

Stuffed Chicken Breasts

Prep period: 15 mins.
Cooking Period: 40 mins.

Procedure of Cooking:

1. For preheating, set your oven at 350 °F (175 °C).
2. Put a bakery paper onto a baking tray.
3. Sizzle oil into a pot on a burner at around medium heat.
4. Cook the onion, bell pepper, and pepperoni pepper for around 1 minute.
5. Add garlic and spinach.
6. Cook for around 2-3 minutes.
7. Stir in oregano, salt, and pepper, and take off the pot from the burner.
8. Put the stuffing mixture into the middle of each butterflied chicken breast.
9. Fold each chicken breast over the filling to make a little pocket and secure it with toothpicks.
10. Lay out the chicken breasts onto the baking tray.
11. Bake in your oven for around 18-20 minutes.
12. Enjoy moderately hot.

Ingredients Required:
Serving: 4

- Olive oil – 1 tbsp.
- Small-sized onion – 1, cut up
- Small-sized bell pepper – ½, seeded and thinly slivered
- Pepperoni pepper – 1, seeded and thinly slivered
- Garlic cloves – 2, finely cut up
- Spinach – 1 C., fresh, cut up
- Dried oregano – ½ tsp.
- Salt and powdered black pepper – as desired
- Boneless chicken breasts – 4 (4 oz.) (110 g), butterflied and pounded

Per Serving: Calories 262, Fat 12g, Carbs 3.7g, Protein 33.5g

Turkey & Spinach Bake

Prep period: 15 mins.
Cooking Period: 18 mins.

Procedure of Cooking:

1. For preheating, set your oven to broiler.
2. Sizzle oil into a cast-iron wok on a burner at medium-high heat.
3. Sauté the onion, garlic, salt, and pepper for around 2-3 minutes.
4. Put in ground turkey and stir.
5. Cook for around 4-6 minutes, stirring frequently.
6. Put in spinach and dried herbs and blend to incorporate.
7. Turn the heat to medium.
8. Cook for around 2-3 minutes.
9. Take off the burner and stir in half of the feta cheese.
10. Lay out the olives on top of the turkey mixture, followed by the remnant feta cheese.
11. Broil for around 2-3 minutes.
12. Take it out of the broiler and enjoy it right away.

Ingredients Required:
Serving: 5

- Olive oil – 1 tbsp.
- Small-sized onion – 1, finely cut up
- Garlic cloves – 2, finely cut up
- Sea salt and powdered black pepper – as desired
- Lean ground turkey – 1 lb. (455 g)
- Fresh spinach – 10 oz. (280 g)
- Dried oregano – 1 tbsp.
- Dried parsley – 1 tbsp.
- Low-fat feta cheese – 8 oz. (225 g), crumbled

Per Person: Calories 360, Fat 24.2g, Carbs 7.3g, Protein 33.1g

Turkey Meatballs & Spinach Soup

Prep period: 15 mins.
Cooking Period: 25 mins.

Ingredients Required:
Serving: 6

For the Meatballs:

- Lean ground turkey – 1 lb. (455 g)
- Garlic clove – 1, finely cut up
- Organic egg whites – 2, whisked
- Low-fat Parmesan cheese – 1/4 C. (28 g), grated
- Sea salt and powdered black pepper – as desired

For the Soup:

- Olive oil – 1 tbsp. (15 ml)
- Small-sized onion – 1, finely cut up
- Small-sized carrot – 1, peel removed and slivered
- Garlic clove – 1, finely cut up
- Homemade chicken broth – 6 C. (440 ml)
- Fresh spinach – 7 C. (210 g), cut up
- Sea salt and powdered black pepper – as desired

Procedure of Cooking:

1. For the meatballs, put ground turkey and remnant ingredients into a basin and blend to incorporate thoroughly.
2. Shape the mixture into balls.
3. Sizzle oil into a large-sized soup pot on a burner at medium heat.
4. Cook the onion and carrot for around 5-6 minutes.
5. Put in garlic and stir.
6. Sauté for around 1 minute.
7. Put in broth and immediately turn the heat to around high.
8. Cook the mixture until boiling.
9. Carefully lay out the balls into the pot.
10. Cook the mixture until boiling.
11. Immediately turn the heat to low.
12. Cook for around 10 minutes.
13. Put in kale and stir.
14. Cook for around 5-6 minutes.
15. Put in salt and pepper, and enjoy right away.

Per Person: Calories 197, Fat 23.7g, Carbs 3.7g, Protein 22.5g

Ground Turkey with Green Beans

Prep period: 15 mins.
Cooking Period: 20 mins.

Ingredients Required:
Serving: 5

- Olive oil – 1 tbsp.
- Medium-sized onion – 1 thinly slivered
- Fresh ginger – 2 tsp., finely cut up
- Garlic cloves – 4, finely cut up
- Extra-lean ground beef – 1 lb. (455 g)
- Fresh lime juice – 2 tbsp.
- Fresh green beans – 1 lb. (455 g), trimmed and slivered
- Fresh cilantro – 1/4 C. (5 g), cut up

Procedure of Cooking:

1. Sizzle oil in a large wok on a burner at around medium heat.
2. Cook the onion, ginger, and garlic for around 4-5 minutes.
3. Put in beef and mix thoroughly.
4. Cook for around 6-7 minutes.
5. Drain off the excess grease from the wok.
6. Blend in lime juice.
7. Cook for around 1 minute.
8. Put in green beans and stir thoroughly.
9. Cook for around 5-6 minutes.
10. Stir in cilantro.
11. Cook for around 1 minute.
12. Enjoy right away.

Per Person: Calories 236, Fat 8.6g, Carbs 9.9g, Protein 29.7g

Meat Recipes

Garlicky Flank Steak

Prep period: 10 mins.
Cooking Period: 16 mins.

Ingredients Required:
Serving: 8

- Garlic cloves – 3
- Fresh ginger – 1 tsp., grated
- Maple syrup – 1 tbsp.
- Olive oil – 2 tbsp.
- Sea salt and powdered black pepper – as desired
- Flank steak – 1½ lb. (680 g), fat removed
- Olive oil baking spray

Procedure of Cooking:

1. Put garlic and remnant ingredients except for steak into a large sealable bag and mix to incorporate thoroughly.
2. Put in steak and coat with the marinade.
3. Seal the bag and place it in your refrigerator to marinate for around 24 hours.
4. Take it out of the refrigerator and put it at room temperature for around 15 minutes.
5. Lightly spray a cast-iron wok with baking spray and sizzle on a burner at medium-high heat.
6. Discard the excess marinade from the steak and place it in the wok.
7. Cook for around 6-8 minutes on both sides.
8. Take the steak out of the wok and place it on a chopping block for 10 minutes.
9. Cut the steak into serving portions and enjoy.

Per Person: Calories 236, Fat 8.6g, Carbs 9.9g, Protein 29.7g

Tomato Braised Beef

Prep period: 15 mins.
Cooking Period: 1 hr. 55 mins.

Procedure of Cooking:

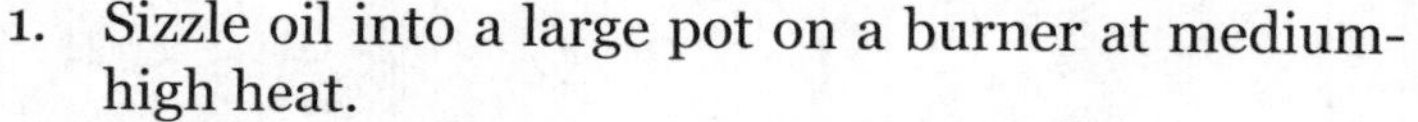

1. Sizzle oil into a large pot on a burner at medium-high heat.
2. Sear the beef cubes for around 4-5 minutes.
3. Put in celery, onions, and garlic and stir.
4. Cook for around 5 minutes, stirring frequently.
5. Stir in remnant ingredients.
6. Cook the mixture until boiling.
7. Turn the heat to low.
8. Cook with the cover for around 1½-1¾ hours.
9. Enjoy right away.

Ingredients Required:
Serving: 12

- Olive oil – ¼ C. (60 ml)
- Boneless beef tenderloin – 2½ lb. (1150 g), fat removed and cubed
- Celery stalks – 3, cut up
- Onions – 2, cut up
- Garlic cloves – 4, finely cut up
- Tomatoes – 6-8 C. (600-800 g), finely cut up
- Homemade chicken broth – 1½ C. (360 m)
- Fresh parsley – ½ C. (10 g), cut up
- Dried oregano – 1 tsp.
- Sea salt and powdered black pepper – as desired

Per Person: Calories 278, Fat 11.7g, Carbs 6g, Protein 36.2g

Braised Beef & Carrot

Prep period: 15 mins.
Cooking Period: 1 hr. 5 mins.

Ingredients Required:

Serving: 10

- Olive oil – 2 tbsp.
- Beef tenderloin – 1½ lb. (680 g), fat removed and cubed
- Large-sized onion – 1, cut up
- Medium-sized carrots – 2, peel removed and slivered
- Celery stalks – 2, cut up
- Garlic cloves – 2, finely cut up
- Fresh ginger – 2 tsp., finely cut up
- Sea salt and powdered black pepper – as desired
- Tomato puree – 2 C. (600 g)
- Homemade chicken broth – 4 C. (960 ml)
- Dried thyme – 1 tsp.
- Dried parsley – 1 tsp.
- Dried rosemary – 1 tsp.
- Paprika – 1 tbsp.
- Fresh parsley – ¼ C. (5 g), cut up

Procedure of Cooking:

1. Sizzle oil into a large Dutch oven on a burner at medium-high heat.
2. Cook the beef cubes for around 4-5 minutes.
3. With a frying ladle, move the beef cues into a basin.
4. Put onion, carrots, and celery into the same Dutch oven.
5. Cook for around 4-5 minutes.
6. Put in remnant ingredients and stir to incorporate.
7. Immediately turn the heat to high.
8. Cook the mixture until boiling.
9. Immediately turn the heat to low.
10. Cook with a cover for around 40-50 minutes.
11. Stir in salt and pepper, and enjoy right away.

Per Person: Calories 225, Fat 14.3g, Carbs 4.8g, Protein 25.4g

Beef & Mushroom Casserole

Prep period: 15 mins.
Cooking Period: 3 hrs.

Ingredients Required:

Serving: 12

- Water – 1 C. (240 ml)
- Arrowroot starch – 3 tbsp.
- Beef tenderloin – 1½ lb. (680 g), fat removed and cubed
- Fresh mushrooms – 1 lb. (455 g), slivered
- Tomatoes – 3 C. (600 g), cut up
- Medium-sized carrots – 4, peel removed and cut up
- Medium-sized onions – 2, cut up
- Celery stalks – 2, cut up
- Fresh thyme – 1 tbsp. (1¼ g), cut up
- Garlic clove – 1, finely cut up
- Homemade chicken broth – 2 C. (480 ml)
- Sea salt and powdered black pepper – as desired
- Ground mustard – ½ tsp.

Procedure of Cooking:

1. For preheating, set your oven at 325 °F (165 °C).
2. Put water and arrowroot starch into a small basin and mix to incorporate thoroughly.
3. Put the beef pieces and remnant ingredients into a large ovenproof pot and stir to incorporate.
4. Slowly put into arrowroot starch mixture, stirring all the time.
5. Cover the pot and bake in your oven for around 3 hours, stirring after every 30 minutes.
6. Enjoy right away.

Per Person: Calories 189, Fat 3.4g, Carbs 13.2g, Protein 26.8g

Ground Beef with Spinach

Prep period: 15 mins.
Cooking Period: 20 mins.

Ingredients Required:
Serving: 4

- Olive oil – 1 tbsp.
- Medium-sized onion – ½, cut up
- Garlic cloves – 2, finely cut up
- Jalapeño pepper – 1, cut up
- Lean ground beef – 1 lb. (455 g)
- Powdered coriander – 1 tsp.
- Powdered cumin – 1 tsp.
- Powdered ginger – ½ tsp.
- Powdered cinnamon – ½ tsp.
- Powdered turmeric – ½ tsp.
- Sea salt and powdered black pepper – as desired
- Cherry tomatoes – 8, quartered
- Fresh spinach – 1 lb. (455 g), cut up
- Fresh lemon juice – 1 tsp.

Procedure of Cooking:

1. Sizzle oil into a large-sized wok on a burner a medium heat.
2. Sauté the onion for around 4-5 minutes.
3. Put in garlic and jalapeño and stir.
4. Sauté for around 1 minute.
5. Put in beef and spices and blend.
6. Cook for around 6-8 minutes, stirring from time to time.
7. Put in tomatoes and greens and stir.
8. Cook for around 4 minutes.
9. Stir in lemon juice, salt, and pepper, and take off from the burner.
10. Enjoy right away.

Per Person: Calories 285, Fat 14.6g, Carbs 11g, Protein 26.4g

Lemony Pork Tenderloin

Prep period: 10 mins.
Cooking Period: 22 mins.

Ingredients Required:
Serving: 5

- Olive oil baking spray
- Fresh rosemary – 1 tbsp., finely cut up
- Garlic clove 1, finely cut up
- Fresh lemon juice – 1 tbsp.
- Olive oil – 1 tbsp.
- Dijon mustard – 1 tsp.
- Powdered Erythritol – 1 tsp.
- Sea salt and powdered black pepper – as desired
- Pork tenderloin – 1 lb. (455 g), fat removed
- Sea salt and powdered black pepper – as desired

Procedure of Cooking:

1. For preheating, set your oven at 400 °F (205 °C).
2. Spray a large-rimmed baking tray with baking spray.
3. Put rosemary and remnant ingredients except for the pork tenderloin into a large basin and whisk to incorporate thoroughly.
4. Add pork tenderloin and coat with the mixture.
5. Lay out the pork tenderloin onto the baking tray.
6. Bake in your oven for around 20-22 minutes.
7. Take the baking tray of pork tenderloin out of the oven and move it onto a chopping block for around 5 minutes.
8. Cut the pork tenderloin into serving portions and enjoy.

Per Person: Calories 157, Fat 6.1g, Carbs 0.5g, Protein 23.9g

Pork with Bell Peppers

Prep period: 15 mins.
Cooking Period: 14 mins.

Procedure of Cooking:

1. Put broth, lemon juice, garlic, ginger, and cornstarch into a basin and stir to incorporate thoroughly.
2. Sizzle 1 tsp. (5 ml) of oil into a large wok on a burner at medium-high heat.
3. Sear the pork strips for around 3-4 minutes.
4. Move the pork strips into a basin.
5. Sizzle remnant oil into the same wok on a burner at high heat.
6. Stir-fry the bell pepper for around 2-3 minutes.
7. Stir in scallion and red pepper flakes.
8. Cook for around 1 minute.
9. Stir in the broth mixture and immediately turn the heat to medium-high.
10. Cook for around 2 minutes, stirring from time to time.
11. Put in cooked pork strips.
12. Cook for around 2-3 minutes.
13. Enjoy right away.

Ingredients Required:
Serving: 4

- Homemade chicken broth – 1/3 C. (90 ml)
- Fresh lemon juice – 2 tbsp.
- Garlic cloves – 3, finely cut up
- Fresh ginger – 2 tsp., finely grated
- Cornstarch – 1 tsp.
- Olive oil – 5 tsp. (25 ml), divided
- Pork tenderloin – 12 oz. (340 g), fat removed and cut into thin strips
- Large-sized bell pepper – 3, seeded and cut into thin strips
- Scallions – 3, cut up
- Red pepper flakes – ½ tsp.

Per Person: Calories 253, Fat 11.5g, Carbs 9.6g, Protein 27.7g

Pork & Beans Bake

Prep period: 15 mins.
Cooking Period: 3 hrs. 20 mins.

Procedure of Cooking:

1. For preheating, set your oven at 250 °F (120 °C).
2. Put the beans into a large pot of water.
3. Cook for around 20 minutes.
4. Take off the burner and drain the beans.
5. Put the beans and remnant ingredients into a large casserole dish and stir to incorporate.
6. Cover the casserole dish and bake in your oven for around 3 hours.
7. Enjoy right away.

Ingredients Required:
Serving: 10

- Dried Great Northern beans – 1 lb. (455 g)
- Homemade chicken broth – 4 C. (960 ml)
- Onion – 1, cut up
- Tomatoes – 3 C. (600 g), finely cut up
- Carrots – 3, peel removed and cut into ½-inch pieces
- Pork tenderloin – 2 lb. (910 g), fat removed and cut into 1-inch chunks
- Fresh parsley – 2 tbsp.
- Fresh thyme – 2 tbsp.
- Powdered allspice – 1 tsp.
- Sea salt and powdered black pepper – as desired

Per Person: Calories 279, Fat 23.3g, Carbs 47.1g, Protein 37.1g

Ground Lamb with Cabbage

Prep period: 15 mins.
Cooking Period: 45 mins.

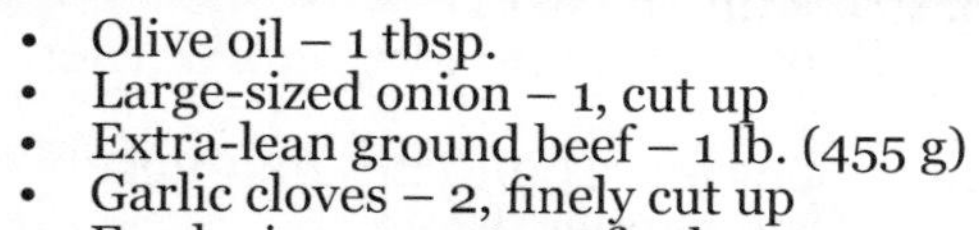

Ingredients Required:

Serving: 8

- Olive oil – 1 tbsp.
- Large-sized onion – 1, cut up
- Extra-lean ground beef – 1 lb. (455 g)
- Garlic cloves – 2, finely cut up
- Fresh ginger – 2 tsp., finely cut up
- Sea salt and powdered black pepper – as desired
- Cabbage – 6 C. (530 g), shredded
- Tomatoes – 2½ C. (500 g), finely cut up
- Dried thyme – ½ tsp.
- Dried oregano – ½ tsp.
- Bay leaf – 1
- Paprika – ½ tsp.
- Powdered cumin – ½ tsp.
- Powdered cinnamon – ½ tsp.
- Homemade vegetable broth – 2-3 C. (480-720 ml)

Procedure of Cooking:

1. Sizzle oil in a large soup pan on a burner at around medium-high heat.
2. Cook the onion for around 3-5 minutes.
3. Put in ground beef, garlic, ginger, salt, and pepper and stir to incorporate.
4. Immediately turn the heat to around medium-high.
5. Cook for around 7-8 minutes.
6. Put in cabbage, tomatoes, herbs, bay leaf, spices and broth.
7. Cook the mixture until boiling.
8. Immediately turn the heat to low.
9. Cook for around 25 minutes.
10. Stir in salt and pepper, and enjoy right away.

Per Person: Calories 229, Fat 8.6g, Carbs 21.4g, Protein 18.8g

Ground Lamb with Mushroom & Onion

Prep period: 15 mins.
Cooking Period: 25 mins.

Procedure of Cooking:

1. Sizzle oil in a large anti-sticking wok on a burner at medium-high heat.
2. Cook the ground lamb for around 8-9 minutes.
3. With a frying ladle, move the lamb into a basin.
4. Put the garlic into the same wok and stir.
5. Sauté for around 1 minute.
6. Add the mushrooms and onion and stir.
7. Cook for around 5-7 minutes.
8. Put the cooked lamb, basil, broth, and vinegar.
9. Cook the mixture until boiling.
10. Turn the heat to medium-low.
11. Cook for around 3 minutes.
12. Stir in parsley and enjoy right away.

Ingredients Required:

Serving: 5

- Lean ground lamb – 1 lb. (455 g)
- Olive oil – 2 tbsp.
- Garlic cloves – 2, finely cut up
- Onion – 1, slivered
- Fresh mushrooms – 2 C. (250 g), slivered
- Fresh basil – 2 tbsp.
- Homemade chicken broth – ¼ C. (60 ml)
- Balsamic vinegar – 2 tbsp.
- Fresh parsley – 2 tbsp., cut up

Per Person: Calories 269, Fat 12.2g, Carbs 3.2g, Protein 29.1g

Fish & Seafood Recipes

Lemony Salmon

Prep period: 10 mins.
Cooking Period: 14 mins.

Procedure of Cooking:

1. For preheating, set your grill to medium-high heat.
2. Spray the grill grate with baking spray.
3. Put garlic and remnant ingredients except for salmon fillets into a large basin and stir to incorporate thoroughly.
4. Put salmon fillets in and coat them with the garlic mixture.
5. Put salmon steaks onto the grill.
6. Grill for around 6-7 minutes on both sides.
7. Enjoy right away.

Ingredients Required:
Serving: 4

- Olive oil baking spray
- Garlic cloves – 2, finely cut up
- Lemon zest – 1 tbsp., grated
- Fresh lemon juice – 2 tbsp.
- Olive oil – 1 tbsp.
- Sea salt and powdered black pepper – as desired
- Boneless salmon fillets – 4 (6 oz.) (150 g)

Per Person: Calories 208, Fat 11.3g, Carbs 0.8g, Protein 26.6g

Glazed Salmon

Prep period: 10 mins.
Cooking Period: 10 mins.

Procedure of Cooking:

1. Put all spices into a small bowl and stir thoroughly. Set aside.
2. Put the salmon fillets, lemon juice, 2 tsp. (10 ml) of oil and the spice mixture into a large basin and toss it all to mingle nicely.
3. Cover and place into your refrigerator for at least 2 hours.
4. Put the maple syrup and soy sauce into a small cast-iron wok on a burner at medium heat.
5. Cook for around 7-10 minutes, stirring from time to time.
6. In the meantime, sizzle remnant oil in a large cast-iron wok on a burner at high heat.
7. Place the salmon fillets in the wok, flesh side down.
8. Cook for around 4 minutes.
9. Carefully flip the side of the fill and put in the maple syrup glaze.
10. Cook for around 4 minutes.
11. Move the fillets onto serving plates.
12. Top with the glaze from the pot and enjoy with the decoration of the scallion.

Ingredients Required:
Serving: 6

- Red pepper flakes – 2 tsp.
- Powdered cinnamon – 1 pinch
- Powdered black pepper – as desired
- Salmon fillets – 6 (6-oz.) (150-g)
- Fresh lemon juice – 2 tbsp.
- Olive oil – 4 tsp. (20 ml), divided
- Maple syrup – 1/4 C. (75 g)
- Low-sodium soy sauce – 3 tbsp.
- Scallion – 1/4 C. (25 g), cut up

Per Person: Calories 297, Fat 13.8g, Carbs 10.6g, Protein 33.9g

Stuffed Salmon

Prep period: 15 mins.
Cooking Period: 16 mins.

Procedure of Cooking:

1. Cook the spinach in a pot of lightly salted boiling water for around 40-60 seconds.
2. Drain the spinach into a colander and immediately immerse it in a basin of ice water.
3. Again, drain the spinach thoroughly and place it into a basin.
4. In the basin of spinach, put the artichokes, sun-dried tomatoes, and feta cheese and stir thoroughly.
5. With a sharp knife, make a horizontal cut in the center of each salmon fillet. (Do not cut all the way through).
6. Season each salmon fillet with garlic powder, salt, and pepper.
7. Stuff each salmon pocket with the spinach mixture.
8. Sizzle a cast-iron wok on a burner at medium heat.
9. Lay out the salmon fillets into the wok, skin-sides down.
10. Cook for around 5 minutes on both sides.
11. Again, flip the fillets.
12. Cook for around 5 minutes.
13. Enjoy right away.

Ingredients Required:
Serving: 4

- Fresh spinach – 4 C. (120 g), cut up
- Canned artichoke hearts – ½ C. (85 g), liquid removed and cut up
- Oil-packed sun-dried tomatoes – ½ C. (55 g), liquid removed and cut up
- Low-fat feta cheese – ¼ C. (30 g), crumbled
- Salmon fillets – 4 (8-oz.) (225-g)
- Garlic powder – 1 pinch
- Sea salt and powdered black pepper – as desired
- Fresh parsley – ¼ C. (5 g), cut up

Per Person: Calories 345, Fat 16.3g, Carbs 4.4g, Protein 47.1g

Salmon & Veggie Parcel

Prep period: 15 mins.
Cooking Period: 20 mins.

Procedure of Cooking:

1. For preheating, set your oven at 400 °F (205 °C).
2. Lay out 6 pieces of foil on a smooth surface.
3. Place 1 salmon fillet onto each foil piece and sprinkle with salt and pepper.
4. Put the bell peppers, broccoli, and onion into a basin and stir.
5. Place veggie mixture over each fillet and top with parsley.
6. Drizzle with oil and lemon juice.
7. Fold the foil around the salmon mixture to seal it.
8. Lay out the foil packets onto a large-sized baking tray into a single layer.
9. Bake in your oven for around 20 minutes.
10. Enjoy right away.

Ingredients Required:
Serving: 13

- Salmon fillets – 6 (3-oz.) (85-g)
- Sea salt and powdered black pepper – as desired
- Large-sized bell peppers – 2, seeded and cubed
- Small-sized broccoli florets – 1½ C. (135 g)
- Small-sized onion – 1 thinly slivered
- Fresh parsley – ½ C. (10 g), cut up
- Olive oil – ¼ C. (60 ml)
- Fresh lemon juice – 2 tbsp.

Per Person: Calories 224, Fat 14g, Carbs 8.2g, Protein 18.2g

Tuna with Olive Sauce

Prep period: 15mins.
Cooking Period: 10 mins.

Ingredients Required:
Serving: 4

- Olive oil baking spray
- Tuna steaks – 4 (6-oz.) (150-g)
- Olive oil – 2 tbsp. (30 ml), divided
- Sea salt and powdered black pepper – as desired
- Garlic cloves – 2, finely cut up
- Tomatoes – 1 C. (200 g), cut up
- Homemade chicken broth – 1 C. (240 ml)
- Olives – 3/4 C. (135 g), pitted and slivered
- Capers – 1/4 C. (30 g), liquid removed
- Fresh thyme – 2 tbsp., cut up
- Lemon zest – 1 tsp., grated
- Fresh lemon juice – 2 tbsp.
- Fresh parsley – 2 tbsp., cut up

Procedure of Cooking:

1. For preheating, set your grill to high heat.
2. Spray the grill grate with baking spray.
3. Coat the tuna steaks with 1 tbsp. (15 ml) of oil and then sprinkle with salt and pepper.
4. Set them aside for around 5 minutes.
5. For the sauce: sizzle remnant oil in a small wok on a burner at medium heat.
6. Sauté the garlic for around 1 minute.
7. Add the tomatoes and stir.
8. Cook for around 2 minutes.
9. Put in wine and stir.
10. Cook the mixture until boiling.
11. Add the remnant ingredients except for parsley and stir.
12. Cook for around 5 minutes.
13. Stir in parsley, salt, and pepper, and take off from the burner.
14. In the meantime, put the tuna steaks over a direct heat.
15. Cook for around 1-2 minutes on both sides.
16. Enjoy the tuna steaks right away with the decoration of the sauce.

Per Person: Calories 468, Fat 10.7g, Carbs 7.3g, Protein 52.1g

Parmesan Tilapia

Prep period: 10 mins.
Cooking Period: 11 mins.

Procedure of Cooking:

1. For preheating, set your oven to broiler.
2. Lay out a piece of heavy-duty foil onto a baking tray and then spray it with baking spray.
3. Rub the tilapia fillets with salt and pepper lightly.
4. Lay out the tilapia fillets on the baking tray into a single layer and top each with Parmesan cheese.
5. Broil for around 10-11 minutes.
6. Take them out of the oven and enjoy them right away.

Ingredients Required:
Serving: 4

- Olive oil baking spray
- Tilapia fillets – 4 (6-oz.) (150-g)
- Sea salt and powdered black pepper – as desired
- Low-fat Parmesan cheese – 1/2 C. (55 g), shredded

Per Person: Calories 173, Fat 4g, Carbs 0.2g, Protein 34.1g

Garlicky Tilapia

Prep period: 10 mins.
Cooking Period: 8 mins.

Ingredients Required:
Serving: 5

- Olive oil – 2 tbsp.
- Tilapia fillets – 5 (5-oz.) (140-g)
- Garlic cloves – 3, finely cut up
- Fresh ginger – 1 tsp., grated
- Low-fat unsweetened coconut – 2 tbsp., shredded
- Homemade chicken broth – 2 tbsp.

Procedure of Cooking:

1. Sizzle oil in a wok on a burner at medium heat.
2. Cook the tilapia fillets for around 2 minutes.
3. Flip the side and stir in garlic, ginger, and coconut.
4. Cook for around 1 minute.
5. Put in broth and stir.
6. Cook for around 2-3 minutes.
7. Enjoy right away.

Per Person: Calories 124, Fat 7.6g, Carbs 2.4g, Protein 26.9g

Shrimp & Tomato Curry

Prep period: 15 mins.
Cooking Period: 20 mins.

Ingredients Required:
Serving: 6

- Salmon fillets – 6 (3-oz.) (85-g)
- Olive oil – 2 tbsp.
- Onion – ¼ C. (30 g), cut up
- Roasted red pepper – ¼ C. (40 g), cut up
- Garlic clove – 1, finely cut up
- Shrimp – 1½ lb. (680 g), peeled and deveined
- Tomatoes – 2 C. (400 g), cut up
- Unsweetened coconut milk – 1 C. (240 ml)
- Fresh lime juice – 2 tbsp.
- Sea salt and powdered black pepper – as desired
- Fresh cilantro – ¼ C. (5 g), cut up

Procedure of Cooking:

1. Sizzle oil into a pot on a burner at medium heat.
2. Sauté the onion for around 4-5 minutes.
3. Put in red pepper and garlic and stir.
4. Sauté for around 4-5 minutes.
5. Put in shrimp and tomatoes and blend.
6. Cook for around 3-4 minutes.
7. Stir in coconut milk.
8. Cook for around 4-5 minutes.
9. Stir in lime juice, salt, and pepper, and take off from the burner.
10. Decorate with cilantro and enjoy right away.

Per Person: Calories 236, Fat 11.1g, Carbs 6.7g, Protein 26.6g

Shrimp with Bell Peppers

Prep period: 15mins.
Cooking Period: 9 mins.

Ingredients Required:
Serving: 4

- Olive oil – 2 tbsp.
- Garlic cloves – 4, finely cut up
- Fresh red chili – 1, slivered
- Shrimp – 1 lb. (455 g), peeled and deveined
- Bell peppers – 2½ C. (450 g), seeded and julienned
- Onion – ½ C. (60 g), thinly slivered
- Homemade chicken broth – ¼ C. (60 ml)
- Sea salt and powdered black pepper – as desired

Procedure of Cooking:

1. Sizzle oil in a large anti-sticking wok on a burner at medium heat.
2. Sauté the garlic and red chili for around 2 minutes.
3. Add in shrimp, bell peppers, onion, and black pepper and stir.
4. Stir-fry for around 5 minutes.
5. Put in broth and stir.
6. Cook for around 1-2 minutes.
7. Enjoy right away.

Per Person: Calories 230, Fat 9.1g, Carbs 9.7g, Protein 27.1g

Scallops with Spinach

Prep period: 15 mins.
Cooking Period: 10 mins.

Ingredients Required:
Serving: 4

- Sea scallops – 20 oz. (560 g), side muscle removed
- Sea salt and powdered black pepper – as desired
- Olive oil – 3 tsp., divided
- Fresh baby spinach – 6 oz. (150 g)
- Garlic cloves – 2, finely cut up
- Fresh lemon juice – 1 tbsp.

Procedure of Cooking:

1. Rub the scallops with salt and pepper.
2. Sizzle 2 tsp. (10 ml) of oil into a large cast-iron wok on a burner at medium heat.
3. Cook the scallops for around 2-3 minutes from both sides.
4. With a frying ladle, move the scallops onto a plate.
5. Sizzle remnant oil in the same wok on a burner at medium heat.
6. Cook the spinach and garlic for around 3-4 minutes.
7. Stir in salt and pepper and remove from the burner.
8. Move the spinach onto serving plates and top with scallops.
9. Drizzle with lemon juice and enjoy.

Per Person: Calories 165, Fat 4.4g, Carbs 5.5g, Protein 25.2g

Vegetarian Recipes

Stuffed Zucchini

Prep period: 15 mins.
Cooking Period: 18 mins.

Ingredients Required:
Serving: 8

- Olive oil baking spray
- Medium-sized zucchinis – 4, halved lengthwise
- Bell pepper – 1 C. (150 g), seeded and finely cut up
- Kalamata olives – ½ C. (90 g), pitted and finely cut up
- Tomatoes – ½ C. (100 g), finely cut up
- Garlic cloves – 3, finely cut up
- Dried oregano – 1 tbsp.
- Sea salt and powdered black pepper – as desired
- Low-fat feta cheese – ½ C. (55 g), crumbled

Procedure of Cooking:

1. For preheating, set your oven at 350 °F (175 °C).
2. Spray a large-sized baking tray with baking spray.
3. With a melon baller, scoop out the flesh of each zucchini half. Discard the flesh.
4. Put the bell pepper, olives, tomatoes, garlic, oregano, salt, and pepper into a basin and stir.
5. Stuff each zucchini half with the veggie mixture.
6. Lay out zucchini halves onto the baking tray.
7. Bake in your oven for around 15 minutes.
8. Now, set your oven to broiler on high.
9. Top each zucchini half with feta cheese and broil for around 3 minutes.
10. Enjoy right away.

Per Person: Calories 59, Fat 3.2g, Carbs 6.2g, Protein 2.9g

Mushroom Curry

Prep period: 15 mins.
Cooking Period: 20 mins.

Ingredients Required:
Serving: 4

- Tomatoes – 2 C. (400 g), cut up
- Serrano pepper – 1, cut up
- Fresh ginger – 1 tsp., cut up
- Unsalted cashews – ¼ C. (30 g)
- Olive oil – 2 tbsp.
- Powdered cumin – ½ tsp.
- Powdered coriander – ¼ tsp.
- Powdered turmeric – ¼ tsp.
- Red chili powder – ¼ tsp.
- Mushrooms – 4 C. (500 g), fresh, slivered
- Water – 1½ C. (360 ml)
- Sea salt and powdered black pepper – as desired

Procedure of Cooking:

1. Put tomatoes, Serrano pepper, ginger, and cashews into a food mixer and process to form a smooth paste.
2. Sizzle oil in a pot on a burner at medium heat.
3. Sauté the spices for around 1 minute.
4. Put in tomato paste and stir.
5. Cook for around 5 minutes.
6. Stir in mushrooms and water.
7. Cook the mixture until boiling.
8. Cook for around 10-12 minutes, stirring from time to time.
9. Stir in salt and pepper and remove from the burner.
10. Enjoy right away.

Per Person: Calories 146, Fat 11.5g, Carbs 9.2g, Protein 4.4g

Tofu with Green Peas

Prep period: 15 mins.
Cooking Period: 25 mins.

Ingredients Required:
Serving: 5

- Olive oil – 2 tbsp. (30 ml), divided
- Extra-firm tofu – 1 (16-oz.) (455-g) package, pressed, liquid removed, and cubed
- Onion – 1 C. (120 g), cut up
- Fresh ginger – 2 tsp., finely cut up
- Garlic cloves – 2, finely cut up
- Large-sized tomatoes – 2, finely cut up
- Frozen green peas – 3 C. (480 g), thawed
- Homemade vegetable broth – 1/3 C. (90 ml)

Procedure of Cooking:

1. Sizzle 1 tbsp. (15 ml) of oil in a large wok on a burner at medium-high heat.
2. Cook the tofu for around 3-4 minutes, stirring from time to time.
3. Move the tofu into a basin
4. Sizzle the remnant oil in the same wok on a burner at medium heat.
5. Cook the onion for 3-4 minutes.
6. Put in ginger and garlic and stir.
7. Sauté for around 1 minute.
8. Add in tomatoes and stir.
9. Cook for around 4-5 minutes, crushing with the back of a spoon.
10. Stir in green peas.
11. Cook for around 3-4 minutes.
12. Stir in broth and tofu.
13. Cook for around 2-3 minutes.
14. Enjoy right away.

Per Person: Calories 231, Fat 11.5g, Carbs 20.7g, Protein 14.8g

Cauliflower & Green Peas Curry

Prep period: 15 mins.
Cooking Period: 15 mins.

Ingredients Required:
Serving: 3

- Water – ¼ C. (60 ml)
- Olive oil – 2 tbsp.
- Medium-sized tomatoes – 2, cut up
- Garlic cloves – 3, finely cut up
- Fresh ginger – 1 tsp., finely cut up
- Powdered cumin – ¼ tsp.
- Powdered turmeric – ¼ tsp.
- Cauliflower – 2 C. (210 g), cut up
- Fresh green peas – 1 C. (160 g), shelled
- Sea salt and powdered black pepper – as desired
- Warm water – ½ C. (120 ml)
- Fresh cilantro – ¼ C. (5 g), cut up
- Olive oil – 2 tbsp.

Procedure of Cooking:

1. Put tomatoes and ¼ C. (60 ml) of water into a clean blender and process to form a smooth puree.
2. Sizzle oil in a large-sized wok on a burner at medium heat.
3. Cook the garlic, ginger, and spices for around 1 minute.
4. Put in cauliflower, peas, and tomato puree and stir.
5. Cook for around 3-4 minutes.
6. Put in warm water and stir.
7. Cook the mixture until boiling.
8. Immediately turn the heat to medium-low.
9. Cook with a cover for around 8-10 minutes.
10. Enjoy right away.

Per Person: Calories 163, Fat 10.1g, Carbs 16.1g, Protein 6g

Stuffed Bell Peppers

Prep period: 15 mins.
Cooking Period: 40 mins.

Ingredients Required:
Serving: 4

- Water – 1 C. (240 ml)
- Uncooked couscous – ½ C. (85 g)
- Large-sized bell peppers – 4, tops and seeds removed
- Parsley – 2 tbsp., fresh, cut up
- Olive oil – 1 tbsp.
- Fresh lemon juice – 1 tbsp.
- Sea salt and powdered black pepper – as desired

Procedure of Cooking:

1. Put water into a pot on a burner at medium-high heat.
2. Cook the water until boiling.
3. Stir in couscous and immediately cover the pot.
4. Remove from the burner and set the pot aside with a cover for around 10 minutes.
5. With a fork, fluff the couscous and let it cool thoroughly.
6. For preheating, set your oven to 350 °F (175 °C).
7. Lightly spray a baking tray.
8. Place the bell peppers onto the baking tray.
9. Put cooled couscous and remnant ingredients into a large basin and blend to incorporate thoroughly.
10. Stuff each bell pepper with the couscous mixture.
11. Bake in your oven for around 35 minutes.
12. Enjoy moderately hot.

Per Person: Calories 151, Fat 4g, Carbs 26g, Protein 4.1g

Lentil with Kale

Prep period: 15 mins.
Cooking Period: 15 mins.

Ingredients Required:
Serving: 6

- Red lentils – 1½ C. (315 g), rinsed
- Homemade vegetable broth – 1½ C. (360 ml)
- Olive oil – 2 tbsp.
- Onion – ½ C. (60 g), cut up
- Fresh ginger – 1 tsp., finely cut up
- Garlic cloves – 2, finely cut up
- Tomatoes – 1½ C. (300 g), cut up
- Fresh kale – 6 C. (330 g), tough ends removed and cut up
- Sea salt and powdered black pepper – as desired

Procedure of Cooking:

1. Put the broth and lentils into a pot on a burner at medium-high heat.
2. Cook until boiling.
3. Turn the heat to low.
4. Cook with a cover for around 20-25 minutes.
5. Remove from the burner and set aside, covered.
6. In the meantime, sizzle oil in a large-sized wok on a burner at medium heat.
7. Sauté the onion for around 5-6 minutes.
8. Put in ginger and garlic and stir.
9. Sauté for around 1 minute.
10. Put in tomatoes and kale and stir.
11. Cook for around 4-5 minutes.
12. Stir in lentils, salt, and pepper, and remove from the burner.
13. Enjoy right away.

Per Person: Calories 257, Fat 4.5g, Carbs 39.3g, Protein 16.2g

Tofu with Brussels Sprout

Prep period: 15 mins.
Cooking Period: 15 mins.

Ingredients Required:
Serving: 4

- Olive oil – 1 tbsp. plus 2 tsp. (25 ml), divided
- Extra-firm tofu – 8 oz. (225 g), pressed, liquid removed, and cut into slivers
- Garlic cloves – 2, cut up
- Pecans – 1/3 C. (50 g), toasted and cut up
- Unsweetened applesauce – 1 tbsp.
- Fresh cilantro – ¼ C. (5 g), cut up
- Brussels sprouts – 1½ lb. (680 g), trimmed and cut into wide ribbons

Procedure of Cooking:

1. Sizzle 2 tsp. (25 ml) of oil into a large wok on a burner at medium heat.
2. Sauté the tofu for around 6-7 minutes.
3. Put in garlic and pecans and stir.
4. Sauté for around 1 minute.
5. Put in applesauce and stir.
6. Cook for around 2 minutes.
7. Blend in cilantro and remove from the burner.
8. Place the tofu onto a plate and set it aside
9. Sizzle remnant oil in the same wok on a burner at medium-high heat.
10. Cook the Brussels sprouts for 5 minutes.
11. Stir in tofu and remove from the burner.
12. Enjoy right away.

Per Person: Calories 218, Fat 14.8g, Carbs 11.6g, Protein 9.8g

Lentils & Quinoa Stew

Prep period: 15 mins.
Cooking Period: 33 mins.

Ingredients Required:
Serving: 8

- Olive oil – 1 tbsp.
- Carrots – 3, peel removed and cut up
- Celery stalks – 3, cut up
- Onion – 1, cut up
- Garlic cloves – 4, finely cut up
- Tomatoes – 4 C. (400 g), cut up
- Red lentils – 1 C. (210 g), rinsed
- Dried quinoa – ½ C. (95 g), rinsed
- Powdered cumin – ½ tsp.
- Red chili powder – 1 tsp.
- Homemade vegetable broth – 5 C. (1200 ml)
- Fresh spinach – 2 C. (60 g), cut up
- Sea salt and powdered black pepper – as desired

Procedure of Cooking:

1. Sizzle oil in a large pot on a burner at medium heat.
2. Cook the celery, onion, and carrot for around 8 minutes, stirring frequently.
3. Put in garlic and stir.
4. Sauté for around 1 minute.
5. Put in remnant ingredients except for spinach and stir.
6. Cook the mixture until boiling.
7. Turn the heat to around low.
8. Cook with the cover for around 20 minutes.
9. Put in spinach and stir.
10. Cook for around 3-4 minutes.
11. Stir in salt and pepper, and enjoy right away.

Per Person: Calories 253, Fat 4g, Carbs 43.6g, Protein 12.4g

Chickpeas & Pumpkin Stew

Prep period: 15 mins.
Cooking Period: 50 mins.

Ingredients Required:
Serving: 8

- Olive oil – 2 tbsp.
- Large-sized onion – 1, cut up
- Red chili powder – 2 tsp.
- Powdered cumin – 1 tsp.
- Garlic cloves – 2, finely cut up
- Sea salt and powdered black pepper – as desired
- Large-sized bell pepper – 1, seeded and cut up
- Medium-sized poblano peppers – 2, seeded and cut up
- Pumpkin – 1½ lb. (680 g), peel removed and cut into small-sized chunks)
- Water – 2 C. (480 ml)
- Cooked chickpeas – 30 oz. (850 g)
- Tomatoes – 3 C. (600 g), finely cut up
- Fresh lime juice – 2 tbsp.

Procedure of Cooking:

1. Sizzle oil in a large-sized Dutch oven on a burner at medium heat.
2. Cook the onion, chili powder, and cumin for around 5 minutes.
3. Put in bell pepper, poblano peppers, garlic and salt.
4. Cook for around 5 minutes, stirring from time to time.
5. Put in pumpkin cubes and stir to incorporate.
6. Immediately turn the heat to low.
7. Cook with a cover for around 5 minutes, stirring from time to time.
8. Put in water and stir.
9. Cook with a cover for around 20-30 minutes.
10. Put chickpeas and tomatoes into the pot of stew and lightly stir to incorporate.
11. Immediately turn the heat to around medium-high.
12. Cook the mixture until boiling.
13. Immediately turn the heat to medium-low.
14. Cook for around 5 minutes.
15. Stir in lime juice, salt, and pepper, and enjoy right away.

Per Person: Calories 290, Fat 5.2g, Carbs 55.1g, Protein 7.9g

Beans & Mushroom Chili

Prep period: 15 mins.
Cooking Period: 1 hr. 25 mins.

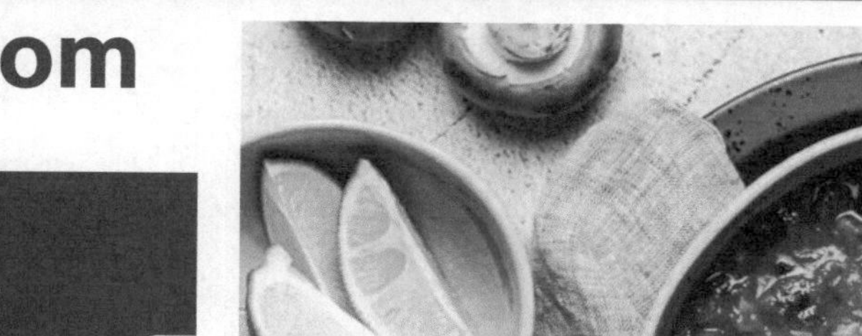

Ingredients Required:
Serving: 4

- Olive oil – 2 tbsp.
- Medium-sized onion – 1, cut up
- Carrot – 1, peel removed and cut up
- Small-sized bell pepper – 1, seeded and cut up
- Fresh mushrooms – 1 lb. (455 g), slivered
- Garlic cloves – 2, finely cut up
- Dried oregano – 2 tsp.
- Red chili powder – 1 tbsp.
- Powdered cumin – 1 tbsp.
- Sea salt and powdered black pepper – as desired
- Cooked black beans – 1 lb. (455 g)
- Tomatoes – 2 C. (400 g), finely cut up
- Homemade vegetable broth – 1½ C. (360 ml)

Procedure of Cooking:

1. Sizzle oil in a large Dutch oven on a burner at medium-low heat.
2. Cook the onions, carrot, and bell pepper for around 10 minutes, stirring frequently.
3. Turn the heat to around medium-high.
4. Put in mushrooms and garlic and stir.
5. Cook for around 5-6 minutes, stirring frequently.
6. Put in oregano, spices, salt, and pepper, and cook the chili for around 1-2 minutes.
7. Put in beans, tomatoes, and broth and stir.
8. Cook the mixture until boiling.
9. Turn the heat to low.
10. Cook with the cover for around 1 hour, stirring from time to time.
11. Enjoy right away.

Per Person: Calories 273, Fat 2.2g, Carbs 69g, Protein 24.5g

Quinoa with Mushrooms

Prep period: 15 mins.
Cooking Period: 30 mins.

Ingredients Required:
Serving: 4

- Olive oil – 2 tsp.
- Uncooked quinoa – 1 C. (190 g), rinsed
- Fresh mushrooms – 12 oz. (340 g), slivered
- Garlic cloves – 3, slivered
- Fresh ginger – 1 tsp., finely cut up
- Water – 1¾ C. (420 ml)
- Fresh parsley – ¼ C. (5 g), cut up
- Cayenne pepper powder – ¼ tsp.
- Sea salt and powdered black pepper – as desired
- Fresh lemon juice – 1 tbsp.

Procedure of Cooking:

1. Sizzle oil in a medium Dutch oven on a burner at medium-high heat.
2. Sauté the garlic for around 30-40 seconds.
3. Put in mushrooms and stir.
4. Cook for around 5-6 minutes, mixing all the time.
5. Put in quinoa and stir.
6. Cook for around 2 minutes, mixing all the time.
7. Put in water, cayenne, and salt and stir.
8. Cook the mixture until boiling.
9. Immediately turn the heat to around low.
10. Cook with a cover for around 15-18 minutes.
11. Enjoy right away with the decoration of cilantro.

Per Person: Calories 197, Fat 4.7g, Carbs 31.5g, Protein 9g

Kidney Bean Curry

Prep period: 10 mins.
Cooking Period: 25 mins.

Ingredients Required:
Serving: 6

- Olive oil – ¼ C. (60 ml)
- Medium-sized onion – 1, finely cut up
- Garlic cloves – 2, finely cut up
- Fresh ginger – 2 tsp. (4 g), finely cut up
- Powdered coriander – 1 tsp.
- Powdered cumin – 1 tsp.
- Powdered turmeric – 1 tsp.
- Cayenne pepper powder – ¼ tsp.
- Sea salt and powdered black pepper – as desired
- Large-sized plum tomatoes – 2, finely cut up
- Cooked red kidney beans – 3 C. (530 g)
- Water – 2 C. (480 ml)
- Fresh cilantro – ¼ C. (5 g), cut up

Procedure of Cooking:

1. Sizzle oil in a large-sized pot on a burner at medium heat.
2. Sauté the onion, garlic, and ginger for around 6-8 minutes.
3. Put in spices and blend.
4. Cook for 1-2 minutes.
5. Stir in tomatoes, kidney beans, and water, and turn the heat to high.
6. Cook the mixture until boiling.
7. Turn the heat to medium.
8. Cook for 10-15 minutes.
9. Enjoy right away with a decoration of parsley.

Per Person: Calories 253, Fat 4g, Carbs 43.6g, Protein 12.4g

Lentil & Veggie Curry

Prep period: 15 mins.
Cooking Period: 1½ hrs.

Ingredients Required:
Serving: 8

- Water – 8 C. (1920 ml)
- Powdered turmeric – ½ tsp.
- Red lentils – 2 C. (420 g), rinsed
- Olive oil – 1 tbsp.
- Large-sized onion – 1, cut up
- Garlic cloves – 3, finely cut up
- Tomatoes – 2, seeded and cut up
- Curry powder – 1½ tbsp.
- Powdered cumin – 2 tsp.
- Carrots – 3, peel removed and cut up
- Pumpkin – 3 C. (735 g), peel removed, seeded, and cubed into 1-inch size
- Granny Smith apple – 1, cored and cut up
- Fresh spinach – 2 C. (60 g), cut up
- Sea salt and powdered black pepper – as desired

Procedure of Cooking:

1. Put the water, turmeric, and lentils into a large-sized pot on the burner at high heat.
2. Cook the mixture until boiling.
3. Turn the heat to medium-low.
4. Cook with the cover for around 30 minutes.
5. Drain the lentils, reserving 2½ C. (360 ml) of the cooking liquid.
6. In the meantime, sizzle oil in another large-sized pot on the burner at medium heat.
7. Cook the onion for around 2-3 minutes.
8. Put in garlic and stir.
9. Cook for around 1 minute.
10. Put in the tomatoes and stir.
11. Cook for around 5 minutes.
12. Put in curry powder and spices and stir.
13. Cook for around 1 minute.
14. Put in carrots, pumpkin, cooked lentils, and reserved cooking liquid and stir.
15. Cook the mixture until boiling.
16. Turn the heat to around medium-low.
17. Cook with the cover for around 40-45 minutes.
18. Put in apple and spinach and stir.
19. Cook for around 15 minutes.
20. Stir in salt and pepper and remove from the burner.
21. Enjoy right away.

Per Person: Calories 263, Fat 3g, Carbs 47g, Protein 14.7g

NOTES

Rice & Lentil Loaf

Prep period: 20 mins.
Cooking Period:1 hr. 50 mins.

Ingredients Required:
Serving: 6

- Water – 1¾ C. plus 2 tbsp. (450 ml), divided
- Wild rice – ½ C. (100 g), rinsed
- Brown lentils – ½ C. (100 g), rinsed
- Sea salt – as desired
- Italian seasoning – ½ tsp.
- Medium-sized onion – 1, cut up
- Celery stalk – 1, cut up
- Cremini mushrooms – 6, cut up
- Garlic cloves – 4, finely cut up
- Gluten-free rolled oats – ¾ C. (75 g)
- Walnuts – ½ C. (50 g), finely cut up
- Sugar-free ketchup – ¾ C. (225 g)
- Red pepper flakes – ½ tsp. (1¼ g)
- Fresh rosemary – 1 tbsp. (1¼ g), finely cut up

Procedure of Cooking:

1. Put the 1¾ C. (420 ml) of water, rice, lentils, salt, and Italian seasoning into a pot on a burner at medium-high heat.
2. Cook the mixture until boiling.
3. Turn the heat to around low.
4. Cook with the cover for around 45 minutes.
5. Remove the pot from the burner and set it aside with the cover for at least 10 minutes.
6. For preheating, set your oven to 350 °F (175 °C).
7. Place bakery paper into a 9x5-inch bread loaf pan.
8. Sizzle remnant water in a wok on a burner at medium heat.
9. Sauté the onion, celery, mushrooms, and garlic for around 4-5 minutes.
10. Remove from the burner and set it aside to cool slightly.
11. Put the oats, walnuts, ketchup, and rosemary in a large basin and stir to incorporate thoroughly.
12. Add the rice mixture and vegetable mixture and stir thoroughly.
13. Put the mixture into a blender and process to form a chunky mixture.
14. Place the mixture into the loaf pan.
15. With a piece of heavy-duty foil, cover the loaf pan.
16. Bake in your oven for around 40 minutes.
17. Take off the foil and bake in your oven for around 20 minutes.
18. Remove from the oven and place the loaf pan onto a cooling wire rack for around 10 minutes.
19. Take out the loaf from the pan and place onto a platter.
20. Cut into serving portions and enjoy.

Per Person: Calories 254, Fat 7.5g, Carbs 38.6g, Protein 11.5g

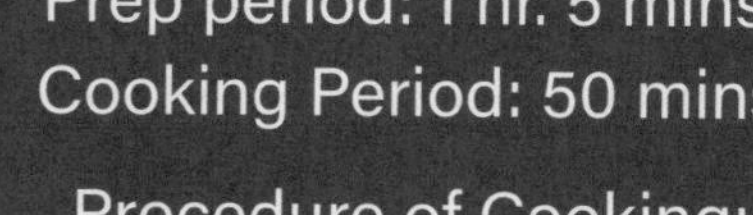

Barley & Veggies Pilaf

Prep period: 1 hr. 5 mins.
Cooking Period: 50 mins.

Ingredients Required:
Serving: 4

- Pearl barley – ½ C. (100 g)
- Homemade vegetable broth – 1 C. (240 ml)
- Olive oil – 2 tbsp. (30 ml), divided
- Garlic cloves – 2, finely cut up
- Onion – ½ C. (60 g), cut up
- Fresh mushrooms – ½ C. (65 g), slivered
- Bell pepper – ½ C. (75 g), seeded and cut up
- Fresh green peas – ½ C. (80 g), shelled
- Fresh cilantro – 2 tbsp., cut up
- Fresh mint leaves – 2 tbsp., cut up
- Low-sodium soy sauce – 1 tbsp.

Procedure of Cooking:

1. Put the barley and broth into a pot on a burner at medium-high heat.
2. Cook until boiling.
3. Turn the heat to around low.
4. Cook with the cover for 45 minutes.
5. Sizzle 1 tbsp. (15 ml) of oil into a large wok on a burner at medium-high heat.
6. Put in cooked barley and stir.
7. Cook for around 3 minutes.
8. Remove from the burner and set it aside.
9. Sizzle remnant oil into another wok on a burner at medium heat.
10. Sauté the onion and mushrooms for 7 minutes.
11. Put in bell pepper and green peas and stir.
12. Stir-fry for 3 minutes.
13. Put in remnant ingredients and stir.
14. Cook for 3 minutes.
15. Put in barley mixture and stir.
16. Cook for 3 minutes.
17. Enjoy right away.

Per Person: Calories 204, Fat 10.1g, Carbs 25.3g, Protein 4.8g

NOTES

Desserts Recipes

Frozen Vanilla Yogurt

Prep period: 10 mins.
Cooking Period: 0

Ingredients Required:
Serving: 6

- Fat-free plain Greek yogurt – 3 C. (750 g)
- Liquid stevia – 3-4 drops
- Organic vanilla extract – 1 tsp. (5 ml)

Procedure of Cooking:

1. Put the yogurt and remnant ingredients into a basin and stir to incorporate thoroughly.
2. Place the mixture into your ice cream maker and process according to the manufacturer's directions.
3. Move the mixture into an airtight container.
4. Cover the container and place into your freezer for around 30-40 minutes.
5. Take the container out of the freezer and set it aside for around 5-10 minutes before enjoying it.

Per Person: Calories 72, Fat 0.3g, Carbs 5.1g, Protein 12g

Spinach Sorbet

Prep period: 15 mins.
Cooking Period: 0

Procedure of Cooking:

1. Put the spinach and remnant ingredients into a blender and process to form a creamy and smooth mixture.
2. Place the mixture into an ice cream maker and process according to the manufacturer's directions.
3. Now, put the mixture into an airtight container.
4. Cover the container and place it into your freezer for at least 4-5 hours before enjoying.

Ingredients Required:
Serving: 4

- Fresh spinach – 3 C. (90 g), torn
- Fresh basil leaves – 1 tbsp.
- Avocado – ½, peel removed, pitted, and cut up
- Unsweetened almond milk – ¾ C. (180 ml)
- Liquid stevia – 20 drops
- Almonds – ½ tbsp., cut up very finely
- Organic vanilla extract – 1 tsp.
- Ice cubes – 1 C. (250 g)

Per Person: Calories 166, Fat 16g, Carbs 5.7g, Protein 2.3g

Strawberry Sundae

Prep period: 10 mins.
Cooking Period: 0

Procedure of Cooking:

1. Put the ricotta cheese and remnant ingredients, except for strawberries and almonds, into a basin and whisk to form a smooth mixture.
2. Put half of the cheese mixture into a serving glass dish.
3. Lay out the strawberries over the cheese mixture.
4. Top with remnant cheese mixture.
5. Decorate with almonds and enjoy right away.

Ingredients Required:
Serving: 1

- Part-skim ricotta cheese – ¼ C. (55 g)
- Organic vanilla extract – 1 tsp.
- Fresh lemon juice – 1 tsp.
- Liquid stevia – 2 drops
- Fresh strawberries – ¼ C. (30 g), hulled and slivered
- Almonds – ½ tbsp., cut up

Per Person: Calories 122, Fat 6g, Carbs 7g, Protein 7.8g

Raspberry Mousse

Prep period: 10 mins.
Cooking Period: 0

Procedure of Cooking:

1. Put the raspberries and remnant ingredients into a food processor and process to form a smooth mixture.
2. Pour the mixture into serving dishes and enjoy.

Ingredients Required
Serving: 6

- Fresh raspberries – 1½ C. (190 g)
- Chilled unsweetened coconut milk – 1 2/3 C. (400 ml)
- Erythritol – 2 tsp.
- Organic vanilla extract – 1 tsp.

Per Person: Calories 114, Fat 9.3g, Carbs 4.5g, Protein 1.1g

Spiced Egg Custard

Prep period: 10 mins.
Cooking Period: 40 mins.

Procedure of Cooking:

1. For preheating, set your oven at 325 °F (165 °C).
2. Spray 8 small-sized ramekins with baking spray.
3. Put the eggs and salt into a basin and whisk thoroughly.
4. Lay out a sieve over a medium-sized bowl.
5. Through the sieve, strain the egg mixture into a basin.
6. Put the maple syrup in the eggs and stir to incorporate.
7. Put the almond milk and spices and whisk to incorporate thoroughly.
8. Pour the mixture into the ramekins.
9. Lay out the ramekins into a large-sized baking pan.
10. Put hot water into the baking pan about 2 inches high around the ramekins.
11. Bake in your oven for around 30-40 minutes.
12. Take the ramekins from out of the oven and set aside to cool.
13. Put into your refrigerator to chill before enjoying.

Ingredients Required:
Serving: 8

- Olive oil baking spray
- Eggs – 5
- Sea salt – as desired
- Liquid stevia – 4-5 drops
- Unsweetened almond milk – 20 fluid oz. (600 ml)
- Powdered ginger – ¼ tsp.
- Powdered cinnamon – ¼ tsp.
- Powdered nutmeg – ¼ tsp.
- Powdered cardamom – ¼ tsp.
- Powdered cloves – 1 pinch
- Powdered allspice – 1 pinch

Per Person: Calories 52, Fat 3.8g, Carbs 1g, Protein 3.8g

Mocha Panna Cotta

Prep period: 15 mins.
Cooking Period: 5 mins.

Procedure of Cooking:

1. Put ½ C. (120 ml) of almond milk into a large-sized basin and sprinkle with gelatin.
2. Set aside until soaked.
3. Put the remnant almond milk, coconut milk, cacao powder, coffee granules, and stevia into a pot on a burner at medium heat.
4. Cook the mixture until boiling, stirring all the time.
5. Remove from the burner.
6. Put the gelatin mixture and hot milk mixture into a clean blender and process to form a smooth mixture.
7. Place the mixture into serving glasses and set aside to cool thoroughly.
8. With plastic wrap, cover each glass and place into your refrigerator for around 3-4 hours before enjoying.

Ingredients Required:
Serving: 4

- Unsweetened almond milk – 1½ C. (360 ml), divided
- Unflavoured gelatin powder – 1 tbsp.
- Unsweetened coconut milk – 1 C. (240 ml)
- Erythritol – 1/3 C. (75 g)
- Cacao powder – 3 tbsp.
- Instant coffee granules – 2 tsp.
- Liquid stevia – 6 drops

Per Person: Calories 136, Fat 12.1g, Carbs 5.8g, Protein 4.4g

Carrot Pudding

Prep period: 15 mins.
Cooking Period: 31 mins.

Ingredients Required:
Serving: 4

- Unsweetened almond milk – 2-2½ C. (480-600 ml)
- Raw cashews – ¼ C. (30 g)
- Olive oil – 1 tbsp.
- Carrots – 2 C. (300 g), peel removed and shredded
- Erythritol – 2 tbsp.
- Powdered cardamom – ¼ tsp.
- Powdered cinnamon – 1 pinch
- Sea salt – 1 pinch
- Mixed nuts – 3 tbsp. (30 g), cut up

Procedure of Cooking:

1. Put the almond milk and cashews into a high-power blender and process to form a smooth and creamy mixture.
2. Sizzle oil in a wok on a burner at medium heat.
3. Cook the carrots for around 5-6 minutes, stirring from time to time.
4. Put in almond milk and blend.
5. Cook for around 10 minutes, stirring from time to time.
6. Turn the heat to medium-low and stir in Erythritol, cardamom, cinnamon, and salt.
7. Put in nuts and raisins and stir thoroughly.
8. Cook partially covered for around 10-15 minutes, stirring from time to time.
9. Enjoy moderately hot.

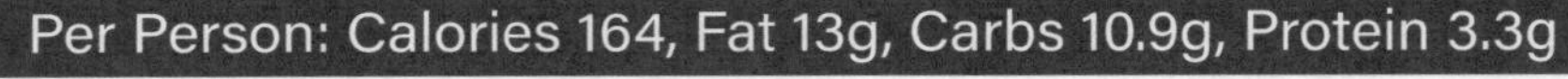

Per Person: Calories 164, Fat 13g, Carbs 10.9g, Protein 3.3g

Peanut Butter Fudge

Prep period: 15 mins.
Cooking Period: 0

Procedure of Cooking:

1. Put the peanut butter and coconut oil into a small pot on a burner at low heat.
2. Cook until liquefied and smooth, stirring frequently.
3. Put in Erythritol and protein powder and stir to form a smooth mixture.
4. Remove from the burner and stir in vanilla extract.
5. Place the fudge mixture into a bakery paper-lined, 8x8-inch baking pan.
6. With a spatula, smooth the top surface.
7. Place it into your freezer for around 30-45 minutes.
8. Carefully put the fudge onto a chopping board with the help of the bakery paper.
9. Cut the fudge into squares and enjoy.

Ingredients Required
Serving: 16

- Creamy, salted peanut butter – 1½ C. (375 g)
- Coconut oil – 1/3 C. (70 g)
- Erythritol – 2/3 C. (130 g)
- Unsweetened protein powder – ¼ C. (30 g)
- Organic vanilla extract – 1 tsp.

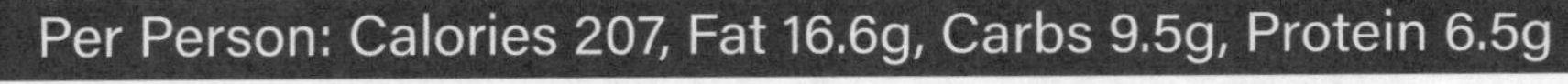

Per Person: Calories 207, Fat 16.6g, Carbs 9.5g, Protein 6.5g

Blueberry Scones

Prep period: 15 mins.
Cooking Period: 20 mins.

Ingredients Required:
Serving: 8

- Flaxseed meal – 1 tbsp.
- Water – 3 tbsp.
- Almond flour – 1 C. (100 g)
- Coconut flour – ¼ C. (23 g)
- Erythritol – 3 tbsp.
- Baking powder – ½ tsp.
- Sea salt – 1 pinch
- Unsweetened almond milk – ¼ C. (60 ml)
- Coconut oil – 2 tbsp., liquefied
- Organic vanilla extract – 1 tsp.
- Fresh blueberries – ½ C. (75 g)

Procedure of Cooking:

1. For preheating, set your oven at 350 °F (175 °C).
2. Place a bakery paper onto a baking tray.
3. For scones, put the flaxseed meal and water into a large basin and blend to incorporate thoroughly. Set it aside for around 5 minutes.
4. Put the flours, Erythritol, baking powder, and salt into a basin and stir to incorporate thoroughly.
5. Put the almond milk, coconut oil, and vanilla extract in the basin of the flaxseed meal mixture and whisk it to incorporate thoroughly.
6. Add the flour mixture and stir to form a pliable dough.
7. Lightly blend in blueberries.
8. Lay out the dough onto the baking tray, and with your hands, pat it into a 1-inch thick circle.
9. Carefully cut the circle into 8 equal-sized wedges.
10. Lay out the scones onto the baking tray about 1-inch apart
11. Bake in your oven for around 18-22 minutes.
12. Take out of the oven and move the baking tray onto a cooling wire rack to cool thoroughly before enjoying.

Per Person: Calories 128, Fat 11.1g, Carbs 3.9g, Protein 0.2g

Chocolate Yogurt Cheesecake

Prep period: 15 mins.
Cooking Period: 35 mins.

Procedure of Cooking:

1. For preheating, set your oven at 35 °F.
2. Spray a 9-inch cake pan with baking spray.
3. Put the yogurt and remnant ingredients into a large basin and stir to incorporate thoroughly.
4. Place the mixture into the pot.
5. Bake in your oven for around 30-35 minutes.
6. Take it out of the oven and let it cool thoroughly.
7. Place it in your refrigerator to chill for around 3-4 hours.
8. Cut into serving portions and enjoy.

Ingredients Required:
Serving: 8

- Olive oil baking spray
- Fat-free plain Greek yogurt – 2½ C. (625 g)
- Liquid stevia – 6-8 drops
- Egg whites – 3
- Cacao powder – 1/3 C. (45 g)
- Arrowroot starch – ¼ C. (30 g)
- Organic vanilla extract – 1 tsp.
- Sea salt – 1 pinch

Per Person: Calories 85, Fat 1.6g, Carbs 10g, Protein 6.4g

Conclusion

As we conclude this culinary adventure, it's important to emphasize the profound importance of taking care of our diet, especially as we journey through the golden years. Our bodies have carried us through a lifetime of experiences, and now, more than ever, they deserve our utmost care and attention. By nourishing ourselves with wholesome, nutrient-rich foods and avoiding those that can harm our health, we honor our bodies and empower ourselves to live our best lives.

Loving your body means more than just treating it well; it means cherishing it, nurturing it, and embracing the unique journey it's taken you on. Each meal we prepare is an opportunity to show gratitude for the incredible vessel that carries us through life's adventures. So, let's continue to make mindful choices, savor every bite, and relish in the joy that comes from nourishing ourselves from the inside out.

As you close the pages of this book, may you carry with you the knowledge, inspiration, and motivation to continue prioritizing your health and well-being. And remember, you're never alone on this journey. Reach out to your support network, lean on your loved ones, and know that you have the power to shape your health destiny.

Here's to a future filled with vitality, happiness, and endless culinary delights. Cheers to loving your body, honoring your health, and savoring the richness of life at every age. Keep cooking, keep nourishing, and above all, keep shining bright.

You've got this!

This page is for your notes

Made in United States
Troutdale, OR
11/15/2024